For Paul &

& Shin-chan

with best wishes

Hosea Hirata

Dec. 93

The Poetry and Poetics of

Nishiwaki Junzaburō

Studies of the East Asian Institute, Columbia University

The East Asian Institute is Columbia University's center for reasearch, publication, and teaching on modern East Asia. The Studies of the East Asian Institute were inaugurated in 1962 to bring to a wider public the results of significant new research on modern and contemporary East Asia.

The Poetry and Poetics of
Nishiwaki Junzaburō

MODERNISM IN TRANSLATION

Hosea Hirata

PRINCETON UNIVERSITY PRESS

PRINCETON • NEW JERSEY • MCMXCIII

Library of Congress Cataloging-in-Publication Data

Nishiwaki, Junzaburō, 1894–
The poetry and poetics of Nishiwaki Junzaburō : modernism in
translation / Hosea Hirata.
p.   cm. — (Studies of the East Asian Institute)
Includes selections from: Chōgenjitsu shugi shiron; Ambarvalia;
Tabibito kaerazu; and Eterunitasu.
Includes bibliographical references and index.
ISBN 0-691-06981-6
1. Nishiwaki, Junzaburō, 1894—Translations into English.
I. Hirata, Hosea, 1952– .   II. Title.   III. Series
PL834.I76A24 1993
895.6'14—dc20   92-42404 CIP

For Catherine

Contents

Preface

The thing is not just something conforming to laws that I discuss objectively (adequately) or, on the contrary, subjectively (anthropomorphically). Beforehand, the thing is the other, the entirely other which dictates or which writes the law, a law which is not simply natural (*lex naturae rerum*), but an infinitely, insatiably imperious injunction to which I ought to subject myself, even when this involves trying to acquit myself afterwards, at the end of a duel, having offered it, with my life and desire, something akin to my signature. . . . [T]his dictate, this inscription can require the muteness of the thing. It gives orders while remaining silent.—*Jacques Derrida*

Nishiwaki is paradisal. Admittedly this is an awkward and remote expression, yet it marks the beginning of this writing as no other expression could.

The paradisal is necessarily remote. Writing begins only from the knowledge of this remoteness and moves toward what has classically been termed *télos,* or *éschatos,* which, in turn, the same remoteness simultaneously shows and hides. This paradox situated at the end of our desire to write can also be described as the "end" of writing: that is, the death of a certain language-movement. Writing is seduced by its own end—paradise. But paradise must exist utterly alone, as the absolute, sovereign region of language, in order to be such. That is, it must refuse writing's entry in order to protect its status. Unless writing dies, unless writing reaches its end, this paradise will never appear as such.

Nishiwaki has written a paradise. That is quite possible; there is essentially no other explanation for the coming-into-being of this writing. Nishiwaki is paradisal. More precisely, the *Nishiwaki-text* is paradisal. This statement, however, belatedly announces a death. Nishiwaki's writing has already died, entombed in his canonized texts, only to be read from afar. As a translator I approach his paradisal text and attempt to resuscitate its textual movement, but now in a foreign tongue. Translation does violence to the mother tongue, to the entombed silence within which his original "poetry" must be heard. The translator knows he or she is violating the purity of the original, knows the translation will never reach the paradise of the original. Yet the translator discovers that in the tomb of the original, in its silence, there never was a sweet mother tongue so overwhelmingly protective of its poetry—its most authentic language. Nishiwaki's language was already translatory. Paradise was translating. I am here only to insert myself in the silent textual movement, which has already begun without me, in the name of the translation that the original demanded of itself.

One Japanese critic does not hesitate to call Nishiwaki Junzaburō (1894–1982) one of the four most important poets of this century, assigning him a place alongside R. M. Rilke, Paul Valéry, and T. S. Eliot (Chiba 1978, 163). Revered in Japan, yet unknown in the rest of the world, Nishiwaki left us with an enormous corpus, including poetry, essays, scholarly papers, and translations, now collected in his twelve-volume *Zenshū* (Collected works). Nishiwaki is often regarded as the father of literary surrealism in Japan, yet his work cannot be so easily confined within a modernism. He was, to say the least, a unique poet and thinker who cultivated a truly original voice unlike any other in the world.

Following a brief introduction sketching Nishiwaki's formative years, this book is divided into two parts. Part One begins with a selection from Nishiwaki's theoretical writings published in 1929 under the title *Chōgenjitsushugi shiron*, translated here as *Surrealist Poetics*. This is followed by my translations of his first collection of Japanese poems, *Ambarvalia*, published in 1933, his second collection of Japanese poems, *Tabibito kaerazu* (No traveller returns), published in 1947, and a long poem, *Eterunitasu* ("eternity"; in Latin, *aeternitas*), published in 1962.

In Part Two, the first chapter provides a brief history of modernist poetry in Japan, on which Nishiwaki left an indelible mark. The following three chapters explore various issues raised by the translated Nishiwaki-texts. Woven through these chapters are the related issues of language, poetry, and translation. If there must be a center, a unifying focus, it is the notion of "nonmeaning." This is a study of the nonmeaning (the silence of the thing that dictates that one speak) to which language, poetry, and translation all aspire.

Chapter 2 presents a reading of *Chōgenjitsushugi shiron* juxtaposed to one of Jacques Derrida's *Of Grammatology*. In an attempt to define poetry, Nishiwaki posits a negative evolution of poetry until its own death. He claims that poetry is essentially an antiexpressive act; that is, an effort not to express. Moreover, according to Nishiwaki, it is an effort to abolish itself. Thus the most advanced mode of poetry is envisioned as that which is closest to its own extinction. Despite his ostensible endorsement of surrealism, Nishiwaki also claims that poetry must be founded on reality. But reality, he says, is "boring" (*tsumaranai*). I argue that if *tsumaranai* is translated as "insignificant" (that is, "lacking meaning"), Nishiwaki's notion of poetry can be seen as a return to this *tsumaranasa*, to the fundamental nonmeaning of reality.

Nishiwaki's radical view of poetry as a self-annihilating textual movement toward the nonmeaning of reality is then examined through Derrida's deconstructive critique of origin. Derrida's grammatology posits a notion of writing that is more originary than the origin, presence, or being. Writing is an indefinite play of traces, a chain of supplements, that reverses the order of mimesis. It does not refer back to the origin, being, or presence that is commonly considered the solid foundation of a text through which we communicate and exchange truths; rather, it is always already at the site of origin. In sum, Nishiwaki's writing appears as the result of the failure of pure poetry, the failure of silence, the failure of his language to attain the ultimate mute reality. Derrida's notion of writing is also this failure of silence at the origin.

My heavy indebtedness to the writings of Derrida may make some readers wonder why one must use a "postmodernist" thinker in order to provide an account of modernism in Japan. My repeated references to Derrida arise from a conviction that Derrida is one of the most dexterous and rigorous readers of modernist texts. We know that Derrida's thought is inextricably bound with various modernist writers, including Artaud, Bataille, Blanchot, Céline, Freud, Joyce, Kafka, Mallarmé, Nietzsche, and Ponge. To put it crudely, one could say that Derrida applies the methods of avant-garde artists to the field of philosophy. Consequently, I find Derrida's writings to be the most useful, if not the easiest, gateway to an understanding of what takes place in modernist texts. Furthermore, his critique of origin helps us see how the workings of translation produced a modernism in Japan by way of Nishiwaki.

Chapter 3 is presented as a detour to the final paradisal destination (poetry). It is a detour of translation. Walter Benjamin's "Task of the Translator" is the focal point here. According to Benjamin, all languages strive to become one in what he calls "pure language." Pure language is a certain absolute state of language in which the separation between signifier and signified ceases, where meaning is no longer necessary, where the word is instantly truth. Benjamin sees translation as the only means to achieve this paradisal unity of languages. What emerges from these notions of writing, poetry, and translation is a certain drive toward nonmeaning seemingly inherent in language itself. In chapter 4, Nishiwaki's poems are shown to be exemplary in manifesting the movement of language on which Derrida and Benjamin elaborate. Nishiwaki's poems attempt to become, without much hesitation but with much duplicity, a pure movement of writing itself.

To translate is to trace a certain paradise. The present study traces this tracing of paradise. The originary paradise is always far removed from any beginning of writing. The present work attempts to approach this paradise of the original. The ecstasy of translation, however fictive, is revealed only at the end of this approach, of this writing, where the original becomes almost touchable, waiting with unprecedented clarity, illuminated, yet essentially remaining an elusive dream.

My translations of Nishiwaki's poems as well as my notes on them are much indebted to the information provided by Niikura Toshikazu in his *Nishiwaki Junzaburō zenshi inyu shūsei* (Collection of allusions in the complete poetry of Nishiwaki Junzaburō). Without Niikura's study, my translations of Nishiwaki's poetry would have been almost impossible. One of the difficulties a translator encounters in Nishiwaki's texts involves the deciphering of foreign words transliterated into Japanese. How could one know, for example, by reading the Japanese text written "hēra hēra hēra," that the word *hēra* derives from the French *hélas*, or in another example, that *sasupēru* derives from an old spelling of Shakespeare, "Saxpere"?

Many people have kindly supported this project directly or indirectly since its inception. First, my heartfelt gratitude goes to my dissertation supervisor at the University of British Columbia, Lorraine Weir, who taught me what it takes to be an intellectual, and to Janet Walker and J. Thomas Rimer, without whose encouragement I could never have finished this book. I am also deeply indebted to my teachers and colleagues: Kin'ya Tsuruta, Leon Hurvitz, Robert Kramer, Peter Quartermain, Marian Coope, and Michael Bullock at U.B.C.; Sam Yamashita, Lynne Miyake, Stanleigh Jones (and the other members of the Beer-and-Pizza Gang) at Pomona College; Richard Okada and Earl Miner at Princeton. I am grateful to the members of the East Asian Institute at Columbia University, especially Carol Gluck and Madge Huntington, for their generous support and for including this book in their Studies of the East Asian Institute series. I would also like to express my gratitude to my editors at Princeton University Press, Robert Brown and Beth Gianfagna, and to my wonderful copy editor, Jane Lincoln Taylor. This work has been in every sense a labor of love. Thus I dedicate the book to the eternal phantasmal traveller, Junzaburō, whom I never met, and to Catherine, with whom I share my life.

Parts of the book have previously appeared in print in a slightly different form. Part Two, chapter 2 appeared under the title "Pure Poetry and *Différance*: Negativity in Nishiwaki and Derrida," in the *Journal of the Association of Teachers of Japanese* 26, no. 1 (April 1992); the first three sections of chapter 4 are scheduled to be published in *Comparative Literature* under the title "Violation of the Mother Tongue: Nishiwaki Junzaburō's Translatory Language in *Ambarvalia*"; the section on *No Traveller Returns* in the same chapter was first published in *Literary History, Narrative, and Culture: Selected Conference Papers* (Honolulu: University of Hawaii Press, 1989) under the title "Return or No-Return: Nishiwaki's Postmodernist Appropriation of Literary History, East and West." Permission to republish these articles is gratefully acknowledged.

All Japanese authors' names (unless their texts were originally written in English) are written in the customary Japanese order, that is, with the family name first. All translations are mine unless otherwise indicated.

Nishiwaki Junzaburō in 1933. (Courtesy of Nishiwaki Jun'ichi.)

Introduction

POUND, JANUS, AND THE NOBEL PRIZE

At Christmastime in 1956, in St. Elizabeths Hospital, Ezra Pound received a package containing a newly published volume of his poems in Japanese translation. Arriving in the same package was a long poem entitled "January in Kyoto." His Japanese translator informed Pound that a Japanese colleague at his university had written it *in English:*

January in Kyoto

Janus, old man,
Your name is damp and grey and too prolonged
A ring to rattle in my verse;
You double-faced, diluted churl of churls,
You corn-dull, poppy-wilted, beaver-brown,
You snow-eater, a parasite on roots and berries,
Iconoclast of gins and perries,
You're really one of the pariah dogs
Yelping, thrash-worth, at the belated gods.
I know the deities would rather inflate
And flow in pipes than in metric odes, but now
You suddenly brought us shy myth,
When we, disguised as Zeus and Hermes, went
Looking for orchids that will hang oblong and dim
At cuckoo-crow at the hell lady's door,
In the Hiei foot-hills by pebbly-purring streams.

We went into a peasant's cottage to see
How one cleans and adorns one's range
With a sprig of rue and a tangle of hips
To honour the bluff god of the kitchen fire.
The old baucis-and-philemon tree rustled its top:
"Reverend sirs, you are early. Well now."
My friend, a Ben Jonson scholar at the university,
And a complete parr angler, could speak

The Yase doric: "Look what we've got,
Such lovely slender buds; may we leave
These things with you by this mercury bush,
As we're going to see Emau Convent up there?"
Again we went out into loam land, dreaming
Of Angels and pottery crystal-beaming:
This time as tinkers we wandered . . .
Post-orchid journey it will be named.
A redolent trek, there was a smell
Of yellow plum blossom in the turnip fields.
"Who is it walking with you, strangers?"
"It is a woman."
She is in holy visibility:
That was an old woman with the help of a stick
On her way from Shu-gaku-in to Iwakura
To draw out money, the account book on her head,
Nicely done up in a peony-patterned cloth
Probably to ransom her helen out of peonage.
She had a leer like a boar
And had a stutter like Darley;
But it might be thunder if she chose to parley.
Excited by our indignation on the boar ravages,
With fury and frothing she made a Delphic utterance:
"It only took them a night to devour
A middlesex acre (as Macaulay says) of your yams;
Last year they shot a huge one, but nobody
Could bear him anyway, so there you are . . ."
So saying she glowered at us and passed by.
Now I come to the second nonnes tale:
We greeted the ancress in a most elegant way;
Unrobed, aproned, head tonsured as azure as
The kingfisher's wings, sweeping up fallen leaves
Among the landscape stones green with moss,
Herself indistinguishable from the blue.
"Good morning, Madame Eglantine, may I
See your garden? Wonderful!
And do you happen to know my relation
Who is a prioress living near Kitano-Tenjin?"
"I wouldn't know, sir. But how odd, when I've been
Of the same tribe nearly all my life.

> Bo tree, that. Very, very rare."
> "Perhaps you could let me have a twig in the spring;
> I'd like to graft it on a stock . . . mulberry it is."
> Enlightenment . . . an entwining of rose and bay.
> "By all means. Secretum secretorum!"
> When we returned full circle to the roots
> Of our orchids, we maundered to sanctify
> Fertility . . . magic jabber . . . over cups of tea.
> The wife decanted golden mead to immortalize
> Our chats and our pseudo-godliness, but we tried
> Hard to hide our mortality . . .   (*NJZ* 9:708–9)[1]

Pound wrote back to his translator (Iwasaki Ryōzō) with his characteristically copious enthusiasm about the poem, which almost belittled the hard work of Iwasaki, the translator:

> It has been a most delightful Xmas, and I have you to thank for two of the pleasant surprises. Your elegantly printed "Mauberley" (& other poems), and J.N.'s Janus Poem, the latter MOST opportune, as Stock has started a magazine which badly needs it. *Edge,* edited by Noel Stock. . . .
>
> Junzaburo has a more vital english than any I have seen for some time. AND if you choose such good company I can well believe you have made a good job of the "Mauberley," and trust if you also write in english or translate your own poems you will send copies both to Stock and my-self.
>
> I have enjoyed that Janus poem more than anything I have come on for some time. (Kodama 1987, 135)

Some time later, he had this to say:

> Dear Ryozo Iwasaki
> No literary prize or jury award can alter the weight of a consonant or change the length of a vowel, but on the practical side, if you have some sort of Japanese Academy or authoritative body, it could do no harm to bring Junzaburo Nishiwaki's work to the attention of the Swedish Academy; I do not recall their having yet honoured Nippon. (Ibid., 141)

Consequently, Nishiwaki was officially nominated to the Swedish Academy as a Nobel Prize candidate. That was in the fall of 1957. We had to wait until 1968 for the first Nobel Prize in literature to be awarded to a Japanese writer. The winner was not Nishiwaki Junzaburō; the novelist Kawabata Yasunari (1899–1972) received the honor.[2] The lack of translations of his work might have cost Nishiwaki the prize. It seems nearly unbelievable that on the basis of a single poem written in a foreign tongue Pound was able to detect a talent worthy of a Nobel Prize, yet he had a special gift for finding talents that were to change the course of modern literature. Indeed, he almost single-handedly molded the career of James Joyce, as well as those of the Nobel laureates T. S. Eliot and W. B. Yeats. The excitement stirred among those who knew about Nishiwaki's candidacy was quite understandable. What did Pound discern in Nishiwaki's poem?

When Pound was praising the Janus poem in 1957, Nishiwaki was sixty-three years old and commanded an uncontested position in the Japanese literary world as the most respected senior poet. One glance at the events of that year reveals the high esteem in which he was held in Japan. In January, he was inducted into the prestigious Nihon gaku-jutsu kaigi (Science council of Japan); in February he was awarded the Yomiuri Literary Prize for his book of poetry *Dai san no shinwa* (The third myth); in March his *Selected Poems* was published; in May, a collection of his essays, *Shatō no meishin* (Superstitions of an inclining tower), was published. In hindsight, what is most astonishing is that at that stage in his career Nishiwaki had not yet reached the peak of his creativity. He was to publish eight more major books of verse before his death in 1982.

Nishiwaki was indeed a Janus, always simultaneously seeing East and West, modern and ancient worlds, surrealism and haiku, the banal and the sublime. No other modern Japanese poet could come close to him in his erudite knowledge of world literature, from ancient to modern. In one breath he could discuss Piers Plowman and André Breton, Henri Michaux's mescaline and a bowl of miso soup. Slurping Japanese *soba* noodles, he quipped, "No wonder Eliot's no good; he's never tasted this stuff."[3] When he died he left an unedited manuscript of over twenty thousand pages. It was a comparative linguistic study of ancient Greek and Chinese, which he had begun at the age of seventy. Janus, old man, who were you?

CHRONOLOGY

On January 20, 1894, Nishiwaki Junzaburō was born, the second son of a well-established merchant family in Ojiya, Niigata Prefecture.[4] The Nishiwakis had a long history of dealing in silk crape (a well-known local product), rice, and eventually banking. When Nishiwaki was born, his father Kanzō, thirty-four years old, was the head of Ojiya Bank. Kanzō and his wife Kisa had four sons (the youngest son died soon after birth) and three daughters. The infant Junzaburō was looked after by a wet nurse.

Nishiwaki's predilection for the arts as opposed to the sciences was evident from an early age. In elementary school he derived the greatest pleasure from his art classes. It was here that his lifelong passion for painting was nurtured. Once in middle school, he became fascinated with English and began to study it in earnest. It seems that his family's collection of foreign books served as an important source of inspiration for him at this time.[5] In due course, Nishiwaki earned a nickname: *eigoya* (English dealer/freak). The title may have been an honorable one, though it could be interpreted that he was perceived as too occupied with English to participate in other boys' activities. Indeed, it seems that Nishiwaki's preoccupation with English was such that he simply had no time for any of his other subjects—with the exception of painting. In those days in Japan, students precociously posed as intellectuals by dabbling in literature and composing haiku or tanka. Along with this "literary" pose came the usual youthful vices: drinking sake and visiting prostitutes. Nishiwaki felt distant from this "world of literature" that his peers were flaunting. He preferred to paint. The writers popular at that time included those of the naturalist school, Shimazaki Tōson (1872–1943), Tayama Katai (1872–1930), and Kunikida Doppo (1871–1908), all of whom Nishiwaki disdained. In fact, his downright neglect and consequent ignorance of contemporary Japanese novelists continued until his death and were often documented in humorous anecdotes. How then did he encounter literature? Nishiwaki said he felt a stirring of love for poetry when he read classical Chinese poetry in class. Thus, when he was still young, it was already evident that he was not interested in what was near him, namely modern Japanese literature; distant matters, a foreign language and ancient poetry, were capturing his imagination. When he began writing theoretical papers on modernist poetry two decades later, Nishiwaki, though perceived to be a modernist himself, would pride himself on proving that there was nothing new about modernism; it was merely a slight extension of ancient Greek rhetoric![6]

In 1911, upon his graduation from middle school, encouraged by his art teacher and with permission from his father, the seventeen-year-old Nishiwaki decided to pursue his interest in painting. In April, he left for Tokyo, where he was immediately accepted as a pupil of the famous Western-style painter Fujishima Takeji (1867–1943). He also became acquainted with other painters at this time, including Kuroda Seiki (1866–1924) and Shirotaki Ikunosuke (1873–1960). Yet despite such favorable circumstances, Nishiwaki quickly began to doubt his resolution to become a painter. In May, just one month after he had arrived in Tokyo, his father died. With his father's death, Nishiwaki's dream of going to France to study painting vanished. Now he felt forced to pursue a more financially stable career.[7]

The period that followed was an oppressive one for the young Nishiwaki. He wrote in his autobiographical essay "Nōzui no nikki" (The journal of a brain): "Once a young man is out of middle school, he has to choose a profession to make a living. Throughout my entire life, there was nothing that made me more depressed than this fact of life. When I became aware that I had to have a profession, I cursed life for the first time" (*ZS*, 1247). One sees a young man emphatically wanting to be released from normal social obligations. Indeed, Nishiwaki carried this unworldly air around with him throughout his life. Many still wonder how such an ethereal man could have maintained an important academic position at a prestigious university. It seems he was freed from many bothersome "realistic" chores of public life by simply posing as an unworldly poet; everyone surrounding him allowed him to be one.

Persuaded by his family, he took the entrance examination for Dai ichi kōtōgakkō (the First Higher School, later to be connected with Tokyo University) in April 1912. Typically, he wrote only the English section of the examination and then escaped to the schoolyard, where he became immersed in Shakespeare's *A Midsummer Night's Dream*. Not surprisingly, Nishiwaki was rejected by Dai ichi kōtōgakkō. In September, however, he managed to enter the preparatory course (*yoka*) for the Department of Economics at Keiō University. It was around this time—when he was supposed to be immersing himself in economics—that Nishiwaki began studying Greek, Latin, and German, and most importantly, began writing poems in English. By choosing to write in a foreign tongue, Nishiwaki was distancing himself from the very concept of modern Japanese poetry defined by the highly elevated literary language of the poets of that time, among them Shimazaki Tōson, Kanbara Ariake (1876–1952), Ueda Bin (1874–1916), and Kitahara Hakushū (1885–1942).

It must have become progressively more clear to Nishiwaki that he was headed for the wrong department. Privately, he longed to pursue his studies of foreign literatures and languages at the university, but the pressure from his family was too great. Continuing on track, he entered the Department of Economics. In his class, he befriended Nozaka Sanzō, who later became a noted Communist leader. Later Nishiwaki would boast that he had read Marx's *Capital* with Nozaka. However, it was clear that Nishiwaki was destined to become neither a politician nor a business executive. He would bring literary books into his classes and read secretly. Among the authors whose works he enjoyed were Turgenev, Tolstoy, Baudelaire, Rimbaud, Verlaine, Flaubert, Maupassant, Symons, Pater, Yeats, Wilde, Dostoevsky, Nietzsche, Verhaeren, and Maeterlinck. Of these, Flaubert, Symons, and Pater left a lasting impression on the young man.

In 1917, Nishiwaki was graduated from the university. His graduation thesis, entitled "Pure Economics," was, amazingly enough, written entirely in Latin. Nishiwaki later recalled that when he submitted his thesis, no one in the department could read it. His professor, Koizumi Shinzō, asked him to write a synopsis in Japanese, which came to about fifteen pages. Soon rumors started: "Nishiwaki was graduated with a mere fifteen-page thesis!"[8] Nishiwaki's first job was with the *Japan Times*, the only English newspaper in Japan, for which he was assigned to write articles in English. This job was, however, rather short-lived. Only months after he began, an illness—a mild case of amyloid infiltration of the lungs—forced him to retreat to his home in Ojiya for a year of rest. He returned to work in 1919, receiving a part-time position in the Ministry of Foreign Affairs. The next year he became a lecturer in the preparatory course of the English department at Keiō University.

It was during the first years following his graduation that Nishiwaki began publishing essays and poems in English in the journal *Eigo bungaku* (English literature). He also read *Tsuki ni hoeru* (1917; Howling at the moon) by Hagiwara Sakutarō (1886–1942) during this time.[9] The book made an indelible impression on Nishiwaki: for the first time he felt it might be possible to write poetry in Japanese. However, absorbed in Keats, he kept practicing writing sonnets in English, and did not attempt to write poetry in Japanese until much later. Nishiwaki's reading of Hagiwara was, to say the least, idiosyncratic. In an interview, he insisted that what he had learned from Hagiwara was the *kaigyaku* (wit)[10] of his style and said that he could not stop laughing as he read *Tsuki ni hoeru.*[11] Anyone who has ever been touched by the morbid sentimentality of Hagiwara would find it hard to conceive of a man laughing while reading *Tsuki ni hoeru.* Nishiwaki's laughter marked the fundamental difference between the two poets. Hagiwara confronted his angst head-on; his spiritual sufferings appeared genuine in his poetry. Nishiwaki's path was always a little crooked, which created the poetic effect of *kaigyaku* everywhere. He projected essentially an elusive and ironic subject (more "textualized" than Hagiwara, as it were). His language deftly eluded the existentialist horror and moved toward eternity along its crooked path.

In 1922, at the age of twenty-eight, his long-awaited chance to study abroad became a reality. Keiō University decided to send him to England to study English literature, criticism, and linguistics. He was aboard the ship *Kitanomaru* that left the port of Yokohama on July 7. On the way, the ship called at Singapore, Egypt, and Italy, reaching England at the end of August. Nishiwaki is said to have taken with him his most cherished books as if they were talismans for the journey: Baudelaire's *Les fleurs du mal,* Nietzsche's *Thus Spoke Zarathustra,* and Hagiwara's *Tsuki ni hoeru.*

Though he had hoped to enroll at Oxford University, he was too late to register for the new term. Thus began a year of freedom in London—perhaps the most educationally valuable year for his development as an artist. Finding lodging in South Kensington, he became acquainted with a number of young writers, poets, painters, and journalists. Among his closest friends was the budding novelist John Collier (1901–80). Nishiwaki seems to have held Collier in particularly high esteem, since he let him see some of the poems he had written in English. To Nishiwaki's dismay, they were utterly dismissed by Collier as too old-fashioned. In an obvious attempt to broaden his horizons, Collier introduced Nishiwaki to *The Waste Land* by Eliot, which was printed in the first issue of *The Criterion.* This was the first time Nishiwaki encountered a modernist text.

Shepherded by Collier, Nishiwaki soon went through a complete conversion from Keatsian Romantic to ardent modernist. The time was ripe, since every avant-garde artistic circle of London was fervently discussing the various schools of European modernism—dada, surrealism, cubism, expressionism, futurism. Together Nishiwaki and Collier would worship Pound, Eliot, Joyce, and Wyndham Lewis. They would study paintings by Van Gogh, Picasso, and Matisse. They would see the Russian ballet by Diaghilev and listen to the music of Stravinsky. At a bookstore that was reportedly also frequented by Eliot, Nishiwaki would buy as many recent publications on modernism as he could afford. The year 1922 also saw the publication of Joyce's *Ulysses*, a copy of which Nishiwaki promptly bought.[12]

In October 1923, Nishiwaki did manage to enroll at New College, Oxford, where he studied Old and Middle English literature. The year at Oxford was marked by several other important events. Nishiwaki went to Paris, where he had a chance to see many paintings by French impressionists. He completed a manuscript of English poems, from which "A Kensington Idyll" was published in the poetry magazine *The Chapbook*, no. 39. (Incidentally, the same issue included a poem by Eliot, "Doris's Dream Songs," an early version of "The Hollow Men.") On July 25, 1924, Nishiwaki married a young British painter named Marjorie Biddle. Nishiwaki was thirty years old; his bride was twenty-four.[13]

In August 1925, Nishiwaki published his first collection of English poems, *Spectrum*, through Cayme Press, London, at his own expense. The book elicited the following reviews:

> The sub-title of Mr. Nishiwaki's book is "The Sick Period: A Novel" and the patient is delirious throughout, as the following typical passage will testify:
>
>> Your prisms dance tropically on my curtain,
>> My purple jar and my Van Gogh chair
>> Guns guns guns of a gun
>> loneliness of existence
>> My soul was blown in flinders
>> I gather it up and blow it
>> Into your red-hot face
>> A pancake to your radiance!
>
> Such verse lacks the art either of sense or of nonsense, but we are relieved to hear, in a moment of coherence, that
>
>> The elastic
>> Of my old catapult
>> Is broken. (*Times Literary Supplement*, October 29, 1925)
>
> Mr. Nishiwaki seeks a standard manner capable of expressing, without modulation, any really modern thing from a cigarette to a fit of delirium. Many

possible plots emerge from his novel, of which the foremost is perhaps this: an Oxford undergraduate, finding that elephants and monkeys perambulate the streets of a place which might be Chelsea, goes to the seaside for a change, and is there obsessed by the belief that he is being maliciously prevented from receiving alcoholic refreshment. But here a warning note should perhaps be struck. It all might well be simply the interplay of symbols, and the book an account of England and war. (*The Daily News*, November 17, 1925)[14]

Nishiwaki also attempted to publish a collection of poems in French, entitled *Une montre sentimentale*, through a publisher in Paris, but was turned down.

What Nishiwaki accomplished in his brief stay in Europe is nothing short of extraordinary, especially when one thinks of the bitter and alienating experiences other Japanese writers, such as Natsume Sōseki (1867–1916)[15] and Takamura Kōtarō (1883–1956),[16] went through during their foreign sojourns. Nishiwaki seems not to have shared their "white complex" or "colonial complex." One might say that he was a self-created "foreigner" even before he went to England. He experienced neither the exoticism nor the blind adoration to which his fellow citizens were susceptible, nor did he fall victim to an inferiority complex vis-à-vis the West. Rather, he seemed to project a curiously "neutral" attitude toward the West, and perhaps more importantly toward the East as well.[17] The elusive Nishiwaki was, as it were, textualized by a "strategy of distance," which he was later to endorse as the essential mechanism of poetry.

Without taking a degree, Nishiwaki left Oxford and returned to Japan with his wife in November 1925. The next year, he became a professor of literature at Keiō University. He was assigned to teach Old and Middle English Literature, History of English Literature, Introduction to Literature, and Introduction to Linguistics.[18] He became acquainted with literature students who were soon to become the central figures in the development of modernism in Japan. The group consisted of Ueda Toshio (1900–82),[19] Takiguchi Shūzō (1903–79),[20] Satō Saku (b. 1905),[21] Ueda Tamotsu (1906–73),[22] and Miura Kōnosuke (1903–1964).[23] Takiguchi was so impressed with Nishiwaki's lectures in his English class that he initiated a study group around Nishiwaki. Satō recalls those days:

Every week after Professor Nishiwaki's lecture, it became our common practice to stay in a café in Mita and discuss poetry. We would only pay for a cup of coffee and stay on for a few hours. But that wasn't enough; we would invite ourselves to Professor's home in Tengenji and talk past midnight. Looking back, I am sure that we must have been a big nuisance, but he always looked glad to talk to us. His room would be filled with cigarette smoke and the light would look dimmed by it. On the desk there were foreign poetry books scattered all over: Lautréamont, Rimbaud, Breton, Goll, etc. We would look at the pictures of African sculptures and endlessly discuss theories of poetry from the ancient to the modern. We did this every week. (*Mita bungaku*, January 1955; quoted in *NJZ* 11:648)

In 1926, Nishiwaki began publishing important theoretical essays in Keiō's own literary journal, *Mita bungaku* (Mita literature). These essays were collected in his first major publication, *Chōgenjitsushugi shiron* (1929; Surrealist poetics). In December 1927, the first surrealist anthology in Japan, *Fukuikutaru kafu yo* (Oh, fragrant stoker), was published under Nishiwaki's leadership. The editor was Satō Saku; the contributors were Nishiwaki, Takiguchi, Ueda Tamotsu, Satō, Miura, and Nakamura Kikuo (dates unknown). Marjorie designed the cover. One hundred twenty copies were printed. With these publications, Nishiwaki was firmly inserted into the history of Japanese modernist movements that had already been flourishing for some time. Before going further with the history of Japanese modernism and Nishiwaki's activities in it, we should look at the primary texts: my translations of *Chōgenjitsushugi shiron, Ambarvalia, Tabibito kaerazu,* and *Eterunitasu.*

PART ONE

Translations

Surrealist Poetics

(Chōgenjitsushugi shiron, 1929)

Profanus

I

To discourse upon poetry is as dangerous as to discourse upon God. All poetic theory is dogma. Even that famous lecture Mallarmé delivered to some English students has become another trifling dogma now.[1]

The reality of human existence itself is banal. To sense this fundamental yet supreme banality constitutes the motivation for poetry. Poetry is a method of calling one's attention to this banal reality by means of a certain unique interest (a mysterious sense of exaltation). An everyday name for this is art.

Custom dulls the awareness of reality. Conventions let this awareness slip into hibernation. Thus our reality becomes banal. Then it follows that the break with custom makes reality exciting, for our awareness is refreshed. What we must note here, however, is that the bonds of habits and conventions are to be broken down not for the sake of destruction itself but for the sake of poetic expression. In other words, this act of destruction, with its consequential process of making reality exciting, must be committed in order to fulfill the aim of poetry. Yet poetry will not appear if in fact one breaks with custom and tradition *in actuality*. Such an act would belong to the field of ethics, of philosophy. Our habitual way of recognizing reality is through our ordinary feelings and reason. When we break down this ordinary order of feelings and intellect, our consciousness, sloughing off custom and tradition, succeeds in recognizing reality on a totally new plane. We all know that many critics have criticized this attitude, saying that modern poetry is keen only on destruction and never on construction of poetry. However, this destruction is in fact poetic construction. Without its destructiveness poetry would not gain creativity. Intellect recognizes reality through reason, whereas poetry recognizes reality by transgressing reason or even by disdaining it.

Pascal remarked that the one who despises philosophy is the true philosopher. Nietzsche also thought in the same vein.[2] Nietzsche believed that any tradition, no matter what great authority it may hold, should not be accepted. Poetic form is also a tradition.

In the nineteenth century, modern consciousness witnessed a conspicuous dissolution of poetic traditions. Baudelaire despised even ordinary people's sense of beauty or morality.

> I get feverishly intoxicated
> With the confused odors of coconut oil, musk, and tar.[3]

Such an expression used to astonish ordinary readers. But today an ordinary poet could easily come up with such an expression. Heine's poetry has become mere children's songs. Similarly, Verlaine's "Il pleure dans mon coeur" has come to represent a banal sensibility.

Human emotions possess a power to harmonize themselves. They move and act like weather. Then they vanish into nothingness. They harmonize with the existence of God. "God is the only being that does not require to be in order to reign."[4] We may discern here two types of harmonizing movement. At times one type moves centrifugally. It becomes scattered like autumn leaves, tattered like wastepaper, and finally returns to nothingness. At times the other type moves centripetally. Like a lens, it gathers the sunlight on a focal point and burns itself out. The former type can be seen in decadent poetry. The latter type is exemplified in *King Lear* or in what Baudelaire expresses as the *explosion* of the soul. In short, this explosion is what Baudelaire calls *l'émotion.*

"Thus, strictly yet simply put, the principle of poetry is man's aspiration toward superior beauty. And the manifestation of this principle can be seen in a certain enthusiasm, excitement of the soul."[5] What is meant by this "superior beauty" is a certain state that absolutely satisfies the human soul. Thus, it indicates a different notion of beauty from that which *la passion* seeks. It is different from Catullus's outburst, "Vivamus, mea Lesbia!" Baudelaire says that *l'amour* is a taste for prostitution.[6] He also writes: "For passion is *natural*, too natural not to introduce a broken, discordant tone into the domain of pure beauty, and is too ordinary and too violent not to shock the pure Desires, graceful Melancholies and the noble Despairs that inhabit the supernatural regions of poetry."[7] "One must always be drunk. That's it. Nothing else matters. . . . But with what? With wine, with poetry or with virtue, whatever you like."[8] Baudelaire knew that poetry had already lost its primitive significance, which was merely to sing out thoughts and feelings. This awareness marks the spirit of modern poetry.

One may claim that poetry is primitive. The nature of primitive languages was poetic. Humboldt says, "[Man] is a singing creature."[9]

This notion of poetry may be useful in discussing the origin of language but it is not the most distinguished idea where poetry is concerned. This notion of poetry could also be seen in what Lessing meant by *Liebhaber.* Mr. Garrod, professor of poetry at Oxford, once said, "It has become extremely difficult to compose a poem. A long time ago, when people wore their hair long, any utterance became poetry immediately."[10]

One may say, then, to represent life is poetry. Plato argued against this notion in the *Republic.* In terms of the expression of human nature, the first naturalist may well have been Homer: his heroes wail in the sand; the hairy Odysseus weeps on an isolated island, longing for his homeland. But this type of poetry, which is a mere copy of human life, did not please Plato. In all likelihood, it was as an attack on Plato's attitude toward poetry that Aristotle wrote the *Poetics.*

Aristotle argued that poetry is not merely a copy of human life, but rather that it expresses man's universal characteristics and tendencies. This theory delimits the mimesis of human nature and emphasizes human "probability," or "necessity."

Plato complained about the lack of critical function in poetry. Baudelaire, who later said "all great poets become, naturally and inevitably, critics. I pity those poets who are guided solely by instincts,"[11] was a *moraliste* like Plato. In general, Aristotle can be regarded as an instinctivist, who shared similar ideas with the Italian Renaissance thinkers and even with the naturalists of nineteenth-century France.

Aristotle located the origin of poetry in man's natural propensity toward imitation and the pleasure he takes in imitated products. This theory of poetic origin encompasses a field too broad to elucidate the characteristics unique to poetry. Other forms of art can easily be subsumed under it. His theory merely shows that poetry is a part of art.

At the beginning of the seventeenth century, Francis Bacon wrote "The Tvvo Bookes of the Proficience and Advancement of Learning, Divine and Hvmane" and offered it to the king. We find some elements of poetics in it. It is truly bizarre that his simple theory of poetry is perfectly represented in modern (twentieth-century) poetry (dada or surrealism). To be sure, his was a theory that was also evident in the metaphysical poets (to use Dr. Johnson's phrase) of the seventeenth century or even in Shakespeare.

Bacon was a poet. If not, he would never have been able to say such insightful things concerning poetry. It is true, as Poe said, that only poets can write poetics. Bacon himself was a poet. By the way, I would like to support the theory that conjectures that Bacon was in fact

Shakespeare. As a writer of theoretical prose, Bacon—more than Montaigne—was thoroughly logical, and there was nothing poetic about him. It is, however, impossible even to imagine an age in which Bacon's work will be forgotten.[12]

Poetry belongs to a mental process called imagination. This classification made by a Spaniard, Huarte, has been recognized as valid since antiquity.[13] But before Bacon, imagination was regarded as representing the abnormal side of poetry. Bacon, however, recognized it as the creative force of poetry. In this sense, he was a modern thinker. The same force was recognized by Coleridge and Baudelaire, as well as by Max Jacob.

Jacob states, "Imagination is nothing but the association of *idées*."[14] This is also noted in Dr. Johnson's criticism of "metaphysical poets": "the most heterogeneous ideas are yoked by violence together."[15] Fundamentally, therefore, imagination opposes what is called *le bon sens* or "common sense." The figure of conceit that appears in Shakespeare, Marvell, or Donne is the manifestation of a certain disdain for a logical manner of thinking. In the old days, imagination was called madness. Recent French poetry by Tristan Tzara, Jean Cocteau, and Yvan Goll demonstrates this technique of imagination. In order to create a metaphor or an association through this kind of imagination, a poet must join elements that are scientifically different in nature, or elements that are usually placed at the greatest distance from each other, temporally as well as spatially. Thus what he produces is an association absolutely impossible in terms of common sense. What Gourmont means by "dissociation" is this type of "association." Such eighteenth-century English poets as Dryden and Pope, who valued the common man, as well as poets like Horace and Boileau, taught ordinary folks to select and join images that are similar in nature in order to write poetry.

Although Dr. Johnson's words "the most heterogeneous ideas are yoked by violence together" were ironically directed against some seventeenth-century poets, they now appear to describe well the dominant technique of modern poetry. This very "violence" was what nineteenth-century poets called *l'émotion* or *la passion*, and it became an important element in the creation of poetry. Mr. Garrod called the mood of this type of poetic creation "a storm of association."[16]

Coleridge, influenced by the philosopher of association, Hartley, clearly regarded the act of imagination as the logic of poetry. In short, the force of poetic creation manifests itself at the point where two opposing images are juxtaposed, harmonized, and balanced. It is like the similar balanced against the dissimilar, the general against the particular, image against matter, the new against the old, ordinary reason against profound passion. After Coleridge, Shelley wrote, "[Poetry] makes familiar objects be as if they were not familiar."[17] For example, a familiar reality such as the mere sight of water flowing through a fountain is rendered by Marvell:

> . . . a fountaines liquid Bell
> Tinkles within the concave Shell.[18]

Similarly, Cocteau writes of the banal existence of the human ear:

> My ear is a shell
> That loves the sound of the sea.[19]

Presently in France there is a movement called *surréalisme*. This rather inclusive name subsumes members of what used to be called cubism or dada, who are now content to be under this name. Also there seem to be subdivisions within the group. André Breton, representing one faction, makes a remark about Pierre Reverdy, who belongs to another faction, with a touch of sarcasm. He claims that Reverdy's imagination is a posteriori. In other words, Reverdy's poetry is formed by associations of still homogeneous images. Of course, as a matter of theory, Reverdy writes:

> The image is a pure creation of the mind.

> It cannot be born from a comparison but from a juxtaposition of two more or less distant realities.

> The more the relationship between the two juxtaposed realities is distant and true [*juste*], the stronger the image will be—the greater its emotional power and poetic reality.[20]

What Reverdy means by *juste* and what Coleridge means by "balance" are the same. Breton is more radical than Reverdy. He does not think much about balance. Consequently, his poetic effects are indeed destructive.

In short, this idea of supernaturalist poetry has always been present in the works of great poets since antiquity and in fact is not particularly a new mode of poetry.

Imagination, however, is not poetry itself, but only a means to create poetry. People like Baudelaire assert that the aim of poetry is poetry itself. A British writer, Wilde, propagating the poetry of *l'art pour l'art* handed down from Gautier, actually believed in it until he died. "Poetry is art" simply means that poetry possesses a means to achieve its own end, and this means is commonly called art.

The previously mentioned importance of imagination for poetry similarly indicates that poetry needs imagination as a means to attain its own end.

What is the aim of poetry, then?

First, in primitive times, it was to express human thoughts and feelings through a "singing mode." Even now, some amateur poets believe this to be the aim of poetry. Aristotle thought that poetry must contain human universalities. It will not be poetry, then, if a doctor writes his medical journal in a "singing mode." At that rate, Lucretius could probably not have been called a poet. Théodore de Banville says that there is neither *poésie* nor *vers* except in singing, and emphasizes the importance of metrical composition.[21] It was Aristotle who judged the appropriateness of poetry in terms of the material represented. These traditions still linger on whenever we attempt to discuss poetry today. In short, the purpose of primitive poetry is to express human thoughts and feelings.

Second, there are points on which Francis Bacon's ideas on poetry coincide with those of modern poets. He writes: "The vse of this FAINED HISTORIE hath beene to giue some shadowe of satisfaction to the minde of man in those points wherein the Nature of things doth denie it, the world being in proportion inferior to the soule; by reason whereof there is agreeable to the spirit of Man a more ample Greatnesse, a more exact Goodnesse, and a more absolute varietie than can bee found in the Nature of things."[22] And poetry's method is to submit "the shewes of things to the desires of the Mind."[23] To translate the above into modern terms, poetry is the desire of man, dissatisfied with actual life, the desire "to transmute [reality] into forms more satisfactory to the mind."[24] This poetic spirit is well elucidated in the works of Rimbaud, who is regarded as the legitimate ancestor of the present-day surrealists. His poetry lacks the sense of actual things. Only a certain desire hovers over his texts.[25] Compared with this idea of poetry, Aristotle's theory seems like a photographic technique. *Laocöon* by Lessing likewise expresses a theory of artistic photography: "Je näher der Schauspieler der Natur kömmt, desto empfindlicher müssen unsere Augen und Ohren beleidigt werden."[26] What he says is that it is better to be a little blurred.

Rimbaud is now called by surrealist poets *apôtre* or *ange*. It is truly a curious phenomenon that Bacon's theory is explicated in Paris today.

This kind of desire is poetry.

Bacon's words "[to submit] the shewes of things to the desires of the Mind" point to the previously mentioned process of "imagination." In short, it is the conjoining of *idées*. To imagine is not merely to fantasize or to dream; rather, the act of imagination must be performed by force of intellect.

The majority of commentators on Rimbaud insist that his poetry is born from the unconscious or from dreams. I believe, however, that they are grossly mistaken. It is true that the surrealist technique of the joining of *idées* creates the extraordinary and projects oneiric forms of the unconscious. But poetry is not a dream. It is the joining of utterly conscious images. It has been said that poetry is thinking with *l'esprit*.

II

Poetry must be founded in reality. But it is also necessary to feel the banality of reality. Why does the human spirit feel the banality of reality? Human existence itself is desolate. I wonder if those dogs running around over there are feeling this banality. As one dissects the human spirit and reaches its very bottom, one finds the essential existence of this desolate feeling. We suffer, for we think.

With imagination poetry somehow transforms the banal reality for us. But in fact it is a very passive act, merely make-believe. There is no truly active being except God. Religion postulates a happiness of afterlife in order to console us for the banality of reality. This, however, is not poetry. Death or sleep would eliminate reality from our minds. But again this is not poetry. It is pleasant to immerse oneself in the world of ideas as Plato suggested. But neither is this poetry. Like some poets of the past, who indulged in alcohol or in opium, we may elude reality. But this is merely a matter of physics, not of poetry. Like Petrarch, we may grow peaches in the mountains and enjoy natural beauties. But that sort of life itself is reality and does not constitute poetry. Also poetry is not created by rebelling against reality, or conversely, by being enslaved and exhausted by reality. The consequence of this sort of act is, like Baudelaire, to end up being unable to escape from ennui, or, like a very lethargic dyspeptic, to end up announcing one's own end listlessly. These acts do not constitute poetry. After all, poetry appears only when we transform reality with our imaginations and, as Bacon wrote, receive some "shadow of satisfaction."

Reality overwhelms us endlessly. Even when we escape to the mountains, we encounter the soft eyes of a Japanese antelope and the roselike snow that torture our senses. Or let us suppose that, after managing a business in a desert for thirty-odd years, a man abandons his wife and goes to a distant land. But he would still encounter reality there—things like citron blossoms in bloom. Here we find the psychological bankruptcy of exoticists who long for foreign climes. We also know of classicism, which, fed up with the present reality, longs for the reality of the past. There are futurists who set their aims on the future as religions do. There is also demolitionism, which negates all and eventually collaborates with death in its own destruction. Yet poetry must acknowledge reality. It must persistently accept reality. Poetry is realism. Naturally, reality becomes unexciting by force of habit. It is as boring as dust. Poetry must continually refresh this boring reality. This is the task of poetry. Without this refreshment, the human spirit would never be able to accept reality.

Poetry must also acknowledge truth. But poetry is what transforms this truth by the power of imagination and then absorbs it into the spirit.

Poetry, therefore, is a method of cognition. By changing reality into unreality, truth into untruth, poetry is what absorbs reality and truth into the spirit. On the surface poetry may appear to be unrealistic and fictive, but in fact it cognizes reality and truth.

Poetry has been recognized as one of the scholarly fields Bacon categorized. In modern terms, we should rather say that poetry is a method of cognition. It is recognizing truth and reality by first transforming them to fit easily into the human spirit.

Some things of nature seem to get absorbed smoothly by the spirit without first being transformed. We read in the *Odyssey* of a breeze that "bears and ripens." This expression simply came about from a certain actual fact: that the Mediterranean islands grow fruits in abundance. But for the northern people, the expression appears poetic. Romantic love—a fragment of man's internal being—is also a wholly absorbable form. However, it is dangerous to turn such an easily absorbable piece of reality into poetry. This sort of act is like swallowing food whole. Eventually it will cause indigestion or some defect in one's poetic cognition. Some poetry, on the other hand, solely emphasizes the transforming of reality and consequently forgets reality itself. This tendency can be seen in some of today's dada or surrealist poetry. Such poetry degenerates into what Coleridge called "fancy"; or it becomes very similar to Poe's mystery tales or to the adventure stories one finds in children's literature.

The orthodox mode of poetry expresses reality through imagination by transforming it for the moment into a form easily absorbed by the spirit.

For example, in order to make a poetical recognition of the physical fact that the sky appears blue to the eye (a very ordinary fact, a banal reality), a poet would say, "your eyes of sky," whereas a primitive poet would have said simply, "the sky is blue," as a representation of the reality itself. The former shows a poetic transformation by a modern poet.[27]

Historically, this method of poetic transformation has changed its modality through the ages and through individual poets. It can, however, generally be divided into two categories.

In the first category, it takes a form that accords with the flow of human emotions. In this category, aesthetic sense becomes cardinal. In *The Golden Ass* by the Roman novelist Apuleius, the golden ass, wanting to become human again, picks a rose. The story tells us that it is impossible to neglect man's quest for beauty. According to "Grandpa" Gourmont, the quest for beauty stems from the principle of preservation of the species. It is the most common mode of poetic transformation of reality. It includes such beautiful images as Verlaine's sunset, Shelley's dawn, the shadow of saffron in Keats, Valéry's world like a ripened fruit, Cocteau's world like a golden watch, the pastoral aroma of Vergil, perfume of Baudelaire, beauty in Wilde that is like an artificial flower. The instances of this mode are simply as innumerable as the number of shirt-buttons in the entire world.

There is also a mode of poetic transformation that kindles *mono no aware* (sorrowfulness of things). It is to transform reality into a certain emotional fluid—somehow sad and lonely. A poet would sigh, "Ah, life is short," or "Love is vain." We can see this mode in many sonnets written right after the Renaissance—for example, Michelangelo's sonnets that were half religious and half sensual.

There are poets such as Musset and Lamartine who are themselves as fluid as a tragedy of the lachrymal glands.

Poor but noble Francis Thompson blows dandelion-fluff by the road. Villon was his great precursor.

Calling rural areas "inartistic," one comes to a big city, sits by a fireplace in a café, and reads aloud in a melancholy tone a swan song in Latin in the rhythm of the-moonlight-flowing. This type of poet can be seen in many English versifiers of the turn of the century.

Next is the most powerful mode of poetic transformation in this category: the fluid of love, instrumental in producing works of the greatest poets of the past, including Dante. For all its power, however, it exerted a bad influence on latecomers. When a poet was at a loss for words, he could immediately take recourse in the adjective *amoureux* in order to produce a poetic effect:

> Hâ que nous t'estimons heureuse
> Gentille cigale amoureuse![28]

Next, a sick person's listless feeling can invoke a flow of emotion with a certain pleasant feeling of convalescence. The examples abound in decadent poetry.

Next, the overflow of feverish emotions is seen in such works as Shelley's. In this case, it is for the most part a feeling of superiority that overflows.

Next, there is a violent passion that is like an explosion of the soul. A moment after the immense torrent has disappeared, only a clear and serene resonance is left. Together with the resonance, our feelings also flow away into eternity. This mode is well exemplified in Baudelaire's poetry.

Next deserving our attention is Wilde's search for the beauty of artificial flowers, rather than that of natural ones, along with Gautier's aesthetic notions, such as the beauty of geometrical lines, or the crystallization of the fluid beauty of colors.

The foregoing has listed the major modes of image transformation.

Poetry, being essentially a mode of singing, or being traditionally thought of as a mode of singing, has established musical rules of voice. This merely aids the mechanism of poetic transformation. It is by no means necessary for the production of poetry. Bacon says that it is no more than "elocution." Many other critics also generally do not regard *vers* as the fundamental essence of poetry. Of course, the melody inherent in words becomes helpful. In short, versification is merely a means to help poetic function. (In fact, recently the status of this old style of poetry writing has fallen apart. There are even a number of poets now who flatly disregard it, claiming that it is rather an obstacle to poetry writing.) Sentence structure and phraseology are also important elements in poetic expression. The English term "poetic diction" indicates a phraseological convention. Once I heard an anecdote in which a child at school was asked to state the difference between poetry and prose. His answer was that "blue violets" is prose, and "violets blue" poetry. In general, poetry has been written in a literary style. In England, the tradition of Milton's diction lasted up to the nineteenth century. Wordsworth attempted the use of "farmer's language," that is, colloquialism. But at that time, of course, his attempt failed. Verlaine simplified the literary language. He put an end to the embellishing of rhetorical language. Later Apollinaire undertook the use of street-language. Osbert Sitwell, disdaining tradition, published a pamphlet propagating the use of "today's language" in poetry.[29] But there are also people who think that it is wrong to use street-language or today's language. They insist that instead a conversational style rarely used by ordinary people should be employed. A poem is not a school composition. In short, traditional rhetoric has been completely explained by Demetrios, who said that it is good to use "beautiful words" that "appeal to the eye and the ear." At the end of the first half of the nineteenth century, Hunt complained that the younger generation's writing style had become prosaic because of the young people's indolence.[30] Hunt's complaint indicates that the breakdown of traditional style was already showing symptoms in his time.

The foregoing has outlined the tradition of poetic transformation up to the end of nineteenth century, subsumed in the first category. Of course, there are many outstanding exceptions.

The second category posits a transformational method contrary to that of the first category. In the first category, as we have seen, poetry is considered an attempt to transform reality in harmony with the flow of innate human emotions. The second category calls for a rousing of the intellect, which tends to hibernate in customs and conventions, by startling it or even intimidating it so that the attention of the intellect can be totally monopolized. Since ancient times it has been said that art "startles." This statement points to a most powerful type of poetic cognition. Its method is first of all to break away from customs, that is, psychological, intellectual, and formal conventions. Many of today's poets employ this method. There are critics who call them mere destroyers. However, it is this very destructiveness that contributes to genuine poetic cognition. Now I will attempt to outline the major methods of poetic destruction.

The first is to smash the habitual consciousness, which is usually called "common sense" or "logic." In order to achieve this, one must join concepts that keep the farthest associational distance from each other. This method is the same as what Bacon meant by saying "to surprise with the unexpected" and is the same as Rimbaud's so-called unconscious method. One can see the method employed abundantly in the works of today's dadaists and surrealists. Many of them, however, are interested only in the method as such and tend to ignore reality, the recognition of which is crucial. They are confusing ends with means. Works of a group represented by Breton and Paul Eluard, together with German expressionism, share a weakness.

> the world
> a ring made for a flower
> a flower flower for the bouquet of flowers flowers
> a cigarette-case full of flowers
> a small locomotive with the eyes of flowers
> a pair of gloves for flowers
> of the skin of flowers like our flowers flowers flowers of flowers
> and an egg[31]

The above is a section of Tzara's poem. The last line astonishes us by its abruptness.

Reverdy, who was called a cubist some time ago, wrote: "In the brook, there is a song that flows."[32] Regarding this line, Breton wrote that it shows "the slightest degree of premeditation."[33] It can be assumed that the line indicates a type of unconscious state.

The second method of poetic destruction is to break down conventional feelings and ideas (ordinary aesthetic sensibility, morality, logic, etc.), or to disdain them, and present an ironic critique of them. Baudelaire's poetry represents this technique. Rimbaud also offers a good example:

> Supple as the Lord of the cedar and of hyssops,
> I piss toward the dark skies, very high and very far,
> With the consent of the large heliotropes.[34]

He is showing his disdain not only for our ordinary moral sense toward God but also for our habitual aesthetic sensibility. The exhibition of his disdain is, however, merely a device of expression. First it startles our hibernatory intellect and makes it aware, and then directs our attention to the existing beauty of reality. By using, as it were, a "bluff" of pissing into a flower, it poetically directs our attention to the reality of the beautiful evening sky and the blossoming heliotropes in the forest. Unlike naturalists, Rimbaud is not interested in the fact of pissing itself. A few years ago, James Joyce wrote a book called *Ulysses*. It was also another example of "bluff." In short, the breaking down of conventions is not the end of the method of poetic expression. Rather, it is its means.

We find very few examples of the above type of poetic expression in modern English poetry. Even when one does find them, they tend to lack gravity. In one of Rupert Brooke's prewar poems, we may find a trace of it, though still not intentionally produced:

> Just now the lilac is in bloom,
> All before my little room;
> And in my flower-beds, I think,
> Smile the carnation and the pink
> And down the borders, well I know,
> The poppy and the pansy blow . . .
> Oh! there the chestnuts, summer through,
> Beside the river make for you
> A tunnel of green gloom, and sleep
> Deeply above; and green and deep
> The stream mysterious glides beneath,
> Green as a dream and deep as death.
> —Oh, damn! I know it! and I know[35]

So he cried out in a café in Berlin in May 1912.

In "The Poetic Principle," citing his own poem "The Raven," Poe argued for the validity of mysticism as a mode of poetic expression.[36] But his kind of mysticism still belongs to the previously discussed first category. It merely exploits man's curiosity in order to draw his attention. It is just like Dante's use of human lust. Mysticism, handed down from Dante to Blake, eventually died in Maeterlinck. There are, however, instances in which mysticism grows extremely intense and eventually turns into something almost like the "grotesque" to be found in Baudelaire or in Stramm.[37] Jean de Bosschère's work, generally labeled *symbolisme malsain*,[38] shows this tendency:

> I was a green kid
> and bitter like husk.
>
> . . . .
>
> The hat of my father was sacred.
> Sure, there were other fathers
> But this one was the only one

Who was such and such.
He smoked his pipe with integrity.
People got really close to him
In order to draw out his human odor through his nose.
. . . .

And my mother was bread and butter
The chilled rosé wine of six o'clock and the cherry.[39]

It seems appropriate to place T. S. Eliot in this group also. In his *Waste Land* mysticism has become more conspicuous than in the poems of his *Blast* era. In "Death by Water" we read:

Phlebas the Phoenician, a fortnight dead,
Forgot the cry of gulls, and the deep sea swell
And the profit and loss.
                        A current under sea
Picked his bones in whispers. As he rose and fell
He passed the stages of his age and your
Entering the whirlpool.
                        Gentile or Jew
O you who turn the wheel and look to windward,
Consider Phlebas, who was once handsome and tall as you.[40]

Showing contempt for formal conventions also belongs to the second category of poetic expressive methods. In France *vers libre* has existed since the time of La Fontaine. It became rampant in the symbolist era. "Free verse," however, has not yet outgrown the conventional "singing" mode. It has merely reduced to a minimum the restrictions imposed by the traditional metric conventions.[41] Therefore, many of today's poets do not use any regular metrical system at all. Their works have become prose, so to speak. It is a great mistake to apply the term "free verse" to this type of writing. On the other hand, theirs is a significant effort to write poetry without resorting to any established prosody, for it shows a conscious effort to go against man's natural tendency to sing out, or against his natural emotional rhythm, and to create an effect of "bluff." Today, those who criticize prose poetry are the ones who do not understand what true poetic expression is. There were times when we called poems without punctuation "cubism." The elimination of punctuation is another instance of "bluff." Today, most of the young French poets employ this poetic style. In the first issue of a surrealist periodical edited by Yvan Goll, we read: "Until the beginning of the 20th century, it was the EAR that decided the quality of a poem—rhythm, sonority, cadence, alliteration, rhyme—all for the ear. Since about 1920, the EYE took its revenge."[42] What so-called imagists have done is nothing but to disregard the "ear." All poetic expressions belong to "imagination." Thus, the name "imagist" is inappropriate.

By postulating two categories, I have attempted to elucidate the psychological motives of poetry. The second category was mainly intended to explicate the psychological operations of poetic cognition unique to twentieth-century poetry. Of course, this does not include the future. It is valid only up to about 1920.

In Herman Bahr's *Expressionism,* we find a discourse on expressionist painters and poets who seek the unprecedented in their works.[43] But when the past has gained enough distance from the present, it returns as something new. It is possible that the ear may again take the place of the eye. The mode of poetic cognition belonging to the first category may someday regain its power over that of the second category.

Poetry is cognition. Its method changes with the development of man's intellect. Man's soul is prone to hibernate in conventions. The noble effort of poets consists in calling back the hibernating soul to the realm of consciousness by means of an ever-renewed method.

A kind of absolute existence, whether it is expressed as God or as infinity, flashes through our consciousness for an instant. The absolute existence, by reflection, makes man's existence insignificant. Then the petty soul of man explodes against the insignificant, boring reality in anger. This is the poetical spirit, elsewhere named "emotion." The spasm of temper disdains reason and becomes "imagination." Through imagination the banal reality becomes interesting. For our consciousness of reality has been renewed. Such is the purpose of poetry.

It is dangerous to discuss poetry. I have already fallen off the cliff.

The Extinction of Poetry

A notification from my friends, Judge Contomen and the cellist, Dobron

It would not be well that all men should read the pages that are to follow; a few only may savor their bitter fruit without danger. So, timid soul, before penetrating further into such uncharted lands, set your feet the other way.—*Isidore Ducasse*

❦

CHAPTER ONE: THE LIMITS OF EXPRESSION

I. It becomes merely subjective and eudaemonistic to evaluate poetry solely by its contribution to the pleasure of the soul (see *Critique of Practical Reason* by Kant). It becomes necessary, therefore, to postulate a theory, or a hypothesis, if one desires a more rational way to evaluate poetry. One may, then, like a legislator, treating this hypothesis as a guiding principle of justice, take the liberty of instituting laws *one after another.*

II. A hypothesis: The realm of poetry expands infinitely and finally disappears. As a corollary (ipso facto) of this hypothesis the following rule is set forth:
   "The most expanded, the most advanced mode of poetry is that which is closest to its own extinction."

III. The extinction of poetry as art occurs when there is no longer any indication of a will to express. "Indication," in turn, means an act of expression. When there is an act of expression but no will to express, the result will not be an artistic expression. Therefore, natural expression is not art. For instance, the following acts of expression are not artistic expressions. They are nature itself:

   A. The act of expression as in the sound caused by the friction of leaves in a breeze.
   B. The "expressive act" of the sun emitting strong colors and rays of light.

C. The "expression" of a dog emitting a cry when beaten.

D. The act of bursting into song due to an overflowing emotion of love. Note: similarly, the "expression" of all other emotions belongs to nature. It is a kind of excretion (the same as the European euphemism "Nature calls").

E. Such an expression as "Oh, Good Heavens!" uttered by Indo-Europeans when they are in trouble. (This shows a case in which a custom has gained the same status as a natural phenomenon.)

F. Expressions manifested in a dream. Dreams such as we read in Baudelaire's *Les paradis artificiels* show a relatively well-developed artistic mode of expression. In short, the book says that if you eat that green jam, you can dream anything you wish.

No expressive acts belonging to any of the above categories are to be acknowledged as artistic. In flat terms, expressive acts become "legally" artistic only when they are intentionally carried out. Therefore, unconscious expression cannot be art; it is merely a blind, unconscious emotion itself. Moreover, just as conscientious objectors are sometimes exonerated from the usual legal obligations, in the poetic legal system, when an author believes that what he has thought or felt is true, he will be exonerated from the obligations of art. In other words, his work will not be considered art.

> The long convulsive sobs of an autumnal violin
> injure my soul with a certain monotonous languor.   —Verlaine[1]

This is a natural expression; it lacks deliberateness. Verlaine is an extremely "conscientious" expresser. His work cannot be "legal." His expressive act lies outside the laws of art that we have established. Neither Goethe, nor Verlaine, nor Valéry can be classified as a "legal" artist. However, the following text shows something different:

> One evening, the soul of wine sang in the bottles:
> "People, to you I send, oh dear disinherited,
> From my glass prison and my vermilion wax,
> A song full of light and brotherhood.
>
> "I know what it takes, on the hill aflame,
> What effort, what sweat and what scorching sun it needs
> To give me life and to give me a soul;
> But I will neither be ungrateful nor harmful.
>
> "For I feel immense joy when I fall
> Into the throat of a man exhausted by his work,

And his warm chest is a nice tomb
Where I am much happier than being in my cold cellars."[2]

This is an excerpt from a poem by Baudelaire, first published in *Le magasin des familles,* June 1850. Readers at that time must have felt much more distance from such a poem than today's readers would. At any rate, Baudelaire's expression here does not seem to be of a kind that came forth naturally. Even the title ["Le vin des honnêtes gens"][3] sounds contrived and exhibits an act of expression deliberately performed rather than a direct expression of actual feelings and thoughts. It is a deliberate act of expression. If the author has actually felt or thought what he depicts, he would not be classified as a "legal" artist. He would merely be one who expresses natural feelings and thoughts. Today, perhaps we no longer feel the "deliberateness" and find only "natural" feelings and thoughts in this poem. But if we go back to the time of its first publication, we can see his "deliberate" mode of expression. A few more examples:

Lace and roses in the forest morning shine,
Shrewdly the small spider climbs his cobweb line.

Dews are diamonding and blooming faery-bright.
What a golden air! What beauty! Oh, what light!

It is good to wander through the dawn-shot rye,
Good to see a bird, a toad, a dragon-fly.[4]

If the poet thinks that it is *actually* good to do the things described above, his expressions cannot be artistically "legal." Since he says them deliberately, they become "legal." In Rimbaud's poetry one can find many instances of the "legal" expressive act.

In a poem by Soupault we read:

If you knew if you knew
The walls close in
My head becomes enormous
Where the lines of my paper disappear

I would like to elongate my arms in order to
Shake the Eiffel Tower and the Sacred Heart of Montmartre
My thoughts dance like germs upon my brain
In the rhythm of an exasperated pendulum
A revolver's shot would be such a sweet melody.[5]

When the resounding noise of the pistol in this poem actually can be felt and thought of as a gentle melody, the expression becomes sentimental, thus not artistic. To say such a thing intentionally becomes the reason whereby the expression can be, artistically speaking, "legal." In sum, artistic expression is a demonstration of the will to express "deliberately."

IV. Poetry appears in various modes from its birth (the manifestation of a will to express intentionally) to its extinction. They can be categorized as follows.

The First Period: The Era of Expression

The poetic mode of this era probably includes the range of poetry from Baudelaire to cubism, metaphorism, and surrealism. Dadaism merely anticipated the oncoming Second Period before itself becoming defunct. Futurism definitely belongs to the First Period.

The Second Period: The Era of Antiexpression

In this period, the poet manifests a will that shows his deliberate wish *not to express*. In the First Period, poetry was still an effort to express, whereas in the Second Period it is to *make an effort not to express*. Good examples of this poetic mode have not yet appeared. But I believe they will soon come out. In terms of expression, this era shows the extreme limit and the most expanded, most advanced mode of poetry. (Tristan Tzara's work still belongs to the First Period. Obviously his poetic spirit has not been firmly established consciously. But in the future, historians will regard him as a prophet. He published *La première aventure céleste de Monsieur Antipyrine* in 1916 and *Manifeste dada* in 1918. He has also published several books of poetry. You, young Rumanian, who wear a conspicuously colorful tie, behold John, whose head has been made a plaything by Salome.)

The Third Period: Extinction

The Third Period is the time when one does not make any manifestation in the form of the First Period or the Second Period. Consequently, the "legal" expression of art disappears. An extinction, however, must always be preceded by a birth. In other words, it must be born before it dies. It should not be confused with those that do not come into existence in the first place (for example, the poetry of Verlaine, or Maeterlinck). Another point that should be noted with regard to the Third Period is "La soirée avec Monsieur Teste," written by Paul Valéry in 1896. At first glance, his treatiselike work may appear to be promoting the extinction of artistic expression. But in fact it merely says "it is illogical to express feelings." In short, he wants poets to express a mature intellect. Thus, the mode of poetry he proposes does not belong even to the First Period (for he is, at any rate, such a perfect symbolist poet). Let us read what he wrote: "Mr. Teste was perhaps about forty. He spoke extremely fast in a muffled voice. In him, everything faded away, his eyes, his hands. He, however, had military shoulders and his regularized footsteps were amazing. When he spoke, he never lifted an arm nor a finger: he was like a dead puppet. Neither did he smile nor say hello or good evening. He looked as if he didn't know the words 'Comment allez-vous.' "[6] So he writes. But he has not even arrived at the birth of the "legal" act, not to mention the extinction of poetry according to the "law."

With regard to the legal system in the artistic sense discussed above, the following summary can be drawn:

A. Prelegal era: description (Goethe—expressionism)
B. Legal era:
   1. Expressive period (dadaist—surrealist)
   2. Antiexpressive period (X)

CHAPTER TWO: THE LIMITS OF THE OBJECT OF EXPRESSION

I. Reality as an Object of Expression

Any phenomenon related to any desire associated with human nature, whether innate or acquired, may become an object of expression. In this case, one may say that humanity is the object of poetic expression. This, however, is not a "legal" expression. Such an expressive act is subjective and relates to the notion of happiness. It is totally illogical. Humanity is the object of expression in the prelegal era. Here are some examples of such illegal objects of expression:

A. To have matters of aesthetics (feelings or thoughts that seek either beauty or nonbeauty) as the objects of poetic expression. The material that manifests them merely expresses beautiful or not-beautiful reality. When it comes to a poet like Gautier, the material of expression became constituted solely by the lines and colors of objects. Jean Cocteau uses metaphoric expressions as the material of his poetry. Expressionists employ any material that is new, such as dynamics, geometry, and philosophical mathematics. However new the material may be, as long as the poetic expression still seeks either beauty or nonbeauty, it belongs to the prelegal era. Beauty or nonbeauty merely belongs to reality. Reality is subjective, and thus illogical.

B. The desire to become human or a flounder, or the desire to become a machine or superman, is subjective, and thus belongs to reality.

C. The desire to live as intuitively as possible. The desire to do only instinctive work as a plant; or to oppose such a desire.

D. The desire to express musical moods, or the beauty of noises, or the spirit of silence, or a jazzlike soul.

E. Feelings and thoughts that seek truths, lies, eternities, or moments.

F. The desire to break down reality, or the desire to be immersed in reality.

G. To have the desire to express or not to express as the object of expression.

All other human subjective thoughts and feelings belong to reality. Thus, to have them as the objects of expression belongs to the "illegal" era.

It is not good at all to confuse the object and the material of expression. The object of expression itself does not change, while the material changes with the progress of the human intellect. Goethe, expressionists, cubists, surrealists of the bad sort, after all, are all realists. The only difference is in the material of expression, namely the mode of expression. Their objects of expression are homogeneous. Today, most of the surrealist poets in fact still remain realists despite their label. Indeed, they are the epigones of realism. For example, Yvan Goll's recent work, not to mention his *Die Unterwelt* period,[7] still belongs to realism despite its label of surrealism. Poets like Picabia and Eluard are also epigones of realism. They are in a transitional period leading to true surrealism. This transitional period has developed from Baudelaire through Apollinaire and Reverdy to recent poets like Soupault. These recent poets still seem to belong to the transitional period, although their poetry lacks the direct expressions of despair or of ennui that we find so abundantly in the poetry of Baudelaire. At least Soupault's object of expression is surreal. Reverdy used to be labeled a cubist, but recently one frequently sees him writing for the magazines of the self-styled surrealists. His poetry seems to liquefy reality and let it flow into the air in abundance. In his *Les epaves du ciel* and *Ecumes de la mer*, we read:

> Goodbye I fall
> Into the gentle angle of arms that receive me
> From the corner of my eye I see everyone drinking
>   I dare not move
> They sit
>   The table is round
> And my memory too
> I recall everyone
> Even those who are gone[8]

or

> In the nook of woods
> Someone is hiding
> One could approach without noise
> Toward the void or toward the enemy[9]

As for Valéry, the last symbolist, one finds a surrealist demand in his attitude toward realism. His "Introduction à la méthode de Léonard de Vinci" is an artistic pronouncement deserving our attention. It manifests a kind of spiritual struggle distinct from Maeterlinck's silentism.

The expressive attitude that holds reality as the object of poetic expression is subjective, and thus illogical. This attitude is in fact very destructive. In order to have a more constructive attitude, one must reach for more objective logical principles of art.

II. Surreality

Here one must posit the objective (a priori) will itself as the object of expression. The objective will (see *Critique of Practical Reason* by Kant) is the force of the will that aspires to its own *perfection* by breaking down the subjective world (that is, reality). It is like assuming the mode of God. It is to be *free* from the subjective world (reality). This type of expressive method of art (or the material to be used in expression) manifests an expression that is contrary to (*alienus*) our realistic feelings and thoughts. Since such an expression as "A revolver's shot would be such a sweet melody" opposes our ordinary actual feelings, it can be suitable material for expressing the force with which the objective will destroys subjectivity. But once this phrase begins to express any actual feelings, it is no longer suitable as material to manifest the objective will. In December 1924, a magazine called *La révolution surréaliste* appeared in Paris. In its introduction, the editor urged us to use dreams as the material for poetry. This may be plausible because dreams are foreign to our actual feelings and thoughts. One may simply argue that surrealist poetry is a poetry that strives to manifest an energy whereby a blind will to be alive forever attempts to become perfect by demolishing the actual world. The will to live is the will of a creator. Man is helpless to deal with this blind will. This absolutely unmanageable will exists objectively in man. The mere existence of such a will, which is so utterly beneath contempt, is the subject of helpless rage. At times one may feel physically throughout one's brain the startling jolt of an esprit that attempts to resist this blind will. This is a strange phenomenon in which an attempt to rebel against a will that created the human race is manifested. It is a rebellion against the creator's will. Or it can be said that in fact the real creator holds a will that seeks to oppose his own creative will. A creator is a self-deceiver. The poetry that attempts to present the energy of an esprit rebelling against the very effort to live, that is, the effort to break down reality, creates the next poetic region.

III. Antisurreality

Poetry of this category is closest to its own extinction. It is also a highly advanced and expanded mode. When the will to live is destroyed in actuality (not in poetry), mankind will perish. It will also mark the extinction of poetry.

IV. The Extinction of Poetry

Poetry dies as mankind dies. The lamp is turned off. But things like kangaroos or cactuses may be still trying to survive, fidgeting here and there. How pitiful.

CHAPTER THREE: A CRITIQUE OF POETICS

The adage *Ars longa* is merely a children's song. It only appears on the surface that art creates. In fact, art is an effort at self-extinction.

*　*　*

So they scribbled down such simple remarks on the corner of a post-card and mailed it to me from an express train between Paris and Budapest. Every Sunday they go to Budapest for a walk. Such an ordinary custom is boring.

Esthétique Foraine (A Critique of Pure Art)

I. PREPARATION FOR THE CRITIQUE

The twilight of anemones descends. Under a purple opera-lamp, a distressed racketeer leans against the marble Aphrodite and grieves. Sometimes he feels a thirst for some soda pop but does not move. He just grieves in loneliness.

A. Divisions within our consciousness (*Bewusstesein*) with regard to art:

1. The world of empirical consciousness.
2. The world of pure consciousness.

Art belonging to the first division is here defined as impure art, and that which belongs to the second division as pure art. The former is a method of constructing the world of empirical consciousness. The latter is a method of constructing the world of pure consciousness.

B. Epistemologically speaking, impure art empirically operates with sensory intuition (*Anschauung*) and so creates a world of actual sensation that holds an intensive magnitude within.[1] In short, it creates a world of actual sensation, that is, reality, whereas pure art *anschauen* purely, thus creating a world in which the degree of actual sensation is zero.

C. "Art is expression" means that art expresses methodological mechanisms for creating the worlds stated above.

D. Impure art creates an empirical consciousness of the self, whereas pure art creates a world born at the instant when the empirical consciousness expands itself to its own extinction. In other words, it is to create the instant when the consciousness of the self disappears. Baudelaire somewhere described this state as the divine and sublime *insensibilité*. It can also be described as the joy of the self merged with the universe, or that of being divine, or that which Poe finds in his cosmology, or that of Neoplatonism found in Claudel's poetics. Of course the pleasure of this state is only poetically sensible. Viewed from a psychological standpoint, when the consciousness of the self disappears, one becomes devoid of senses. This state itself, therefore, cannot be sensed as either pleasant or unpleasant. One may, however, actually sense the joy a moment after this state has passed. In short, pure art is a method of creating the joy or the beauty of this state.

E. Art is a method whose purpose is the creation of beauty. In terms of impure art, then, one creates a state similar to the world of actual sensation, in which one feels the beauty of actual sensation. In terms of pure art, one creates a state in which the world of actual sensation has vanished. Such a state lasts only for a moment. The next moment will bring back the world of actual sensation, and in it one feels the beauty of the state that existed a moment ago. In short, in pure art, one creates a state in which the world of actual sensation has vanished. Paradoxically, however, one does so in order to feel the type of beauty that must be perceived by the actual senses. What Baudelaire meant by "sublime beauty" is probably the beauty of actual sensation.

F. It is an epistemological mistake to talk about the beauty of actual sensation, or the beauty in which there is no actual sensation. Since beauty is nothing but a sensation, it always belongs to the world of actual sensation. Aesthetics studies the world of actual sensation as its subject. It is absurd for an aesthetician to say "pure beauty" or "the pure mode of beauty." Purity of beauty requires the disappearance of the actual sensation of beauty. Yet it may be possible to admit the concept of purity as a principal formula for constructing beauty, or as a state in which the intensive magnitude of beauty has increased to its maximum limit. Also, it is absurd to say "to purely *anschauen* beauty," for beauty is produced through the operation of empirical *Anschauung*. It is possible, however, to *anschauen* a material phenomenon or a mental phenomenon either purely or empirically.

G. Teleologically speaking, art has the aim of arousing aesthetic sensations. One cannot create art merely by announcing one's ideas and feelings. The aim of both pure and impure art is to arouse aesthetic sensations. If a natural phenomenon arouses an aesthetic sensation, then it is a "divine art" (Coleridge). A beautiful apple is a work of art by God. If man himself is God's work of art, then a work of art created by man is a certain development from it. Beautiful aspects of social phenomena are, then, social art. Macaulay says that art declines as civilization progresses. Ruskin disliked locomotives. Prudhomme said something to the effect that the beauty of windmills and sailboats is good because the force of nature is associated with it (Guyau). But as long as a product makes the beholder sense beauty through its expressive method, it deserves to be called a work of art (according to Croce).

H. What fundamentally distinguishes pure art from impure art is their mechanisms. In impure art, a mechanism to construct aesthetic sensations exists in the object expressed in the work, whereas in the object expressed in a work of pure art, there exists a mechanism that *does not allow* any construction of aesthetic sensations. In other words, the mechanism to construct aesthetic sensations *does not exist* in pure art.

Let us suppose "A is B" is a poem that exhibits a theory of pure art. In this case, the following critiques become possible:

1. Viewed from the standpoint of impure art, the poem appears comical. There is no aesthetic value in it. In terms of aesthetics, it can be said that it fails to construct beauty, for aesthetics most often deals only with impure art.

2. Viewed from the standpoint of pure art, it appears to express neither a thought nor a feeling that is "A is B." Therefore, it can be said that it belongs to the antiexpressive era.

3. It is not a metaphorical expression in which A is compared to B.

4. It is neither comical nor ironical.

It can be claimed, however, that it is an attempt to construct a mechanism to break down the world of reality and to enter momentarily into the world of pure consciousness. It exemplifies a theory proposing that empirical consciousness can be destroyed by means of the conjoining of two objects that stand at the farthest distance from each other on the axis of associational relation.

In a poem in which Baudelaire worships Satan,

1. he does not express thoughts or feelings of actually worshipping Satan;

2. he does not present sarcasm for the sake of sarcasm.

He worships Satan simply to construct a mechanism for transcending reality. When he says that the essential nature of art is the supernatural and irony, we are given an external explication of this mechanism. In actuality, usually our feelings toward "Satan" and toward the image of "worship" are directed to two opposing ends. Thus, by conjoining these two, it is possible to construct a mechanism that breaks down the world of actual sensation. Viewed from the standpoint of impure art, however, pure art may appear sarcastic, comical, and not beautiful. Champfleury says, "Since Baudelaire knew from the beginning that so few souls would understand this perfect comedian, he kept *Les fleurs du mal* from publication for fifteen years."[2]

I. Thus, pure art turns an a posteriori aesthetic world into an a priori world. In this sense, this type of art is purely a priori.

J. In the relation between the beauty aroused by pure art and that aroused by impure art, the former becomes the first cause of the latter. Thus, the former is the fundamental beauty (see Kant's *Critique of Pure Reason*). This type of beauty is difficult to find in material phenomena. It may be something like "an infinite, still unconstructed pleasure" as Poe describes it in *Eureka*.[3] It may be described as an unknown beauty or a minimal beauty. It is almost certain that the mechanism of impure art cannot produce such beauty. Moreover, this type of beauty has rarely been dealt with in aesthetics. In modern times, probably Poe's *Eureka* and Claudel's *Art poétique* are among the few aesthetic theories that deal with it. (A digression: I wonder if Plato's philosophy presents not an epistemology, as is commonly thought, but rather a mechanism to construct this type of beauty. It may well be so.)

K. Like criticisms in the other arts, the principles of literary criticism hold the following duties:

1. To distinguish between pure and impure art.
2. To establish a value system as a standard of criticism.

    a. The value of pure consciousness: as a work of art makes the state of our consciousness approach more closely the extinction of its empiricalness, the work of art increases its value as pure art. It is a value in a negative mode.

    b. The value of impure art: as a work of art moves the state of our consciousness farther away from the extinction of its empiricalness, the work of art increases its value as impure art.

L. The extinction of poetry is merely a figure of speech intimating a method of purifying poetry. Pure poetry is a mechanism that aims to construct fundamental beauty by making the world of actual sensation extinct. The vanishing of the world of actual sensation is, therefore, only its method.

M. The constitutive factors of the mechanism of pure art:

1. In the aesthetic realm, to conjoin two distant elements of empirical consciousness.

2. A powerful survival force. An *excessive force* that seeks beauty is required. Without this force the mechanism of pure art ends up merely having a comical effect.

N. By means of the above methods, empirical consciousness vanishes. At the moment of its disappearance, what Poe calls "an infinite, imperfect sense of pleasure" appears.[4] The qualification "imperfect" indicates the existence of an empirical consciousness that is unclear and impossible to express. If, however, the sense of pleasure should become perfect, the consciousness becomes no longer pure but empirical. In a word, it is *joie*. *Joie* is of course an ordinary sense of pleasure. Thus Baudelaire says somewhere that a sense of pleasure does not belong to beauty, for, of course, Baudelaire's beauty is that of pure art. The definition of art as a sense of pleasure is valid. But the sense of pleasure evoked by pure art is different in nature from that evoked by impure art.

O. The "infinite and imperfect sense of pleasure" may be the sense of beauty one finds in the Buddhist world of nirvana or in the Christian heaven. In this sense, pure art becomes identical with what religion seeks. Although one may admit that pure art and religion have an identical end, one will find that they possess different mechanisms. Religion is nothing but a mechanism, just as art is a mechanism. Then what is the mechanism of religion? It is "faith." But with the development of science this important mechanism of religion has become fundamentally invalid. This opinion forms an important factor in the literary criticism of Professor Richards at Cambridge. Only art is still possible. Of course, from Ruskin's standpoint, art becomes impossible with the progress of science. It may seem that art is also following the demise of religion. But pure art holds absolutely no relation to science; thus, it is not to be persecuted by science.

P. To sum up, pure art is a mechanism that abolishes the world of empirical consciousness, or the world of *moi*. The extinction of the world of *moi* can be translated into ordinary terms as the extinction of the self, that is, the infinite expansion of the self. It is the self merging with the universe, thus forming an infinite mode of itself (see Claudel's cosmology as poetics in *Art poétique*). The psychological impression of this extinction may be the faint sensation of an obscurely infinite pleasure as one momentarily loses one's empirical consciousness, or one's sense of existence. We may experience this state of mind when we look at some excellent Buddhist paintings and statues. In my opinion, they definitely belong to pure art.

Q. Going back to the field of literary and art criticism, we may observe that the recent trend in European art criticism has begun to see pure art as holding the true value of art. Looking at works of art themselves, and more specifically at poetry, we find Baudelaire's poetry as a forerunner of pure art. Of course it is plausible to see the influence of Poe and Sainte-Beuve on Baudelaire at the level of ideas. Poe's poetry, however, did not develop into pure art. Although Baudelaire's poetics in his "Théophile Gautier" seems almost a copy of Poe's poetics, his thoughts found in "Journaux intimes" form a true manifesto of pure art. Poe's poetics is so similar to that of Coleridge, the leader of the English Romantic movement, that it cannot escape being regarded as a case of plagiarism.

R. Pure art is a mode of art that inevitably develops from impure art. Impure art generates the world of empirical consciousness and deepens it by stimulating it. It is commonly thought that art makes us appreciate our life more profoundly. This merely reflects a view from the standpoint of impure art. It is natural for impure art to hold that its ultimate goal is to stimulate our empirical consciousness as much as possible. But if our minds receive too much stimulation on the empirical side, we will, in fact, feel melancholic or lonely. In other words, the psychological state of melancholy or loneliness is the state in which our empirical consciousness is stimulated to an extreme degree. It is the case in which the world of empirical consciousness is losing its equilibrium. In order to control this imbalance biologically, we cry, shedding tears. When we see or feel something beautiful, we certainly feel a sense of loneliness. Sometimes it even leads us to tears. A work of art that controls such imbalance can be regarded as an instance that shows a biological genesis of pure art. It is what Baudelaire calls *hygiène*.[5] As a clinical psychology, it establishes pure art. In the case of Baudelaire, it is like suppressing a poison with another poison. It is a type of bacillus therapy. Therefore, pure art is effective only on those who possess a world of *moi* that has become unbalanced due to a highly developed sensitivity. Conversely, impure art is effective for those who seek stimulation because of the dullness of their sensitivity. In short, this is the biological origin of impure art. For these reasons, it must be theoretically recognized that pure art holds a greater sensitivity than impure art. The above is a further explanation of section M.

II. THE MECHANISM OF PURE ART

A. In order to explain the mechanism of pure art, I shall first discuss the world of empirical consciousness as a possible aesthetic realm. Let us look at the diagram drawn by Zeising (?) (based on Hartmann's history of German aesthetics).[6]

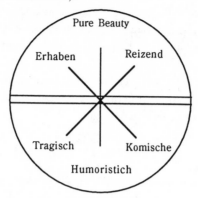

The upper and lower hemispheres represent the two opposing empirical realms. If we use algebraic terms, they can be said to represent the realms of plus and minus. In terms of dynamics, they represent the positive and the negative energy forces. When these two forces are joined, a certain harmony is created. In terms of algebra, it can be demonstrated as $(+) + (-) = 0$. Theoretically the mechanism of pure art suggests this synthetic principle. It creates a harmony in the realm of sensibility. In other words, it postulates a state in which the realm of senses has vanished. Baudelaire calls this state "divine numbness," or more sentimentally, "supreme beauty." Baudelaire's aesthetic system postulates the following theoretical factors.

To the positive realm belong such elements as God and beauty. To the negative realm belong Satan, evil, prostitution, and other grotesque elements. By joining two opposing elements, one constructs the first mechanism previously discussed in section I, subsection M. Evil becomes simply a constituent of this mechanism. By means of the workings of these elements, one constructs "the extinction of empirical consciousness," which is the aim of pure poetry. In other words, it is a construction of an infinite self. "The taste of infinity is all manifested in Evil itself," says Baudelaire.[7] The meaning of this saying is well explained in his poetry. He was interested neither in representing evil nor in enjoying it as an actual sensation. He simply incorporated evil as a constituent into the mechanism so as to create an infinity of the self. Let us call this infinite self "God" for the moment and define it as a metaphor representing the zero degree of the empirical consciousness. God is a world devoid of empirical consciousness. Spinoza explained the notion of God in terms of geometry: "God does not possess passion. Therefore, he is not affected by either pleasant or unpleasant emotions."[8] Baudelaire calls this nature of God *insensibilité*. He also says somewhere that poetry is an emotion that does not hold passion as its aim. Such thinking clearly indicates that his poetry belongs to pure art.

B. We have seen that the mechanism of pure art involves the joining of two distant elements. In geometrical terms the mechanism can be indicated by the summit of a triangle.

In aesthetics generally, this diagram is used to demonstrate a constructive principle of beauty. It is necessary, however, to distinguish the triangle from that which is employed in aesthetics to illustrate forms and rhythms of material phenomena. In short, the triangle does not represent a unifying principle of manifoldness. In general, aestheticians apply the form only to the world of empirical consciousness. The diagram here, however, is simply intended as a metaphysical symbol.

1. The concept of pure art described by the diagram concurs with Pythagoras's aesthetic theorem.

2. After Pythagoras, Alexandrian philosophers showed their belief in such a concept.

3. Then Scholasticism inherited the concept.

4. Francis Bacon, after praising Seneca's words, "Bona rerum secundarum optabilia; adversarum mirabilia," wrote: "We see in needle works and embroideries, it is more pleasing to have a lively work upon a sad and solemn ground. . . . Certainly virtue is like precious odors, most fragrant when they are incensed or crushed."[9]

5. Coleridge says that imagination reconciles opposing and discordant qualities.[10]

6. The poetic mechanism found in seventeenth-century English meta-physical poetry employs such imagination.

7. Shakespeare's poetic genius is also based on the same mechanism of imagination (see *The Background of English Literature* by H.J.C. Grierson).

8. Paul Claudel in *Art poétique* says that in a pine forest he thought of a new theory of cosmic construction, which is the very operation of two op-posing elements conjoined and existing simultaneously. So he shouted out that the shining sun was the apex of a triangle. He writes, "Truly blue knows the color orange, . . . truly and really the angle of a triangle knows the other two in the same sense that Isaac knew Rebecca."[11] This illustrates the mechanism of pure art by using two opposing colors. After all, Claudel wrote his cosmology as a treatise on pure art.

As the above examples show, the concept of pure art has come down to us from the ancient past. From this point of view, therefore, one must claim that today's dadaism is firmly founded on classical aesthetic theory.

C. The construction of the mechanism of pure art: the joining of the negative and positive worlds.

1. The joining of two discordant qualities—Coleridge.

2. Coleridge specifies imagination as the joining of the two most associa-tionally distant elements. Poe writes in his "Marginalia," "The pure imagi-nation chooses, from either Beauty or Deformity, only the most combin-able things hitherto uncombined."[12] But Poe's theory is still vulnerable. He had to say "combinable," for he was still dealing with the art of the expres-sive era, an art that attempts to express a certain object. A Greek teacher of rhetoric in his treatise on metaphor posited a theory similar to Poe's.

3. The construction of the mechanism of pure art involves the breaking down of the world of experience. In other words, it involves the act of as-tonishing just as it is manifested as an important aspect of Baudelairean art. Of course this act of astonishing is not carried out merely for the sake of astonishing someone; it is produced simply as a result of the mechanism of pure art. Why does the breaking down of the world of experience construct the mechanism of pure art? Because experience belongs to the world of em-pirical consciousness.

4. The construction of the mechanism of pure art involves the breaking down of the world of common associations. This breakdown is accom-plished by the method of joining two distant qualities.

5. Bacon calls the effect of this mechanism "unexpected."

6. The unexpected, in turn, produces mystification. In fact, mystification is an impression of the unexpected.

7. In Baudelaire's poetry, both his Satanism and his irony contribute to the construction of the mechanism of pure art.

8. Contrary to Poe's theory, the construction of the mechanism of pure art involves the juxtaposition of "uncombinable" things, without any regard to their interrelations. In "The Philosophy of Composition," Poe writes: "Beauty of whatever kind, in its supreme development, invariably excites the sensitive soul to tears. Melancholy is thus the most legitimate of all the poetical tones."[13] So he concludes: "When it most closely allies itself to Beauty: the death, then, of a beautiful woman is, unquestionably, the most poetical topic in the world."[14] Among as yet "combinable" qualities, beauty and melancholy may be considered comparatively "distant" ones. But seen as elements of the mechanism of pure art, they are still imperfect. Today, such subjects as beauty and melancholy seem cheap and banal to us. Poe's aesthetics belongs to impure art; it merely explains a mechanism of stimulating the world of empirical consciousness. We have already discussed how melancholy is produced by giving aesthetic stimulation to the world of empirical consciousness. In short, Poe's poetic world is that of actual sensation. It was with Baudelaire, therefore, that the modality of art shifted for the first time from the old mode of art to which Poe still clung. In Baudelaire's aesthetics, art no longer aims to present the world of actual sensation. Aloof from reality, he presents a mechanism that joins utterly "uncombinable" elements. The mechanism of pure art can be compared to parallel lines that intersect at an infinite point. In elementary geometry, when two straight lines do not intersect on a plane, they are said to be parallel. But when we introduce the notion of infinity to our consideration, it may become possible to think of parallel lines intersecting at an infinite point. Thus, pure art holds infinity as its object. Poe's poetry is still finite. (Although he cries out the word "infinite" often, when we look at his poems, it becomes clear that his poetry still stands in the world of empirical consciousness.) In contrast with Poe's, Baudelaire's aesthetics belongs to higher mathematics. Poe's is that of junior high school. Pure art is to impure art as higher mathematics is to elementary mathematics. In sum, one must recognize pure art as a higher mode of art. Next, one must note that it is possible to suggest parallel lines that intersect in infinity by using the parallel lines of elementary geometry. The juxtaposition of two elements that never meet characterizes the mode of art that has developed from Baudelaire to dadaism.

D. Pure art is supernaturalism. This, however, does not mean that supernaturalism opposes scientific natural phenomena or human nature. It simply means that pure art as an artistic mechanism transcends

empirical consciousness. By means of this transcendence pure art ful-
fills its aim. In the final analysis, what is meant by supernaturalism is
the construction of a mechanism that breaks down the world of experience or of actual sensation. In terms of the ethical concepts Baudelaire
so habitually uses, the natural becomes "vulgar." Thus, passion, which
belongs to the natural world—the world of actual sensation—becomes
vulgar. A concept that opposes the natural is what Baudelaire calls "artificial." It follows that the artificial is noble and aristocratic. Baudelaire calls the artificial the "Dandy," and the natural, "woman."
Woman is vulgar and the Dandy aristocratic. We must, however, note
here that Baudelaire praises the Dandy not because he actually feels
that the Dandy is praiseworthy but merely in order to explicate the
mechanism of pure art. After all, any poem that expresses actual and
natural feelings is vulgar (see Baudelaire's essay on Heine). It is as an
inevitable development from Baudelaire that surrealism has become a
prevalent mode of art in recent years. In the final analysis, surrealism
and supernaturalism are the same and share a classical tradition of art.
Surrealism transcends reality defined as *Empfindung* in terms of empirical *Anschauung*. In other words, surrealism reduces the degree of empirical consciousness to zero. Surrealism, therefore, must share the
same aesthetic operation and purpose as Baudelaire's aesthetics.

Although in the first issue of *Surréalisme,* edited by Yvan Goll,
someone claims that the term "surrealism" was invented by Apollinaire
and himself, the spirit of this pure art is a classical one. The following
is an outline of the tradition of pure art:

1. Plato (see *Phaedrus, Symposium*, etc.)—his notion of poetry as madness.

2. Horace: with regard to madness, refer to his *Ars Poetica*.

3. Bacon: Poetry recites things that are manifold, full of changes, and
sudden (that is, unexpected). He says, "There is no excellent beauty that
hath not some strangeness in the proportion."[15]

4. Baudelaire (see his ideas on poetry found in various parts of "Journaux intimes").

a. The mixing of the grotesque and the tragic is pleasant to the
mind.[16]

b. Two fundamental literary qualities: supernaturalism and irony.[17]

c. Molière. In my opinion, *Tartuffe* is not a comedy but a pamphlet.[18]
. . . The glory of a comedian. . . .[19]

d. I don't say that joy cannot be joined with beauty, but I say that joy
is one of the most vulgar ornaments.[20]

e. Things that are not even slightly deformed have the air of insensibility. Then, it follows that irregularity, in other words, the unexpected, surprise, astonishment are the essential parts and characteristics of beauty.[21]

5. Mallarmé: Art is hyperbole.[22]

6. Tzara's dadaist method.

7. Breton's group: surrealism, dream.

8. Aristotle: One should avoid using idiomatic expressions as much as possible and should adopt, as it were, the style of a foreign language (in the *Rhetoric*). (In general, I believe that the ancient Greeks produced excellent literature. Our writing should never become like a composition. Schoolteachers' writings would never do.)

In simple terms, these proverbial words suggest methods of constructing the mechanism of art, as well as actual sense impressions that one receives from the mechanism. They are not expressing, however, the authors' emotional or theoretical truths.

E. Pure art and aesthetics.

Aesthetic theories in general have dealt almost exclusively with empirical consciousness. Thus, it follows that the mechanism of pure art blocks the operation of such an empirical aesthetic notion as empathy as defined by the aesthetician Lipps.

F. Pure art and the theory of rhythm.

Pure art rejects rhythm. It does so not because rhythm is not beautiful, but rather because it is beautiful. Due to its beauty, it is an inappropriate material with which to construct the mechanism of pure art. Poe, being an elementary artist in his poetry, of course valued rhythm. At first glance, Baudelaire's poetry may seem to value rhythm highly. Compared with the works of later symbolists, however, Baudelaire's poetry exhibits a lack of the desire to "sing." His poetic rhythm is thus rather prosaic. He had the throat of a medieval monk.

G. Expressionism (impure art) requires a mechanism that asserts the subjective self, whereas supernaturalism must possess a mechanism that abolishes the self. Supernaturalism does not merely express supernatural phenomena, nor does it express the Deus ex machina (see *The Homer of Aristotle* by David Samuel Margoliouth). In order to abolish the self, one must abolish the constructive elements of the self. "Cogito, ergo sum" can become "Percipio, ergo sum." Thus, one must construct a mechanism that does not allow *percipio*. Since *Wahrenehmung* belongs to empirical consciousness, in order to avoid *percipere* one must transform empirical consciousness into pure consciousness.

H. The object of expression in pure art is nothing but the mechanism that generates pure consciousness. Only the mechanism has to be expressed. Pure consciousness itself cannot be directly expressed, for it exists in our psyches. Once it is expressed, it is no longer pure consciousness. On the other hand, impure art is able to express empirical consciousness directly. Thus, it is possible to distinguish pure art from impure art by the nature of the object of expression. Although the objects expressed in Baudelaire's poems are elements, or mental phenomena, that belong to empirical consciousness, we must treat them as constituents of the mechanism of pure art in order to form a valid aesthetic criticism. Someone like Anatole France seems to lack so thoroughly any sense of pure art that his criticism becomes laughable. For example, France said, "Baudelaire is a very bad Christian," and "As a human being, he is despicable."[23] These words exhibit a criticism directed at the exterior of Baudelaire's poetry, or at his life. Baudelaire's life was, however, solely constituted by an activity called "poetry." In short, we may say that his poetry and life formed a certain aesthetic mechanism; his "life" and "poetry" are not to be equated with his true self. This becomes clear when Baudelaire says, "They condemn me for all the sins I merely wrote about."[24] In the same vein, in an appendix to "Marginalia," Poe made fun of some Shakespearean critics. Poe argued that they do not take Hamlet as a mechanism within a play, but take him as an actually existing ethical being separate from the play itself. Both France's criticism of Baudelaire and the above criticism of Hamlet commit the fallacy of biographical criticism. A critic named Séché said, "Baudelaire had a fictitious Baudelaire on the surface of the true Baudelaire. He hides behind the former."[25] This fictitious Baudelaire was indeed his art, that is, his mechanism of pure art.

I. Works of pure art.

Works of supernaturalist art do not directly express the "joy of spirit" that is born out of pure consciousness. They merely possess a mechanism that generates pure consciousness. A work is a mechanism—a machine. In literature, if the reader does not know how to operate the machine, he will not be able to appreciate the work. A producer of pure art simply exhibits the machine. The reader operates it as he wishes and categorizes it as decadent, comic, or nonsensical. The machine is so delicately built that even its manufacturer is not able to explain how to operate it. After all, only the manufacturer is able to use it. Thus, there is no other way of appreciating pure art than to become its manufacturer. It is impossible to comprehend it fully unless one constructs it. Pure art manufactures such a mysterious pipe organ.

III. RHETORIC

A. It is not an animal with lanky legs. A singular blond man runs, holding the belly of a crucian carp, grazing the side of an angelic sergeant who holds an apple and a saber in a field where pansies bloom. We define a lady who comes out of a lump of cheese with her shoulders bared as allanpoépoépoépoé. A dragoon cavalry soldier, who is cooling off his back inside a sponge, takes a smooth, unused pipe out of his tightly sealed palate, and with his party shoe smashes his temple where melancholy is precipitated. It rings like a seven-string harp. Outside a café, a gluteus maximus breathes like a pearl. A pair of narrow glasses, a forest, and two hands guide his vest and comb by inserting a tube into a transparent stratum that has accumulated on a piece of stake. Stuffing a petunia in the ear, pointing at the center of heavens, I let people take a picture of me as I was coming out to a fruit orchard, after lifting a handle of the back gate of the Vatican, but I found myself in the yard of a bottle collector. Courbet. After stuffing a bottle with bread and cigarettes and pulling it up to the library clock using a pulley, we do not pass under it. But I put my head through a hole I made by breaking the stained glass with my head, and look out. There is no one to blow a steam-whistle. Only a chef is running, holding an ornamental hairpin. A barber, who was late for the final judgment, is kicked out of the cathedral with the resounding sound of the pipe organ, and jumps onto the twilight. But he left his wool vest behind, so he goes back in there to retrieve it. As I move to the beach on foot, I find it boring to see a sailor's pink eyebrows or coal tar reflected on my silk hat. So I give it away to a woman. The sky is still pagodite. The skulls of trees are not as alive as one may want to drop God's colorless boots upon them. Gilded breasts of Aphrodite. Upon a golden rain tree, I pitch a tent and pretend to be an icteric. Since there isn't a barber nearby, it feels weird to have saffron growing down my temple. As I run into a house, a gentle man is sleeping soundly on a billiard table. He doesn't know that the earth has become a grape seed, or that his friend with golden buttons is waiting for him outside with his sailboat. Dawn is a wanderer. The sun is not the task of raisin bread. Although it is the noon of a spring field as beautiful as the label of vermouth, as Anacreon blows his horn, the fat torso of evening descends. And Mephistopheles was actually a champagne cork. Water flows through a marshmallow flower. I lie down wearing a pair of narrow black satin pants and enamel shoes. A bird neck is unloosed. Dolben.

    B. Greek rhetoric finally had an amazing development.

Ambarvalia

(1933)

LE MONDE ANCIEN

The Song of Choricos

O Muse, arise.

Of late thou hast been submerged too deeply in Poesy.

The music thou blowest forth reaches not the Abydos[1]

May the curve of thy throat be the heart of the Abydos.

GREEK LYRICS

Weather

On a morning (like an upturn'd gem)[2]
Someone whispers to somebody in the doorway.[3]
This is the day a god is born.

Shepherd in Capri

Even on a spring morning
I hear the noise of autumn
In my Sicilian pipe, retracing
The longings of thousands of years.

Rain

The south wind brought a soft goddess,
    moistened the bronze,
    moistened the fountain,
    moistened the wings of swallows and the golden hair,
    moistened the tide,
    moistened the sand,
    moistened the fish.
It quietly moistened the temple, the bath, and the theater.
This serene procession of the soft goddess
Moistened my tongue.

Violet

Though the cocktail-maker is a poor penny-shaker,
The Greek mix makes a golden noise.
Try a bar called "The Grey Violet."
As the blood of Bacchus and the nymphs' new tears are mixed,
A life, dark and immortal, frothing,
Emits an aroma
With a flounder as large as a wheel.

The Sun

The countryside of Karumojin produces marble.[4]
Once I spent a summer there.
There are no skylarks and no snakes come out.
Only the sun comes up from bushes of blue damson[5]
And goes down into bushes of damson.
The boy laughed as he seized a dolphin in a brook.[6]

Hand

The spirit's artery snapped, God's film snapped—
When I grope for the darkness of lips,
        taking the hand of inspirited ether
        that still dreams within the withered timber,
A honeysuckle reaches out
        spreading fragrance on rock,
                killing a forest.
A hand reaches for a bird's neck and for the twilight of gems—[7]
In this dreaming hand
                lies Smyrna's dream.[8]
A rosebush flaring.

Eye

July, when white waves pounce upon our heads,
We pass through a lovely town in the south.
A quiet garden lies asleep for travellers.
Roses, sand, and water . . .
Heart misted by the roses.
Hair engraved in stone.

Sound engraved in stone.
The eye engraved in stone opens to eternity.

Platter

Long ago when yellow violets bloomed,
Dolphins lifted their heads
    toward the heavens and toward the sea.
A boy sailed across the Mediterranean Sea with a gem merchant,
Washing his face in a decorated platter
In which
Dionysus sailed, dreaming
On a sharp-pointed ship adorned with flowers.
That youth's name has been forgotten.
Oblivion's glorious morning.

Chestnut Leaves

As pea-flowers blossomed
Our eyes grew narrower.
The night came.
The fish and I all slept.
In the whispers of chestnut leaves
I hear Maud's voice.[9]
A nightingale is singing.
The day is dawning.
My head becomes the shadow of a rose upon marble.

A Glass Goblet

The luminescence of a white violet,
Its light travels around a peninsula
And the world of my ring sinks into the darkness
—laughter from a wooden cup.
A pointed flower opens between the toes,
And the white hands held out
—now hidden within a ray of light from a pansy—
Embrace a goddess.
Image shifting into image,
Her cheek in the spring of a glorious mirror reflected
On a glass sycamore leaves reflected

On her blue shaven eyebrows
Polyanthus flowers reflected
On a gem tears reflected.

When the day goes out to the ocean
And the night enters the land,
Thy hair turns invisible.
Thy hand is reflected on every window.
Bliss, Carman.[10]

The woman of bliss strolls[11]
Within thy words.
They are the unopened morning of May.

The Head of Callimachus and Voyage Pittoresque

I

To the sea, to the sea, to the land of Tanagra,[12]
But exhausted,
Stealthily like a jewel thief
I landed on an unknown land and took a rest.

My smoke rose
And wafted into a garden where amaryllis bloomed.
An aborigine's dog shook its ears violently.

This is the land where
The cries of plovers and dogs echo loneliness.
Water splashes over gemstones.
Reminiscence and sand undulate.

Let it be known that this is a terra-cotta dream.[13]

II

I was following after an eternal light
That ran along the angles of a gemstone, or
Reading Aeschylus in search of gods and heroes,
Forgetting the "cycles" of time,
Playing neither a flute nor pipes for a long time,
I climbed up the tree of knowledge in a classroom filled with a
    worldly smell.
I went out to a town, went through a town,

Into a forest where warblers used to sing.
My heavy heart and legs wandered afar.
Leaves awoke like amaryllis,
Put their fingers on my shoulder, as if to whisper.
My heart moved smoothly like a tiger.
O 'tis autumn, Callimachus!
Thou, woman of candle,
Makest swell the hazelnuts and the cheeks of shepherds
With thy flame and fragrance.
When a golden wind rocks thy stone,
Bless me.

LATIN ELEGIES

Elegy

Rose, thy color is sorrow.
My hair trembles.
At this sunny noontime, a breeze undulates.
A starry ring trembles.
My heart also trembles with an invisible star.
Kalos tethnake meliktas.[14]
Red lilies, *tamarix*, blue violets, the smoke from Mt. Aetna,
All adorn the altar with the waves around the isle Asteria.
This neck under the sunny sky, this sleep of summer,
This Ptolemy[15] breathes among the grass and flowers of summer.
His dream blows out music that curves along
The echo within the shell of Triton.[16]
His eyelids atremble in dream,
The spirit is breathing in the golden climate.
Thou, the season of mists and ripened fruit,[17]
Once more, return to summer,
And cast the marigolds moistened with icy stars
On the lips numbed by a slumberous eternity
And the whispers of dolphins.[18]
His silent longings, like a silent gem,
Quietly play the pipes from the Dorian Sea.[19]
His thoughts form a silent gem.
The sound of his pipes drops a silent gem.

His sleep is a silent gem.
He left the Seas of Albion and those of clamorous Hibernia
And still lives in the Sea of Doria.
This morning, I lament the sea.

rosa, color tuus est murex aurora doloris,
ah! mota aura, ista tremitque coma.
ecce, dies medius tranquillus sparsit flatum;
ventum potantes astra tremunt calices.
atque meum vertit cor cum astris aestivis,
                    —kalos tethnake meliktas.
fragrans ara in asteriae undis est facta;
aetna colit, tamarix et vapor et viola.
en! dormit pulchrum caput tempestatis crudae,
en! ptolemaeus ita spirat in auriculas.
cantitat quem calamum palpebram quae tremit ample;
gemma serena gelae est sua mundities.
mens ejus melos est umbra tritonis pictum;
acta abducta, murmurat oceanus.

LE MONDE MODERNE

A Fragrant Stoker

David's duty and his jewels pass through between Adonis and legu-
mina and rush toward their infinite extinction. Thus, behold! How the
smooth *quercus infectoria*[20] frolics, leaning against the magi who generally came from the east.

In a collective sense approximately very purple and extremely justifi-
able postponement! Velázquez and game birds[21] and all other things.

In an effective era when kingfishers gabble, viewing the Acropolis in
the far distance,[22] what refreshes the nails and stretches the infantile
legs is not in a single walnut but is above a single ragman's head.

Continuously bless the water buffalo that attempts to climb up a
maple tree!

When someone tries to call out to me by hitting the palate, I try to
leave the scene furtively. But again there are some people who throw
coins into the mouth. I try to shout, but my voice is merely a visit by
Angelico.[23] I kneel down, yet eternity is too noisy.

I saw someone showing his ankles from a colorful gable. I called out
and asked his name. As expected he was a cook from Sicily.

As I descend the embankment, there is someone who blows my
neck like a flute. It is my servant. Thou must immediately return home
and love thy wife!

There is someone walking under the wisteria trellis. Hey, that's not
a passageway.

Or there is someone behind the curtain holding up his hand over his
eyes, but sleep is rosy-colored and merely something like a vine.

I put on my necklace, violently light my pipe and run to a wheat-
festival.

For I solemnly push my chin out of the water. I hide the *kariroku*.[24]
A man who holds a wild pink within a cylindrical house!

It is not to make a public speech about a lampshade, but it is an
attempt to write a note with regard to an envoy. It is to pull the legs
of an atrophy patient as a gillyflower,[25] who is taking a rest leaning
against a window as music.

O god of procreation! May you create a cliff in front of a somnambulist! The fire of oleander flowers.

Smothered by pink eternity, one is about to fish. When the bishop
Benbo[26] whispers like a woman, a gondola glides.

Thou, sudden flower of acacia! I drank eau de Cologne.

Farewell death!

On a Friday that possesses a virtuous continuity, when I am about to
go to a view-point after offering a water pipe, since there is someone
up on the bridge calling me, hurriedly I raise my legs completely upon
the ambrosia. All is a chin. Man attempts to be perfect just like a chin.
I wrap a forehead that smiles without rest in velvet.

I call the servant as soon as the melted cosmetic gets in the eyes.

From the tower toward a chicken cutlet the brain shudders eternally. Soon again someone knocks my head with an apricot. There is
someone reflected on a vase. That's the heel of Pietro who just came
back from dinner. I try to see this with some pity, but my eyes are too
amarante.[27]

Come, fire.

A Picture Card Show, Shylockiade

Prologus:

Whispers from my eyes reflected upon a hazelnut, are they known
as the shadow of the evening sun blowing at a spring in hell?
A woman lies down in the grass, burning.
Will her tears reach the distant land, dripping?
My two eyes are two Apollos.
The grief of Apollo has disappeared into the grass.
Ye, begone. The play has ended.
This morning I kindled some violets and warmed my cold
necklace.
The warm crystal is the dream that longs for thee.
Ye, return. The play has resumed.
The northern Saxpere misunderstands mine history.[28]
I am the one who tells the true mythos.
But, Aristotle and Plato, ye begone.
Dionysus also is no more than a dream in the fields.
Behold my golden tongue that swears by the Sphinx and
Aristophanes.
Shepherd, thou shalt also fly over the sea. Be the dream of El

Greco's saint, together with Sappho and purple seaweeds.
Both the Renaissance and a Celtic milkmaid are merely
digitalis[29] and a will-o'-the-wisp. There is also the story of
Troy, but it is no more than a blind man's light reflected on a
   sycamore leaf.
My musicians do not know people like David or celestial
musicians or Orpheus or Scheherezade or Stravinsky.
My dancer is a Tartary illusionist, and someone like the
Northerner Mars is merely a drunken beggar.
My theater curtain is heavier than St. Peter's Cathedral, but
its movement is lighter than the breath of the sleeping Adonis.
And its fragrant beauty is superior to the dusk that envelops the
   city of Cairo.
Ye, who blow out dandelion-fluff that grows at the wharf of
   Carthage,
Ye idlers, throw away the roasted chestnuts and applis[30] and hurry
   to my theater.
My memories shiver like anemone in my heart.
My language is not Dorian but Altaic and has a mixture of
colloquial and literary styles just like the poisonous monkshood
   herb.[31]
Ye, classroom-compositions, take flight. But the fact that
ladies, like wild boars, love this poisonous herb is an eternal
   custom.

Shylock:
   Accursed Venice, yet as a storm is gradually calmed,
   my mind has become quiet now.
   Rather, I can send off my breath to Venice with a smile.
   I can even play a gondola, as if playing a mandolin.
   Those who frolic with economics are also far away now.
   Legenda Aurea[32] is all a lie. I am the one who murdered
   Antonio. Taking Jessica with her jewels, I escaped to
   this city of Carthage that resembles one large gemstone.
   "Sin is born out of embracing a woman." This saying
   soaks my heart like April rain. There was a time when I threw
      away
   all my treasures like beer-froth into the ocean, sailed up the
   Nile and cried with Jessica as we leaned against a pyramid.
   I also worshipped the Sphinx with the sun. Its eternal riddle[33]

turned out to be water.
I intend to throw away a gem named Jessica also into
the ocean someday. My "Punch and Judy" play that collects
money from the sailors of Carthage is my sustenance, but
this also I intend to throw away into the water.
Hélas, hélas, hélas![34] Now the tragedy of King Oedipus[35] is
about to begin. Jessica, blow thy horn.

Jessica (ventriloquy):
    (Oedipus)[36]
    Antigone, child of the blind man. What land is this? What
    people, what city's gate have we reached?

    (Antigone)
    Oedipus, my father, I see a beautiful city in the distance.
    This must be the place to worship the gods. There are
    blossoms on the laurel trees, on the olive trees, and on the
    grapevines. Among them, many nightingales are flying and
    singing. Because you have trudged so far to reach here, you have
        aged much.
    Upon this rugged rock, stretch your legs
    and take a rest.—

The Ghost of Antonio:
    I was listening intently to the whispering sound that came
    from here, thinking that it was from the Nile;
    but it was thee, Shylock. Hast thou fled the Venetian laws and
    survived? Thou, accursed Shylock.

Shylock:
    O methought, around here, 'twas the shadow of an ephemera,
    the wings of a swallow; but then, 'tis the ghost of Antonio.
    Thou, the enemy of Jews, dost thou still desire a piece of
    flesh? I have already dried out thy flesh like sugared dates
    and tricked a Sicilian shepherd into eating it.

The Ghost of Antonio:
    I did not come here to claim my flesh. Hand me thy daughter
    Jessica. I was the first to have an eye on her, earlier than
    that youth Lorenzo. My melancholy was not born of the
    oriental trade but of thy daughter.

Shylock:
    Thou, Naturalist. I had no idea that thou possessed such a
    sweet soul. But I still intend to throw all my treasures
    into the water, rather than offering them to thee.
    Hélas, hélas, art thou the one who is followed by an
    ephemera?

The God Jupiter (as deus ex machina):
    Shylock, thou shalt be an abalone. (Shylock dies.)
    Jessica, thou shalt be a breeze and visit my garden.
    (Jessica dies.)[37]

Paradis Perdu

GENESIS

Behind the chemistry classroom
a singular object,[38] a talipot palm,[39] is growing
without emitting any resounding noise.
The chalk and the corn-floss vibrate.
As if it were midnight, every spring is boiling.[40]
Everyone prays that his own soul won't be like that.
He passes across a wooden bridge,
smoking a Golden Bat.[41]

Still an old pencil is left.
By a single[42] large river teeming with salmon,
we, Fouquet and I, lay down like two snakes.
A lone poplar tree was clamorous like a woman.
A mountain made flaccid by mulberry forests flowed into our eyeballs,
as it played on a pipe about the love in our hearts.

We talked about France,
and again returned in the direction of our European lamp.
Oh, what a beautiful old brush!

Further from the honeysuckle-covered house of Miss Aeschylus,
but near my house, an honest man
sounds his steam in order to investigate a smoke pipe that is to be
    repaired.
All my friends have moved beyond the railroad crossing.
There you will find a photograph of Thomas Caldy,[43]
also a very large muslin floor-cushion,

and a kerosene heater.
And on the desk, there is a perennial blue[44] and
a practically CRUSHED pocket watch.

But I
will purchase the surface rights
on the slope of a little hill
pulled by various mechanics and kindergartens,
and I will construct for myself
a dangerous rattan chair.

It is still pitch-black.
My toes bump against the trunk.
The icy chill of the air knocks against the trees.
Turkeys announce the arrival of the sun.
Wearing a woolen shirt, a turkey farmer chops wood.
Extremely frugal.
An old-fashioned aurora opens its rosy fingers.
When I open a shabby window,
I see a singular[45] garden as narrow as my hallway.
The soapy water dripping from the chicken coop
assassinates my imagined cactus flowers.
No fountains exist there.
No wrens, no lawyers, no cigars.
Neither are there the reliefs of choirboys by Luca della Robbia.[46]
There is nobody in the heavens.

The city of lilies is also far.
I only close my eyes before a mirror.[47]

JOURNAUX INTIMES

There is one fresh bicycle.
A singular[48] Isarago[49] man has become a commission salesman of
    soap—
soap that is soft and has arteries and speckles and is scented.
In order to advertise it, he strikes a gong.
This *ding-ding-dong-dong* is the afternoon of shepherds living in my
    birthplace.[50]
Within a piece of sweet bread,[51]
my soul forms a Persian carpet, one profile, and one mint leaf.

It is bad
to be so BAGGY and bluish

because it doesn't have creases like
the trousers of the young man in Millet's Angelus.

When the evening comes
trees breathe softly,
or we see a garance-rose horizon from the *balcon*,[52]
or things like stars cast warm words upon us.

One of my friends is marrying at this moment.
He revealed a double-cased gold watch to me.
When you pull out a button,
within it
ring the bells of the Angelus.
The desire to possess it rises like the sun.

The bells of the abbey ring
ting-kang, ting-kang, toward Rome.
This makes men blow whistles.
The evening sun is in my breakfast.
A scarlet toy-Daruma.[53]

Upon my own slope I alone
stand perpendicularly.
Beyond many worthless roofs
I see a singular[54] yellow house with a strange aura about it
upon a very chic forest GAUDILY decorated.
Such a forest makes me think of a life far away.
But the soft soil, in order to grow a plant that resembles a sorrowful
    thought,
lets the graceful orange-colored cows transport feces
from beneath the cities to the agricultural regions.
How pitiful it is to grow salad
with man's decomposed melancholy.
However, around here,
a youth, who is fond of love,
is walking alone.
Blow the trombone!

I buy a pair of extremely colorful suspenders and
leave the capital, and in three days
I find myself in a sandy isthmus.
All day looking at the lighthouse,
I smoke lots of cigarettes in blue legumes.

If not,
moving away from those lovers of arts and culture as far as possible,
I furiously strike a match
in a city famous for cucumbers and cockscomb flowers.

Again the church announces a quarter of an hour.
GIACONDA.
STRAWBERRY.
Behind a painted hotel building,
I enter a breathing autumn
that is cold as well as extremely pitiful.
Fleshless evergreens loiter about before the horizon.
Things like spinach are quiet.
I feel all has turned into bedroom slippers.

Feeling some chocolate inside my spinal cord,
putting dandelions and violets in my lungs,
I read Mme Guyau's schoolbook.
Where are the silent double lips?
The shooting range is nearby.

APPLES AND SNAKES

My spirit's fur wore a cloak that was really ticklish.
My shadow pours phlegm onto the roadside.
My shadow upon daisies seems truly impoverished.

On a train, a merchant
sleeps soundly as if being at home until he slips into a soft sleep.
What an irregular begonia flower!

On a shaky balcony in deathly twilight
a singular[55] cook
shudders in awe like a mimosa tree.
What sort of grove my childhood is!

At 12 P.M.
the train turns around along the cemetery.
In the interior there is a greenhouse.
Those mouths that gobble up our sleep are Venus's-flytraps.
They are dreaming of a great syringe
sprinkling perfume.

People love cherry blossoms more than dandelions and
eat tempura sea-eels *resplendent* as false teeth.

Tooth powder is the halo of an icon.
The eyeball crawls up the demolished church spire
and follows the sun running
across a green field that spreads out beyond the tin roof.
What mortification!
Lonely people put on their embroidered shoes
and go out to see trees rot like milk.
However, their watches dig the strata of time
accurately.

Hanging shirts in a citron forest
people bathe in hot water and without risking death
roast their fatigue.
Thou, extremely good-natured prawn!
God bless thee.

The chorus of goats!
Me? I'm the god of wine.
Since I've got no goats with eyeballs like raisin bread,[56]
please do eat an antelope born in Africa.
Send up a flare within my poor lonely brain, and just to please it,
    give me an alcarraza water jug.
Oh, in a distant college town,
thrushes are singing.

Adorning my curly locks with marigolds,
I see the festival of Comellon,[57] but
the glory of my brain is heavy.
Browning's pomegranates and bells.[58]
The black hair glittering with so much camellia oil
belongs to a woman forty-five years of age.
Her pipe is as thin and as long as a pen-shaft.
Her train is crossing an iron bridge.
The basin is icy and cold.
When she smiles, her gums feel chilly.

These people are all boring.
I shall hang my seven-string zither
on an almond tree
growing on a slope in paradise.
Fifteen o'clock was rung.
Shall we run?

ROSE DES VENTS

Putting a hat on lightly
I walk on a street of the Latin races
beneath the leaves, over the leaves.

Within the pupil that grows all confused and scared
behold the fuchsia flowers that multiply in violent profusion.
That young Parisian
bends his fingers strangely
in his striped hat.
There are only a post office and trees.

The *ramune* bottle is blue.[59] In front of my face
the master of a bookstore on Kléber[60] is grieving quite *handsomely*.

Then putting an alcohol lamp in Central Europe,
I heat up some café au lait
while listening to the beggar's accordion in a pasture.
An orange-colored roof and blue trees in the distance
spur my mind.

And yet the sea is dead wine.[61]
People want to climb up a hill and
remain dead-still
beside an acacia tree with a great green shadow.
The sun,
gum trees,
a light railway,
tigers,
money
construct a republic of music.

Without a doubt you are the one,
you, beautiful octopus,
who lifts my hat in front of Demeter in London.[62]
Your tender soul fishes for the shimmerings of codfish
in the lethargic afternoon that never flows away.
But occupation-wise, you were a god.
The goddess of *coquelicot*.[63]
The goddess of wheat.
The manicurist of pears.

But now you imbibe
grease out of the local female students
and dust.

Beyond the playground
in the forest of ships, flowers bloom.
At the global noon,
which is all the stockholders' delight,
a merchant starts to walk toward a hotel.
In the sun, a man
wearing a bulky vest and an apricot loincloth
eats a cigar marinated in vinegar
and extremely passionately
thinks of the god of Brahman, of the decoration medal, and of
the snake,
and laughs.
And then he makes a clarinet out of a coconut
that is as big as his skull
by putting a mouthpiece in it.
And when he plays it *crouching* on the ground,
there comes the head of a cobra dancing out from a basket.
What a beautiful cactus!
It oscillates like a metronome.
Yet people walk on the shady side.
One of his friends has become the manager of a branch office.
Wearing a *really nice* hat
he is walking on the peninsula *very very vigorously*.

Under *ravenalas* trees,[64] they are playing violins,
waiting for the rain to fall from love.
People are sticking their smiling chins
out of the window of a mosque.
Beneath that, tranquil lake-water reflects
distant mountains that look like large rice bowls.
(Actually these bowls were your backs.
In short, loincloths dry really well.
Acacia flowers are so beautiful that
they make me melancholic.) So says a traveller.

In the Suez Canal
jellyfish are running beautifully.

The horizon is full of sand.
There is a tent dogs are playing with.
A Moor pursues the evening sun and some change.
And there is a starry night.
But things like vocational schools are not here.
Crouching on the banks, exiled people
keep watch on their burned fingers in a cool silence.
There isn't anybody like a guarantor.
The reckless workers are talking
within the night tightly sealed.

Here is a flexible and taciturn city.
At the storefront a plover and a gemstone can engage in a
    conversation.
In the yard of the police station, hibiscus are flowering like your
    blood-congested hearts.
The local people walk barefoot like cats.
The two men who were just now talking anxiously while chewing
some unknown leaves and lime
are gone somewhere.

When the ships arrive,
they grab gold coins under the sea like fish.
Putting those coins behind their ears or in their mouths,
again they are gone somewhere
travelling along the railroad track.
Without seeing the destiny, until the path disappears into
the bush of bergamot,[65] I think of extremely sublime matters.

Like a camel I want to crawl into the sand
and try some algebra with passion.
And when I turn forty,
I will search out local markets
and eat some dusty grapes.
And just one more time
as I started to run
toward my soul,
I loitered along a sycamore avenue
with a medical doctor whom I met in Cairo,
and together we grieved at our lack of sleep the night before
due to the excruciating noise from the fountain.[66]

Leaning against a pyramid
we fall asleep into the most beautiful dawn in the world.
Meanwhile the camel-rider gets excited by the sound of silver.
What a supple and smooth reality!

ROMAN DE LA ROSE

It was ten years ago at noon when I parted from John.[67]
In October I was to go to university, and John
went to hell.
The two of us ran through foggy London,
got scolded for climbing up on the roof of the British Museum.
Later John's picture appeared in a literary magazine.
Surrounded by pencils, he jutted out his cheekbones with a grand air.
When crocuses burst out from rocks in the park,
when trees bore crooked yellow pears,
everyday we talked in bars, in cafés, and among Italians.
John slept in an attic in a dirty town south of the river Thames.
Since there was no electricity, we put candles into five or six
beer bottles like flowers and lit up our faces a little.
Then we put Donne's poetry and Lewis's pictures into the beer-box.
Around that time I was living in a hotel with a rose-patterned
carpet on Brompton Road in South Kensington.
We called this hotel *Roman de la rose.*
Sometimes we bought some roasted chestnuts under the moon and
    went into the *Roman de la rose.*
Together we grieved under the electric light.
We sometimes visited a blind young man who was writing a novel
for a proletarian magazine. He was the brave man who burned his
beard and eyes lighting fireworks at a celebration party
for the armistice treaty. His wife was most kind and always hospitable
    to us.
There was a pub under their apartment. After ten o'clock, a flautist
    would appear
and play some popular songs, *pyuko, pyuko,*
pyuko. . . . One night we invited him in and had a talk. (He
was planning to play his flute but ended up talking.) Sipping
beer and munching on some sausage, he complained that
he couldn't make much money, for times had changed so much since
the war.

MAY

Adorned with a garland of marigold
my hair curls and waves in gold
in a May breeze.
I see Themistokles' procession of death.[68]
My white surplice is also billowing.
Is it
the bird-singing sea?
the shadow of a fruit?
the explosion of a necklace?

TRAVELLER

Thou, traveller of *explosive* temper,
thy feces have flowed forth and polluted the sea of Hibernia,
the North Sea, Atlantis, and the Mediterranean.
Get thee back to thine own village.
Bless the cliff of thy homeland.
That naked soil is thy dawn.
An akebi-fruit hangs like thy spirit[69]
all summer long.

THE PRIMITIVENESS OF A CUP

Along a luminous riverbank
where flowers of Daphne blossom,
a blond boy runs
passing by an angel who holds an apple and a saber.
His fingers firmly grasping
a fish named red-belly[70]
just above its eyes of milky light—
a golden dream curves.

BARBER

The smoke from the mine looks volcanic.
Above a mountain stream, at the foot of a cliff
where gold-banded lilies bloom,
a barber opened an art studio.
On the bed a laborer's beard and pollen of lilies
are mixed and piled up.
Beneath the portrait of an actress posing for a beer commercial,

between newspaper and a bamboo flute,
this artist
smiles like the god of *beriberi*.

CEYLON

Natives are all inside the houses.
In the hot sun I walked alone.
A lizard on a drainage tile.
Shining eggplants.
Burning violets.
The hot sand on a violet-leaf
pours onto the back of my hand.
Ceylon's ancient past.

DENTIST

The beard of Corbière[71]
chases out snakes by burning rubber.
Water flows into the heavens.
This autumn of Penang.[72]
I was only a boy
wearing a Lamaite robe
and was happy.
From the tip of an iris leaf
the lama peeped into the mouth of my heaven.

A MAN READING HOMER

Silently, dawn and dusk
like two sides of a gold coin
reached his throat every day
through a tamarind tree.
Around that time, he was lodging
at a dyehouse on the second floor and reading Homer.
Around that time, he had a coral pipe
with a picture of a pansy.
All the Gallics laughed (Your pipe
is like a girl's letter, or a Byzantine romance novel—
ouuu aeee . . .).
Yet its phosphorescent smoke travels around a cockscomb,
around the goddess's nose and hips.

No Traveller Returns

(Tabibito kaerazu, 1947)

FOREWORD: WOMAN AND THE PHANTASMAL MAN

When I analyze myself, I find four worlds within: the worlds of intellect, of emotion, of senses, and of flesh. These may be approximately divided into two worlds: that of intellect and that of nature.

Next, I find various kinds of people lurking within myself. First, there are the modern man and the primitive man. The former is expressed through modern sciences, philosophy, religion, and letters. The latter is expressed through the studies of primitive cultures, primitive psychology, anthropology, and so on.

However, there is still another one lurking in me. He probably belongs to the mysteries of life, to the eternal mysteries of the universe— the one who cannot be resolved or comprehended by common logic or sentiments.

I call him the "phantasmal man" and think of him as the eternal traveller.

This "phantasmal man" comes and goes at various moments of my life. Perhaps he is a miraculously retained memory of preprimitive men. It must be the memory of the people who were closer to the eternal realm.

By eternity I do not mean the conventional concept posited as the antithesis to nothingness or extinction; rather, I mean the eternal thought, which necessarily acknowledges nothingness or extinction.

It seems that what makes me feel something like an infinite memory in the seeds of roadside grass is the workings of this "phantasmal man" lurking within myself.

In the realm of nature within myself, I find both man and woman residing. In the realm of nature, humanity's raison d'être is the continuation of the species. Since a pistil is female, and so is the fruit that nurtures the seed, woman should be the center of human's natural realm. Man is only a stamen, a bee, a wind of love. In this sense, woman is closer to the "phantasmal man" than man.

These views are contrary to such notions as "superman" or the "woman-as-organ" theory.

This book of poems collects records of life viewed from the standpoint of the "phantasmal man" or of "woman."

1

O Traveller, await.
Before thou wettest thy tongue
in this faint spring-water,
O think, traveller of life.[1]
Thou art also merely a water-spirit
that oozed out from the chinks of a rock.
Neither does this thinking-water
flow into eternity.
At a certain moment in eternity
it will dry out.
Ah! jays are too noisy!
Sometimes out of this water
comes the phantasmal man
with flowers in his hand.
'Tis only a dream
to seek life eternal.
To abandon thy longings
into the stream of life ever-flowing
and finally to wish
to fall off the precipice of eternity
and disappear . . .
O 'tis merely an illusion.[2]
Thus says this phantom water-sprite[3]
who comes out of the water to towns and villages
when water plants reach for
the shadows of floating clouds.

2

On the window,
a dim light—
how desolate,
the human world.

3

Desolate, the world of nature.
Desolate, our sleep.

4

A hardened garden.

5

Sorrel.[4]

6

Plum-resin.
Oil of life.
Oil of love.
The pointed tip of a bitter old tree.
On a summer evening,
projecting my soul
onto the lotus-pen,
onto the sky of shimmering stars,
I write a sorrowful letter.
The thought of eternity lingers.

7

Sticking her head
out of the window of a house
adorned with autumn bellflowers,[5]
a frowning lady
ponders something.
How lonely, the one who lives
at the deep end of the alley
where zelkova leaves fall.[6]

8

That whisper,
the darkness of a honey nest.
How lamentable,
the realm of women.

9

It is already December
Along a path that curves around

the foot of Nagoe Mountains,[7]
upon the edge of a pale protruding rock,
a seafern grey green
trembles.
A dandelion bud.
A thistle bud.[8]
Buried in sand, the roots of a spearflower[9]
that barely hold its few small red berries,
tremble among fallen leaves and moss.
In this stillness of mountains
I pay reverence to the early setting sun.

10

Late December
I wander into the woods of fallen leaves.
On bare branches already I see leaf-buds
of many shapes and colors.
No one in the capital knows about this.
On a vine entwined around a bare tree,
billions of years' longings ripen;
there, numerous nutlets are growing,
there, a seed more ancient than human life is buried.
In this little nutlet, dimly
lurks the ultimate beauty,
ultimate loneliness perceptible to humans,
trembling faintly.
Is this trembling poem
the true poetry?
This nutlet must be poetry.
Even the story of the lark singing at a castle isn't poetry.

11

I just cannot remember
how to write "rose."
How lonely,
this window
through which I stick out
my sorrowful head
at pitiful dawn whenever

I try to write "rose" and
have to look it up.

12

At night
when flowers bloom
on floating weeds,[10]
I put a boat on the water.
A cloud covers the moon.

13

Around the time
when pear blossoms scatter away,
pushing aside pine branches
I went to visit a monk in a mountain temple.
He was gone to see a woman in the capital.
I drank some sweet sake a sexton offered me.
Lonely is my life.[11]

14

Dusk falling
      as if not falling . . .
Spring in my heart.

15

Faint,
      this road,
      a sound   of
      a warbler.

16

The passion of jade
the world of women fading . . .

17

An autumn day fading into
a coral bead . . .

18

Clad in white Chinese robes
those pine branches . . .
among them sing bulbuls.
How desolate,
the night.

19

The night of cherry blossoms dawning,
roosters crying,
a departing traveller shedding
tears . . .

20

Around the time
when flowers bloom in bushes,
a heart grows misty.

21

Ancient days.
A wild rose on a plate.
Lunch in a ruined garden.
Black gloves.
Mallarmé's spring ode.[12]
The memory of a white dewdrop
floating on a tip of grass.
An infinite sentiment.

22

Around that time
to view cherry blossoms,
I was in a boat on the upper waters of the Ara River.
I read Maupassant.[13]
Loneliness—
a clog floating among reeds
in the evening sun.

23

A three-inch clay pipe in his mouth
a hoarse-voiced lyricist said,[14]
"Eventide of gems"[15]
and gave a glass ball-cap of *ramune*-drink
to a woman.

24

A peony holding raindrops—
it will be food for the devils.
An ancient story says[16]
women should not eat it.

25

"Much of the country we passed through,
just touched with the beginning
of autumn beauty, was very lovely.
Having lunched at Fontainebleau
we did not arrive in Paris till noon."
So reads a passage in a novel.[17]
If I had read this to a dead friend,
he would have been very pleased
and might have babbled something.

26

Is the violet
the heart's shadow?
Loneliness of soil.

27

An ancient pledge.
Around the time
when the rain falls
upon cockscomb flowers,[18]
passing through some old gardens,
through a half-rotten temple gate,
I approached the capital.

28

Being unable to study,
unable to paint,
in the depths of Kamakura,[19]
I spent a lonely summer
walking up a slope to the Buddha Temple.
In a rocky tunnel,
I was picking up the head of a stone *jizō*,[20]
or picking weeds.
Near the tunnel,
of all places,
way up on a mountain
I met two men
who had followed eels upstream
from far below.

29

Pale things.
The apples of Cézanne.[21]
The belly of a snake.
Eternal time.
A chipped plate
remaining in an abandoned paradise.

30

A garden
where deutzia flowers bloom in spring,[22]
where horse chestnuts fall in autumn.[23]
A garden
where one finds a small waterwheel
by a stream running from a pond.
Nobody lives there.
Wagtails live
in an ancient plum tree
that, after all, never blooms.
Its bark caved in
deep with moss,
dampened by eternal desolation.

31

Under a bright autumn sky
dogs are playing happily
on the Kōshū Highway
that runs
far into the distance.

32

A rock caved in.
A mind disconsolate.
Brightness of an autumn day.

33

On a day when oak trees stand crooked,[24]
when thin clouds drift fast,
how desolate they appear,
those woman's socks, .
to the lovers' whispers wandering through a field.

34

Longings tremble
in autumn fields.
To the people in the capital
my longings run.
I saw spikenard blossoms blooming.[25]
The city people do not know about these blossoms.

35

The tip of a green acorn
is turning copper colored.
My disconsolate mind
lost.

36

Around the time
when the hazel eyes grow moist[26]

with dew . . .
How pitiable,
the day of truth.

37

A heart love-stricken
on a day when the night seems
never to arrive.
On a slope in a mountain village,
a longing for acorns . . .

38

Around the time when
the dead zelkova leaves gathered on windowsills,
I left for a journey;
around the time when
the nettle-flowers bloomed by the road,[27]
I came back.
A razor blade had rusted.

39

Early September
from a rock by the avenue
a green acorn hanging . . .

Desolate is the window.
Inside there is someone's voice.
How desolate, the sound of human speech,
"Hey, mistah, dis time I hear you goin' a pilgrimage
to Konpira, eh?[28] Please take dis wid ya.
No, no, it's nothin' mistah, just a partin' token.
Take it, take it."

"I can no longer write poetry.
Poetry exists where there is no poetry.
Only a shred of reality becomes poetry.[29]
Reality is loneliness.[30]
I feel loneliness, therefore I am.
Loneliness is the root of existence.

Loneliness is the ultimate desire for Beauty.
Beauty is the symbol of eternity."

40

A flowering Indian lilac[31]
holding out its crooked bark,
as if falling onto a window . . .
Someone is boring a hole in it,
something is being done . . .

41

I went for a hike to Koma Mountain
with a teacher from a higher teacher's school.
In a blacksmith's garden by the road,
we saw a dusty holly.[32]
Taking a few berries from the tree
we ate them.
"I used to eat these often when I was a child,"
said this taciturn teacher.
For the first time that day
he spoke.

42

I go up the Tama River
from Noborito toward Chōfu.[33]
For ten years I have abandoned my studies.
I have walked around
the Musashi Plain near the capital[34]
or the land of Sagami,[35]
looking at zelkova trees.
I have enjoyed the winter also,
fascinated by the crooks of those trees
or by the configuration of the branches.

43

One autumn afternoon
in the hallway of an English school in Kodaira,[36]
an unbelievably impertinent woman from my hometown asked me,[37]

"Professor, could you please write something
for *Tsuda bungaku?*"[38]
Later when I met her again, she said to me,
"Professor, why did you give me such a boring piece?
How mean of you!"
I was quite disappointed.
But it couldn't have been helped,
because from around that time
I was interested in boring things.
When autumn comes to the Musashi Plain,
thickets make the noise of lovers' ghosts.
Oak trees are bending their gnarled branches—
how desolate . . .
Colored in patinated gold
those deeply serrated, long leaves
rustle softly.

44

Crossing Kodaira village
a road runs like a self-absorbed runner
white and straight.
On a nice sunny day
wearing Western clothes and Japanese clogs,
carrying a black umbrella,
an East Indian walks alone;
sometimes buys a pack of Bats[39]
in a lone house by the roadside.

45

How desolate,
an open window.

46

Around the time when I was wandering
on the Musashi Plain . . .
Every time autumn came,
I thought of the ancient days, hearing
a yellow aged sigh

in the noise of withered oak leaves under my feet,
and thought of it as a pledge for tomorrow.
There were times
when I took home a few leaves of *kunugi* and *nara*[40]
and put them on my desk,
just to reminisce about the fields.
Or when I looked at a dry twig closely,
I could see a reddish sprout cowering out.
Spring is already lying deep
in early winter.
Loneliness
of a sprout . . .

47

I wonder how Mr. Umanosuke of Mogusaen[41]
is doing.
It was still early spring.
Nuptials took place in a house
at the foot of a mountain.
As I walked up a slope,
I saw white magnolias blooming.[42]
The Buddha clouds tattered;
the sunlight on the western mountains.

48

About something
that happened around that time:
along the road which runs
from the edge of Musashi to Chōfu,
a narrow face,
a knotweed,[43]
a foxtail . . .[44]

49

Cries of crickets.[45]
Astonished, my heart is hurried.
I dream of an ancient woman.

50

Tenderness of an acorn.

51

I desire a bronze,
a five-inch bronze of Neptune
wet and glistening
with ocean-drips,
stretching its arms wide,
standing with its legs apart.
It is about to throw
something.

52

An Indian lilac blooming
under the blazing sun.
Its naked trunk.
A heart curving, leaning.
A scarlet hair-comb.
Losing my way
in the darkness of the road ahead,
beneath this traveller's
bamboo
hat . . .

53

Loneliness of
rocks.

54

On a night when lady-flowers bloom,[46]
I sit in the light from a paper lantern
at an autumn night inn.
Crickets' echoes rise.
I read a letter.
Loneliness in the fields.

55

I peek into a thicket
full of spider webs.

56

Green acorns of an oak tree.
Loneliness . . .

57

I lose my way in an alley
where honey locusts bloom.[47]

58

A phantom of soil,
unable to bear the thought of leaving,
leans against the parapet of a bridge.

59

A shriek of a kite
echoes in my heart.
Unnoticed,
cherry blossoms bloom
in the mountains.

60

The smiling face of a sleeping woman.[48]
The color of a dayflower.[49]
Loneliness of the *Man'yō* people.

61

One day in September
my mind wandering off . . .
The morning after a typhoon passed,
I tottered out.
Autumn had arrived overnight.
In the evening I reached Chitose village.[50]
Branches, leaves, and berries had fallen.

I visited an old garden.
There was a guest in the teahouse.

62

My disquieted heart.
In the mountains
upon a red-clay cliff
lies a pinecone.

63

Abundant black hair hanging over his forehead,
this worker of hell
waits desolately in the dreaming rain.
The spring of an ancient savage god[51]
in a ginger field . . .[52]

64

On an uphill path, I hear
the cry of a pheasant.

65

From Yose[53]
I walk down the road by the Sagami River,
and think of the ancient soil on which
someone once asked directions
of a child with a heavy load on his back.

66

Out in the fields
desolate winds were blowing.
Only the noise of a waterwheel was echoing.

67

The crying of crickets has ceased.[54]
The haunted tune from the hautboys[55]
seducing evil spirits
traverses the fields and flows away.

68

In a crooked tree growing out of a rock
there are no longer *tsukutsuku-bōshi* cicadas.
A woodpecker knocks,
imbibing the sweetness out of the ancient tree.

69

A fan tinted with the light green[56]
of an evening-face[57]
hides a face
whose eyes lie
in the crevice of a damson[58]
where the waves of an autumn day
ripple.

70

One morning I was walking down a street in the capital.
A woman passed by leaving the aroma of bay rum.
This was in a novel.[59]
I forgot who wrote it,
though it wasn't long ago.

71

Upon a purple-willow leaf[60]
a long-horned beetle walks.
Loneliness of summer . . .

72

Long ago a *katsura* tree was praised[61]
in a book a Buddhist priest wrote.[62]
Since I wanted to see that tree,
I wandered around the Musashi Plain
but could not find even one.
However, beside a school latrine
this poor tree was standing alone, crooked.
Loneliness
of such comedy . . .

73

On the sandy shore of a river
thousands of unknown grass stalks are growing,
hiding the nests of reed-warblers and larks.
Those hearts' shadows . . .

74

A long time ago on an autumn day
I was walking down a village road on the Musashi Plain.
An evening shower started.
I took shelter in the doorway of a farmer's house.
In its hedge I saw some red berries
that looked like the sweets called *kanoko*.
"Eureka!" I thought.
They are called *sane-kazura* or *binan-kazura*.[63]
They often appear in our ancestors' books.
I asked a woman in the house to give me a branch.
The woman laughed, "Such a worthless thing."
But
the heart is so far
and so near.

75

Who forgot it here
this precious stone,
this auroral love?

76

Those were the days!
when we could watch baseball
climbing up a tree—

77

Traveller, who goes across the Musashi Plain,
do you not know the land
where green walnuts grow?[64]

78

Toward the end of summer at the Koma station,[65]
I bought some pears from a peasant woman.
Instead of thanking me, she made me
laugh doing some funny things
hoping that would please her customer.
I wonder if there is a scholar
of the local history around here . . .
Myths remain,
how desolate . . .

79

When it becomes September
a wild chestnut tree
extends its long lithe branches
from a bush.
How desolate, the chestnut tree.
How lonely, the nuts.
Peeling its white soft skin
I eat this yellow watery nut, uncooked,
tasting this sorrow lurking
within the mountain chestnut.

80

Alone on an autumn day
I stand on the Musashi Plain
under a sumac tree.[66]

81

How sorroful, the days of the past:
a dusty knotweed,[67]
the cigarette I smoked on a wooden bridge,
a lily left in the teahouse . . .

82

In an old garden
where tiger lilies bloom[68]
a forgotten
broken watering can
lying . . .

83

Around the time
when the waters were mirroring the clouds
I walked up a slope to Yōgō Temple.[69]
In autumn when people counted the curls of *Yakushi*[70]
I ate some cakes in a field of pampas grass.[71]
On the way home I bought a talisman
for safe childbirth from a temple
and gave it to a graduate student in art history.
By what curse I don't know
but I caught a cold.

84

I place a silver coin behind my ear,
a half-finished butt behind my ear,
put on *kasuri* underpants and then boots,[72]
hold a tin box
when cherry blossoms bloom
in the people's ancient capital.

85

At daybreak
when little bindweeds blossom[73]
in a bush of mugwort,[74]
invited, I hurry to a breakfast of *soba* noodles.[75]
A dewy travel through a heartless cosmos.
Our living time
gathered between the Sun and the Moon[76]
passes on
again
today.

86

I walked
curving along that narrow landscape
where red knotweeds tilted[77]
at the bend of a rotten bridge.

87

Irreality.[78]
A yellow violet blooming
in the hollow of an old tree—
a spring morning.

88

A Chinese painting of a harlot-goddess
looked like the portrait of an Edo actor.
Hundreds of autumns had been accumulating
within that silk-bound book . . .
Memories of autumn in Shiba.[79]

89

On a path on the Musashi Plain
where bamboo blades droop,
I meet
a slant-eyed woman
who may have been drawn by Kunisada,[80]
I dream
of the sentiments of autumn leaves
tonight—
on a mouldering bridge
red knotweeds
fading . . .

90

How desolate,
a woman crouching
at a ferry.

91

A woman brought a painting by Gauguin
and Chinese bellflowers[81]
for me—
an autumn day.

92

On an autumn day around then,
I was learning Latin
from a Jesuit priest
who had renounced the cloth
in order to marry his lover.
Dante's *De monarchia* in my pocket
I walked toward Sangen Teahouse:[82]
those noodles smelling too much of soy sauce,
a glass bottle, broken,
patched up with paper,
cigarettes sold from that bottle . . .
Cosmos bloomed
around a jerry-built rented house.

93

With three poets
I ate trout from the Futagotama River
on the second floor of a dark inn.
That was the inn
which appears in a novel by Doppo.[83]
It had an entrance on Ōyama Highway.

94

Jōdo Lost is hell[84]
described by a blind man.
Even the light damask of stinking bark[85]
is invisible, but only
a grapevine,
gourds,
barley

are the ornaments of this garden,
trembling.

95

A Rococo woman—
if she finds any room left
she will fill it with more gold.
Tears drop between the roses and the lilies.[86]
A misty heart,
a misty gem.

96

It was still early spring.
When the mountains appeared light yellow,
pine forests dark and hazy,
I walked through the hills of Tama[87]
with my teacher Mr. Ishikawa.
In a dale, a waterwheel was revolving.
"It's beautiful to paint such a landscape
or describe it in a literary work. But, boy,
who could actually live in a place like that?"
said he, opening his lunch of cheese.
We went down a hill
and walked through vegetable fields.
"When I was hiking in the Kiso Mountains[88]
I found a house that looked perfect
for a lunch-rest.
I went up to the house and called.
Nobody came out.
So, I just opened the *shōji* screen,
climbed into the room
and took a nap on the *tatami* mats.
Later I found out that
it was a quarantine hospital for the village,"
said he, laughing.
A warbler was singing by the road.
"How awfully that bird sings!
There is an errand-boy for a greengrocer near my home
who can easily outperform that warbler,

whistling a warbler song on his bike."
We went home without even visiting the Fudō.[89]
It was desolate
like the day when quails cry.[90]

97

There was a time when
a wind
went around the garden,
shook a crooked yellow pear,
entered through a small window, and
extinguished a candle flame.

98

Moist with dew
a black stone, cold—
a summer dawn.

99

Loneliness of the Gobelin tapestry.
A naked woman
woven in
the tapestry—
loneliness.

100

A spring
hedge—
loneliness.

101

A town where sky-blue gourds hang . . .
A townsman's craft,
a three-inch ivory—
engraved so shyly,
these naked women are all
associated with the bath,

hanging a basket
full of toilet articles
for the *shimada* coiffure . . .[91]
This waterfowl,
this mandala of a public bath . . .

102

Grass seeds
in a puddle that
reflects
the crook
of a dried stem . . .
A loner
leaving . . .

103

In the garden
an empty cicada shell—
how sorrowful,
the daybreak
of a summer night's shell.

104

At the end of August
already pampas grasses comb their silver hair
in the mountains.
Lady-flowers sprouting from rocks
curve in gold.
They are the signposts of my native land.
A traveller hurries homeward.

105

Crickets' songs
fill the plain.
I stand alone on a rock
in the autumn of this short eternity
that hurries toward
a link between lives

where neither stars nor night exist—
How sorrowful, my heart
listening
in this infinite field . . .

106

Above a grain field
where desolation grows,
a pitiable crucified man
wearing the straw hat from
Van Gogh's self-portrait,
and a blue shirt,
this suspended *Ecce Homo*—
the color of life's twilight
pierces him . . .
Here, a man
is attempting to say
something.

107

Beneath the shop-curtain
patterned with fringed pinks,[92]
I see
garden stones,
clogs lying upside down . . .
Nobody is there.
Something
is happening.

108

Around the time
when *muku*-nuts rain down on a slope,[93]
I open a Gobelin tapestry,
open a sorrowful window
and watch waterfowls fly
toward the fading distant mountains,
or a ferryman smoking a cigarette.
Then the characters from the novels

I read a long time ago begin to appear
like living spirits:
they get together and again they part,[94]
avoid evil spirits,[95]
difficult predicament,[96]
lemon farm,[97]
razor teeth,[98]
his monkey wife.[99]
So they come one after another.
Real people over there
begin to look like ghosts.

109

An old man
burning acacia wood
in a hearth
forgetting . . .[100]

110

Around the end of August
coming ashore
I took a walk in a town.
Yellow sycamore leaves were on the ground.
A travelling actor was resting in a café
leaning against the back of a chair
without ordering anything.
As I walked down a back street
I saw people selling patterned handkerchiefs
that were just becoming fashionable.
A portrait of Chaplin was hanging.
I bought a French novel for the first time in France.
As I walked up a hill
the sea shone in light green.
At the top of the hill
I saw a house with blooming canna flowers.
I entered the house
and found a middle-aged woman
quietly reading a book by Maeterlinck[101]
called something like

"The Spirit of a Beehive."
I suspect that this is incorrect.
There wasn't much time left.
So I returned to the ship, taking a coach.
His face looking like a pink[102]
standing in a Buddha's cinerary urn,
a young Greek laughed.
He had promised to give me
an old coin
with the head of Venus
imprinted on it.

111

The beauty
of a lady lurking
in oak.
How bitter, its powder.
How bitter, the passion of a crucifix
redeeming mankind from sin.

112

A light pink phantom is
reflected on a mountain thistle flower.
Eternity flows away.
How lonely, our misty silhouette.
'Tis our irreality,[103]
so far away.
On this mountain shadow,
on this swelling of soil,
trembles
a color.

113

I become stranded on a muddy street
where red knotweeds bloom—
the beginning of a new *Divine Comedy*.[104]

114

A few oak leaves.
The ghost of a past lover.
A shaft of light
from a distant past.

115

He wondered whether he should go to
hot-springs in the eastern land
or in the western land.
The man at the Mugiwara Inn
finally decided on Shūzenji.[105]
This man often visited with me at the inn.
Around the time when the temple bell rang,
when pine leaves shone in gold,
we took a bath together
watching a toy waterwheel turn
in a stream from a pond.

116

When I was weary of travel,
resting under a tree,
which villagers called *yosozome,*
I began thinking.
I thought of a monster-dipper.
We certainly had some great mythmakers
among our ancestors.[106]
When I stood up
the autumn was almost gone.

117

Watching the rainy heavens I thought:
I like that "man of ocean"
in *The Thousand and One Nights.*
Somehow, suddenly I stopped my walk
then again began to think.
I crossed a bridge and went to a town.
There, summer had already come.

118

Somebody said that a great novel
was started in a children's notebook
with a pencil.[107]
I recalled it
lying in a field of goldenrod.[108]

119

The sound of musical instruments
flows into the human voice.
This moment
is the swooning of autumn.

120

How desolate, the world of colors—
the color of the leaf-edge,
nameless small flowers blooming in a field . . .
The biology of color, the evolutionary theory of color.
Colors flow ceaselessly.
Our feet do not get washed by the same current:
the Heraclitus of colors,[109]
the Bergson of colors . . .[110]
Through Chavannes's landscape,[111]
through the cover of an old book,
through a pack of Golden Bat,
through a woman's lips,
through the apples of Cézanne,
eternity flows within colors.

121

Lost in thought,
a female spirit—
in her narrow landscape
a windmill turns.

122

In early December
foxtails already withered,
golden dreams gone,
only the shells
of dreams
tremble.

123

Camellias in the mountains
never bloom all year.
Those white buds at the tips of branches
are leaf-buds.
Rather than flowers,
the beauty of leaves is heightened
in their blackened green . . .
Someone takes a leaf
that emits a hard gleam,
rolls it and whistles.
Look at those round cheeks . . .
This sorrowful noise
echos through the mountain spirit.
The stillness of winter mountains.

124

The transience of
a shadowless mandala's[112]
scarlet
grass seeds.
Loneliness of the purple . . .
Desolate shapes
hanging from dried twigs,
spilt into a winter day . . .

125

From over there
a man comes riding on a cow
looking like a *Tenjin*-god.[113]

126

One day
I was walking along a river bank
where honey locusts bloomed.
A woman was squatting,
fishing in silence.
What a rare sight that was!

127

Through the twilight of lovers
bats fly.

128

A gem
thrown by someone
hits a harp,
becomes an ancient song.

129

Amethyst—
a fossil of love?

130

Carved on a peach tree,
a child's smiling head.
Lonely is the sweet tea
of our sorrowful life.

131

The philosophy of clothes[114]
is the philosophy of women.
How sorrowful,
a woman's one-piece sash . . .

132

The roundness of a teacup,
that desolate curve,
karma turning,
reflecting an autumn day.

133

Brocade,
how sorrowful . . .

134

An old nettle tree[115]
crumbling in decay
on this beautiful spring day.

135

Flowers in a thorn hedge.[116]
Who dwells . . .

136

With wild chrysanthemums
I adorn
an unknown phantom
of stone.

137

Into the goldenrods of autumn
recedes
the back of an angler.

138

The darkness of a wildflower
shadows her heart.
No one knows
the longing for her husband
flowering
in the field of mind.

139

In a garden
where peonies bloom,[117]
the water reflects
a lover's lips pouting
with the thought
of waterfowls leaving.

140

I draw closer
the sorrowful hand of autumn night,
or let it make fluttering music of oak leaves;
yet my heart is hurried.
As if to take in the starlight
goblets are raised high—
they are althea flowers[118]
blooming in the hedge.
Lonely is the one
who waits for a serene visit,
leaving the hedge gate open . . .

141

The shadow of a heart
reflected
on a wildflower—
its light purple . . .

142

Dyeing my clothes
in twilight,
tomorrow I depart.[119]

143

Someone
casts a shadow over my heart.
I look back—
a woman of an autumn day;
a dragonfly

alighting on
a bamboo hat.

144

In the swoon of an autumn day,
a dream of a luscious spirit
hangs from the tip of a rock:
dandelion fluff,
half-disappeared crescent moon—
how glorious
thy dream.

145

A village madman all naked
gobbles up
lady-flowers and crickets.

146

How lonely, the ancient ritual,
boring a hole through an eggplant
to look at the harvest moon.

147

An autumn day,
in a corner of a garden
imperceptibly
a stone
mouldering . . .
Hanging a horizontal scroll by Mokkei,[120]
I wait in silence
for the one who does not come.
On a water-mirror
studded with long stemmed reeds,
the heart of woman is reflected.
Man is only the shadow of woman.
Soil dreams of eternity.
We are a vine on a journey
temporarily growing over that soil.
Only the evening sun remains on the stem.

A grass seed is the heart of woman.
The heart's shadow
is the field's shadow.

148

His golden hair waving in the wind
a boy holds a fish in one hand,
an apple in the other,
and runs among angels over the clouds.[121]
I wonder if it was a painting
hung on some restaurant wall . . .

149

Summer days—
sadness in green plums . . .
Born in the land of knotweed,
I lose my way on a path full of thicket.
I go on tottering
through the grounds of a bell-less temple,
passing by a hedge of blooming morning-glories,[122]
through a village where shrikes sing,
taking a rest in a rainy town . . .
In the country of trailing plants
we drink tea together—
a murmuring
brooklet,
a woman's
sentiments
flowing on . . .

150

Facing the glowing sun directly
I hurried along a road
where tiger beetles crawl around.
It seemed that I would never reach
the town with a steeple.
Only hedges of tea leaves and mandin berries continued.[123]
Later
I asked directions of a woman,

who stuck out her head
from a roughly woven wood fence.
I had walked in the opposite direction!
"Thou must go straight back."

151

The barbed tongues of a husband and a wife
quarreling often, unnoticed by others
return to eternal darkness.
A thought of ancient soil . . .
Uttering not a word,
treading on fallen leaves . . .
A bulbul sings
in the garden
both have nurtured.

152

Plucking field horsetails[124]
the one who lives in this village—
loneliness.

153

A glorious
sentiment's
curve.

154

Down the hallway,
in a dim light,
on a closed *shōji* screen,
the shadow of a camellia[125]
set in a vase—
loneliness.

155

Uttering something obscure,
a rueful but curiously funny
female carpenter's whisper,

so *amer*,[126]
somehow pierces my mind.

I wander among withered trees,
How lonely
my thoughts on the moss
I touch.

156

Putting breadcrumbs in my bosom,
tea in my gourd,
I was walking up a hill
with a persimmon cane.[127]
A woman traveller
suddenly looked back
sticking out her slick tongue.
"This is still a theater of life.
Our lives belong to that hazel.
Oh, c'mon, poetry? Painting?
They don't mean nothin',"
so saying
she stuck out her scarlet tongue again.

157

When we set out on a journey
we take something in our bosom,
not for reading
but as a charm
to ward off evil spirits.
One man, a long time ago,
carried *Une vie* to Jōshū.[128]
A revolutionary in a certain country[129]
took *Paradise Lost* with him
to work in the fields.

A maid from Shimousa[130]
hides in her wicker trunk
a picture of Greta Garbo.

When I set out on a journey
in order not to fall in love

nor to starve,
I put a foxtail
between the pages of Dante's "Inferno" . . .
There is lots of food in the mountains.

158

Journey returning to journey,
dust to dust . . .
Once this urn is broken
it becomes a piece of eternity.
The journey flows away.
If I try to scoop it up with my hands,
it becomes dreams and bubbles.
Beneath this bamboo hat wet with dreams,
an autumn light
spills in.

159

For the one
whose eyes grow misty
at the sight of nuts gathered
in a hollow of the mountain soil,
transience is not
that of antiquity.

160

The color of grass.
The crook of a stem.
The crumbling of a rock.
A chipped bowl.
The dozing of soil
lying in the crack of a heart.
How sorrowful,
an autumn day.

161

On an autumn night,
the shadow of a flower on the bed.
Our conversation never ending.
My heart growing pale,
how lonely . . .
"In the genre painting
on the old folding screen,
the foxlike dog,
the eyes of a woman visiting a mountain,
the roofs of temples and shrines
half-visible above cherry blossoms and clouds,
the grass leaves looking like autumn eyelashes,
these things remain in my mind."

"There is a woman
who said
she wanted to see a woman's belly button
in the age when people wore Chinese robes.
The sadness of an autumn day . . ."

Somebody is eavesdropping.

"As for the portrait of a poet[131]
who left a poem called 'Ode to the West Wind,'
I had long disliked him for his too feminine look.
But later I found out that
that portrait had been painted by a woman.
Oh, I see. Woman was coming out of it.
Seeping out of a rock,
a woman's heart—
a dandelion."

"Who painted the portrait of a child[132]
with a pageboy hair cut,
holding a camellia?"

"Once a stockbroker but
now a farmer,
this guy bought some radish seeds beneath a bridge.
Waiting for the change

he laughed 'Hee, hee, hee . . .' and said
'People say that women give shelter to men's seeds.
But that's a myth
Seeds are *in* women, don't ya see?
Men? Yes, sir, we men are merely a ray of light
or somethin' like that, you know.
Like bees and winds!'"

162

An autumn night rain
forming a puddle
on a steppingstone—
a scent of chrysanthemum in the air,
this scent of the distant past . . .

163

To witness the revelation of a miracle
I went up to the capital,
hiding in the shadow of a shepherd's wrinkled robe.[133]
I dozed off
in a forest of zelkova—
desolate, withered.
I dreamed of a woman of dawn
among the whispers of falling leaves and twigs.
Reflected on the plaster,
the gap of Orion
turning pale in the morning grey—
is it the condensation of a morning wind?
the joy of breaking out of darkness?
wood-spirits awakening
from the deep embrace of Saturn?
one afternoon?
The fission of a spirit.
A glorious space.
The severance of a sexless holy tree.
However, since you are the flesh of the planet Venus,
you are the goddess of human procreation,
The light that presides over the festival of life.
Even that irreality between husband and wife[134]

is lavishly embraced by you.
That instant when a woman turns into a doll.
That instant when a doll becomes a woman.
That spirit at the instant of coming out of the body.
That instant when a rose-crept window opens at dawn.
That curve of her finger.
A woman's spirit is lost in thought,
her foot not yet leaving the ground though ready to walk.
As the water-spirit rises,
my heart steps into a blooming field—
beneath the passing dawn,
within a stone,
faintly . . .

164

Just like a man who dreams of awakening,
I could not sleep.
Before the daybreak I set out on a dewy journey.
I did not know whose mountain house it was.
I went through its white painted gate
and went up a slope.
I could see a mountain leaning toward the southeast,
celadon-green mountains looking small
forming a line on the horizon.
On the terrace
I found a dried-out fountain,
in its middle, an old rusty Triton
crouching alone,
like a waterless gourd,
like an empty perfume bottle.
It was a May morning when spears rusted . . .[135]

All the windows of the house were closed
except one upstairs.
Surrounded by a blooming thorny vine,
the window was open.
I could see the back of a mirror-stand.
Who lives there?
Is this the dwelling of the woman

who ties her dreams to the spire of skylarks
when a thistle-color trembles at dawn?
In this ruined house
she was combing her hair,
awakened so early—
after a joyful dream?
or not being able to sleep?
If I could know her . . .
Perhaps it was a honeymoon bed so long ago . . .
By the entrance steps I saw
young lovers carved in stone—
moss hanging from their embrace . . .
Yellow violets blooming—
this heart-rending spring.
A sorrowful sight, panting on a hill
a woman picks field horsetails.
She does not say a word.
Its birth near,
a rose-fruit's,
this beloved life's fruit's,
whispers' whispers
knocking on the leaves—
a thought of eternity.

165

The heart's roots entwined,
the soil's dark distant eternity
sleeps in silence.

Again seed returns to seed
through flowers,
through fruit.
Man's seed also returns to man's seed
through the flower of a maiden,
through the ovarian orchid fruit.[136]
In sorrow the eternal water mill turns.
The water flows,
the wheel turns,
again

the water
flows
away.

The journey of our lives
begins at a certain time in the infinity of the past
and ends at a certain time in the infinity of the future.
Every moment in this world
is also a part of the eternal time.
A seed of grass is also
a part of the eternal space.
The finite existence is a part of the infinite existence.
In this small garden
I see an old plum tree, an Indian lilac,
an oak tree, a camellia, bamboo grass . . .
The succession of birds' memories?
of warblers', of meadow buntings',
those birds that visit here all through the year?
This place used to be Hiroo Field[137]
where pampas grasses pushed forth their whitest tufts.
Next to the water mill
there was a teahouse
where they used to roll bean-paste dumplings.
In this mandala village
young waterfowls rise in the air,
seeking not fruit but flowers.
Yet flowers seek fruit.
It is merely that
flowers exist only for fruit.

166

A country of young leaves.
A world of scarlet
weakens.
Fading
damask colored
luscious thoughts . . .
The sorrowful look
of the phantasmal man . . .

167

Around the time
when I came near a village
after coming down a mountain
and crossing a mountain stream,
I saw
at a road bend . . .
What! Is it spring, now?
A big white rhododendron tree
was in full bloom.
As I picked a branch to see,
I found that it was just frozen snow.
This is a dream of irreality,[138]
not a dream of a poet.
Even in dreams
seasons haunt his mind—
How lonely
the phantasmal man.

168

Touching the roots of eternity,
passing the field's end
where the heart's quails cry,[139]
where wild roses burst into bloom,
passing a village where fulling blocks echo,
passing a country where a woodsman's path crosses,
passing a town where whitewashed walls crumble,
visiting a temple by the road,
viewing a mandala tapestry with reverence,
walking over crumbled mountains of dead twigs,
crossing a ferry where reed stalks are reflected in long shadows,
passing a bush where seeds hang from grass leaves,
the phantasmal man departs.
The eternal traveller never returns.

Eterunitasu

(1962)

Eterunitasu

I

Symbols are desolate.
Words are symbols.
When I use words
my brain turns symbol-colored
and leans toward eternity.
Let me return to the season of no symbols.
I must think
with the frost of broken glass,
must move into a season
wherein I am obliged to seek
a woman's autumnal face[1]
inside a piece of concrete.
Every being leans
toward the world of quivering reflections.
The temple bell resounds in the water.[2]
Along the upside-down spire
runs a dace.
A meadow of clouds
flows quietly
where water lilies bloom.

The autumn-grey of a table is mirrored
within a summer apple.
Only the seven lamps of ambiguity in language[3]
light the human brain.
From the top of an Ōya-stone wall
a stalk of yucca juts out.
The past juts out
onto the future
passing the present.
"Oh dear, what shall we do?"

A fish keeps its eyes open under a rock.
Still more terrible things are happening.
A woman's surprised words
sound like a reflex—
an exclamation from the flattered Cleopatra
serving more wine.

A teacup abandoned in a puddle,
a trace of children's play,
a crest imprinted upon the back of a loach,
a madman crossing a bridge,
the nervous flurry of a stone thrown into a bamboo thicket,
the scream of a meteorite struck by a plow,
a louse left on a traveller's hat,
the movement of Pound's Adam's apple,[4]
a man
on the run
chewing
a soil-crusted bitter root
of nipplewort[5]—
these things do not symbolize.
Things that do not symbolize
attract us more.
To be alive
is to listen to things one cannot hear well,
to see things one cannot see well,
to eat things one cannot eat well.
It is simply to run toward the ultimate X.
Existence is destined.
Symbols are tragic.
"Oh dear, what shall we do?"

Stillness
within a penny.

The evening sun
transgressing the boundaries of a cup
recedes into infinity.
The contour of a black cup is left.
The contour of a goddess
wanders round inside a cat's pupil.

To the eye
of a man pouring wine
into the twilight,
the goddess's blue
returns.

They are here again:
like vine leaves

the whispers of Jacques Bonhomme,
a letter from the blonde of the century:
"Please forgive me, won't you?"—

The portrait of Dorothy Osborn[6]
in the traveller's notebook
is enough to bring the summer to an end.
In the sesame-colored background
decayed leaves are hiding gems.

The yellow letter from the woman
moves
into the transition
to the ultimate transformation,
into El Greco's
magenta.

The only orbit toward eternity
is marked by the footprints of a somnambulist
who, walking along a river,
dreams a dream
in which he has awakened
from a dream
in a dream.

It's getting a little hot.
Let's go inside.
A breeze passes
the purple of an eggplant
shimmering black on a table.
An open window is mirrored.
Poussin's landscape is mirrored.[7]
And Phocion's funeral is . . .[8]

It seems
autumn is already here.
Like a woman gathering firewood,
it is collecting bones.[9]
Let me hang the crown of bindweed[10]
on the thumb of a man
who hanged himself.
"Oh dear, how terrible!"
The sorrel vine is the link

between man and ape
which Darwin overlooked.
By injecting past memories
into the present,
we make a comedy of the present,
make the past present.
It is the "Fearful Joy."[11]
This cottonweed also[12]
is a fleeting laugh of God
within our endless reminiscence.
This inkstone also
is left lying
in the infinite wasteland of reminiscence.
Consciousness is always in the past.
The flow of consciousness is
the murmuring stream of reminiscence.
The flow of time is
the flow of consciousness.
It never progresses nor regresses;
it only changes.
The consciousness of existence is
the consciousness of reminiscence.
"The present" is merely an illusion
discovered by grammarians.
It is the location of the "speaker."
Eternity is not time.
Time is merely the consciousness of man.
That which man is unable to conceive is eternity.
"The more cultured you get, the less you are able to get it up."
Voluptuous impotence.[13]
That much we approach eternity;
that much we recede from dogs.

I want to depart
from the time called man.
Thinking does not produce eternity.
The more one thinks
the further one recedes from eternity.
Eternity denies every existence.
Not to think of eternity
is the only mode

in which eternity can be expressed.
There is no other way
to merge into eternity
but to destroy the brain.
Eternity is an infinite space.
Nature is only renting that space
through the power of love.
Nature is not a part of eternity.
"Oh dear, what shall we do?"
Just don't think.
Let us go to the Dutchess of Ormond's cocktail party.[14]
Lady Chatterley will be there, too.
A white iris also
will be a husk
beside a grey stone.
The lover's path may seem a shortcut,
but you should avoid it.
Sometimes you find
the corpse of a dog there.

I do not want to construct an enigma
with ambiguous *objets*
and think what it symbolizes.
To wander around
the world of symbols
is Odysseus's Penelope's
epos's Homer.[15]
It is time to return somewhere.
On my way back
I want to land on an island
hidden by the grey wine-dark sea,
watch the rosy-fingered dawn
and eat pomegranates.
What I would seek
wouldn't be Mallarmé's *objets,*
but something more banal.
I would seek loneliness:
conversations I hear in the streets,
a stone on which the shadows of grass are cast,
the weight of a fish,
the shape and color of corn,

the thickness of a column.
I would prefer things that do not symbolize.
Upon the banal existence
infinite loneliness
is reflected.
Loneliness is the last symbol
of eternity.
I want to abandon even this symbol.
Not to think of eternity
is to think of eternity.
Not to think is the symbol
of eternity.
I want to abandon even this symbol.
To want to abandon it
is the ultimate symbol of eternity.
We cannot see this symbol.
It is the cosmic ray
that pierces the brain.
Such
taranbō's[16]
blue thorn
shall be
black.

II

When one tries not to symbolize eternity,
eternity will be symbolized for the first time.
The young man's face I see
past the man with a Panama hat talking there
conjures up eternity.
The less one pursues eternity,
the closer eternity approaches.
I send off a man
leaving for the meadow,
raising a goblet high
for the annihilation of symbols.

When the sun nears the horizon,
I shall go back somewhere,
putting on a blue mantle,[17]

stepping on the long shadow of a gas tank.
Tomorrow also
I must discover
a new cliff,
a new puddle.
Man's last desire
is that of *éternité*.
I want to see the blueness of an *akebi*-fruit.[18]
Can we tell how much Priapus resembles[19]
the sunken blue cup?
Desire does not exist in eternity.
The wish to abandon desire
is another desire.
A potato lying under the starlight
is also the goddess of desire.
A potato striving to become a potato
is again the tragedy of desire.[20]
As for glory,
not to wish for glory is glory.
Glory does not attempt to become glory.
To abandon glory is glory.
Truly,
why must man propagate?
The more we pursue eternity,
the more it flees like Amanda.[21]
Why is the preservation of the seed necessary?
The more we pursue eternity,
the more the animal in us disappears.
Animal's "only lyricism is
copulation."[22]
Cultured men are
as ambiguous as animals in the jungle.
Even a table manifests[23]
the desire of the carpenter
in its form and color.
Beauty appears
where there is no desire.
The invisible table is
more beautiful than the visible table.[24]
To break existence is

the beginning of beauty.
Where there is no beauty
stands a goddess.
An existence that is neither beautiful nor ugly
like the moisture on a lead pipe is
"Oh, how beautiful!"
The brain of a traveller
treading on acorns
is beautiful.
It is the joy of *éternité*.
The consciousness of the goddess
walking
far from eternity
walking
eternally distant from eternity
is the consciousness of an infinite space.

A brain drawn to the center of the earth
is the weight of an apple.

The sound of bells
echoing through the villages:
"Do not forget to turn off the gas-cock before you go to bed,"
so announces the transience of life.
It is the sound of water from a gourd
shared by
tormented mankind.
It is the joyous covenant
wherein we all cry our:
VÉRITÉBONTÉBEAUTÉ . . .
The bells toll in the plain.

I wonder
what Toynbee is thinking now.[25]
Is he still on the journey,
wearing that wonderful tweed cap?
He sent me *A Study of History*.
Alas, all is history.
History repeats.
Eternity has no history.
It alone holds both
plus one and minus one—

an existence that is willing to contain existence.
I talked all day in the train.
Mulberries, wheat, and peaches
reminded me of northern Italy.
I thought of the poet of Tang
who lamented the past splendor of a vanquished people
whenever he heard the whispers of corn.

A dog is tottering
after a traveller.
The evening sun
colors his shirt
rosy.
At the end of the town
I bought a pastry
and a dried cuttlefish.
The click of my purse
vanished into the fields
with the wind.[26]
Again I stumbled over a stone.
Again half of the dream
was severed.
Oh, Cynara![27]
I recalled something about sesame and lilies.[28]
Like Ruskin,
like Hopkins
I must begin to study clouds again,
I must begin to love stones again:[29]
that stone jutting out from a tea plantation,
that stone I found under a Japanese pepper tree by the Tama River,[30]
that milestone
buried in a bamboo thicket,
and that stone of Venus in the waning light . . .[31]
Ah, again I stumble over a stone.
Ah, again
without knowing
I am using the deluxe words
of man . . .

Already there are no more Chinese milk-vetches,[32]
no more rape blossoms.[33]
Again I have come to the riverside.

A bus is running in the distance.
A man is fishing
wearing a cat-colored cap.
The face of a man watching him
is green
like sorrel.[34]
From beneath a collar of briar,[35]
Ecce!
H
O
M
O
.

.

.

PART TWO

Modernism in Translation

Modernist Poetry in Japan

The birth of modernist poetry in Japan is usually traced back to "Japanese Futurist Manifesto" (1921) by Hirato Renkichi (1893–1922), *Dadaisto Shinkichi no shi* (1923; Poems of dadaist Shinkichi) by Takahashi Shinkichi (b. 1901), or the publication of the journal *Aka to kuro* (1923; Red and black). The dates of the above publications suggest the fortuitous but subtle connections between the rise of modernism in Japan and the impact of the great Kanto earthquake and fire that occurred on September 1, 1923.[1] The earthquake destroyed half of Tokyo and most of Yokohama and took approximately one hundred thirty thousand lives. In the confusion and terror created by the earthquake, modernity, with all its chaotic energy and insidious violence, took root in Japan. As the foundations of everyday life collapsed, there seemed to surface two extreme energies: a terror and consequent expulsion of the "other," and an emboldened leap toward the completely new. In the streets everywhere, the uncontrollable mob lynching of Koreans became rampant. At the same time, the latent fascism of the police state was taking shape, which resulted in the mass arrests and murders of Koreans, anarchists, and socialists. One of the most well known among such incidents was the murder of the noted anarchist thinker Ōsugi Sakae (1885–1923), along with his wife Itō Noe (1895–1923)[2] and his young nephew, by a captain of the military police, Amakasu Masahiko. This and other such atrocities did not, however, stop the spread of the anarchist revolutionary spirit among intellectuals and poets. The natural calamity became a catalyst for the radical social and cultural changes that had been felt in a more abstract way before. Tokyo was rebuilt from the ground up, with many sections now resembling cities of the West. The appearance and the consequent acceptance of modernism in Japan shared in this social transformation.

Any modernism begins by rejecting the contemporary establishment that attempts to enforce an orthodoxy and to conserve tradition. However, mainly due to the brief history of modern Japanese poetry (as opposed to the tradition of haiku and *waka*), until the late 1910s there was no central, unified organization that yielded power in this newly established genre. In 1917, an effort to bring together poets from different coteries was initiated by the poet Kawaji Ryūkō (1888–1959) and others. The result was the establishment of the Shiwa-kai (Society of poetry talk), whose intent was to "spread poetry into society at large by calling for a major unification of all the poets without discrimination" (quoted in Harazaki 1980, 90). It started with nine poets, but the society soon attracted most of the major poets and began to assume the status of *shidan*—an official establishment of modern Japanese poetry.

Yet because the eclectic collection of poets had differing ideas about poetry, the unity of this establishment was suspect from the beginning. The main friction was felt between two schools, the *minshūshi-ha* (people's poetry coterie) and the *kanjōshi-ha* (emotional poetry coterie). The former was organized around the journal *Minshū* (The populace), first published in 1918, and around the poet Shiratori Seigo (1890–1973), who was much influenced by the "democratic poetry" of Walt Whitman. The *minshū-shi* group advocated the use of a plain colloquial diction that would appeal to the masses. The other group was gathered around the journal *Kanjō* (Emotion), first published in 1916, which included works by such aesthete poets as Hagiwara Sakutarō, Murō Saisei (1889–1962), Kitahara Hakushū, Yamamura Bochō (1884–1924), and Takamura Kōtarō. In short, one school was more socially oriented and the other more artistically oriented. The disputes between them sometimes became heated to the point where members angrily defected. Kitahara Hakushū was one of them. He left the society with his friends after severely criticizing some of the members' "artless" products. Nonetheless, with the financial backing of the publisher Shinchō sha, the Shiwa-kai founded the journal *Nihon shijin* (Japanese poet) in 1921. *Nihon shijin* offered a timely stage on which the *minshū-ha* and the *kanjō-ha*, whose chief theorist was Hagiwara Sakutarō, could engage in critical debate. It was against this rather confused yet sufficiently authoritative establishment of modern Japanese poetry that more radical avant-garde movements rebelled. When finally the Shiwa-kai disbanded and *Nihon shijin* folded in 1926, the avant-garde poet Yoshida Issui (1898–1973) was beside himself with excitement: "*Nihon shijin* went bust! *Banzai!* Serves them right! Now come out as one person, one party!" (quoted in Chiba 1978, 137).

In sum, the modern Japanese poetry scene of the early 1920s through the mid-1930s can roughly be divided into four camps: (1) the established poets associated with *Nihon shijin*; (2) dadaist and anarchist poets; (3) proletarian poets; and (4) intellectual formalists and surrealists surrounding Nishiwaki and the journal *Shi to shiron* (Poetry and poetics.)[3] After the Manchurian incident in 1931, the Fascist government's oppression increased and in 1934 the *Nihon purore-taria sakka dōmei* (Japan proletarian writers' federation) was forced to disband. On the other hand, reactionary, nationalistic journals, such as *Nihon romanha* (Japanese romanticist), first published in 1935, began to appear. As the proletarian literature weakened and *l'esprit nouveau* of *Shi to shiron* lost its newness, another "mainstream" poetic style was instituted in the journal *Shiki* (Four seasons) in 1934. *Shiki* helped form what is considered the principal lyricism of modern Japanese poetry.[4]

FUTURISM

In December 1921, Hirato Renkichi stood on a busy street in Hibiya, Tokyo, and distributed copies of a leaflet to passersby. The leaflet was entitled "Nihon miraiha sengen undō" (Japanese futurist manifesto movement). The text began:

> The trembling god's heart, the central action of humanity, issues forth from the core of a collective living. A city is a motor whose core is dynamo-electric.
>
> God's possessions were all conquered by the hands of Man. Today, God's engine becomes the city's motor and contributes to a million human activities. (Quoted in Nakano 1975, 46–47)

Futurism was announced by F. T. Marinetti on the front page of the Paris newspaper *Le Figaro* on February 20, 1909, insisting that the art of the past was dead, that the artist must now concern himself or herself with the vital, noisy life of the industrial city. Although Hirato's manifesto lagged behind Marinetti's by nearly a decade, his tone was similar. Actually, Marinetti's manifesto was quickly translated into Japanese by the novelist Mori Ōgai (1862–1922) and was published in the neoromanticist journal *Subaru* in May 1909.[5] The introduction of futurism and cubism to Japan was continued by such writers as Takamura Kōtarō,[6] Kinoshita Mokutarō (1885–1945),[7] Yosano Hiroshi (1873–1935),[8] Horiguchi Daigaku (1892–1981),[9] and Moriguchi Tari (1892–1984).[10] The poet Yamamura Bochō's innovative book of verse *Seisanryōhari* (1915; Sacred prism) was referred to as "the futurist poetry of Japan" in Hagiwara Sakutarō's enthusiastic review (Chiba

1978, 111). The influence of Marinetti's futurism could also be seen in the establishment of Miraiha bijutsu kyōkai (The association of futurist artists) in 1920, as well as in a one-person show of the work of the poet/painter Kanbara Tai (b. 1898) in 1921 and his manifesto "Dai ikkai Kanbara Tai sengen sho" (1921; The first manifesto of Kanbara Tai), considered the first avant-garde manifesto in Japan.[11] Kanbara was inspired by a futurist art exhibit held in October 1920, organized by David Davidouich Burliuk (1882–1962), a leading Russian futurist who took refuge in Japan. Burliuk's exhibit caused a sensation among young artists and poets who had been dreaming about European avant-garde art movements (Chiba 1971, 46). Hirato's futurist manifesto was born in such a milieu, announcing that artistic activities were no longer to be confined to a private space; they must now move into the streets: "Already many graveyards have become useless. Libraries, art museums, and academe are not worth the sound of a car gliding through a street. Try smelling the awful odor of an accumulated heap of books. Compared with that, the fresh aroma of gasoline is many times sweeter" (quoted in Andō Yasuhiko 1978, 6). In fact, what was shocking to the poets of the day was Hirato's distribution of the manifesto in the street, announcing a new way of being a poet, radically different from a writer's usual solitary, bookish existence.

However, a noticeable difference between Hirato's futurism and Marinetti's must be addressed: the former utterly lacked the latter's belligerent political involvement and remained within a formalist aestheticism. While Marinetti's illogical advocacy of both militarism and anarchism inevitably split the movement into fascism in Italy and communism in Russia (as seen in the case of Vladimir Mayakovsky), Hirato's manifesto appeared merely as an introduction to a new form of artistic movement divorced from political implications. Similarly, most of the modernist movements in Japan were to remain strictly in the domain of aesthetics; those who were more politically inclined turned to the proletarian literature movement.

DADA

On May 15, 1916, the first dada publication came out of Cabaret Voltaire in Zurich. On August 15, 1920, dada was introduced to Japan in the newspaper *Yorozuchōhō*. The article "Kyōrakushugi no saishin geijutsu: Sengo ni kangei saretsutsu aru dadaizumu" (The hedonistic newest art: Dadaism popular after the war) was written by

Wakatsuki Shiran (1879–1962), who later became known as a playwright and scholar. There was another article, entitled "Dadaizumu ichimenkan" (A view on dadaism), signed "Yōtōsei (羊頭生),"[12] which criticized dada as mere hedonism born of a whim of degenerate literati, in contrast to expressionism, which emphasized civilization's progress and power. Both articles referred to Tristan Tzara's dada manifesto of 1918, printed in the periodical *Dada 3*, and summarized the movement as a transformation of futurism, advocating nihilism, hedonism, and absolute individualism.

These articles were to change the life of at least one young man in Japan, who later developed into an important poet embracing the spirit of both dada and Zen.[13] Takahashi Shinkichi, then nineteen years old, was convalescing from typhoid fever in a rural town in Shikoku when he read these articles. He recalled that what impressed him most was the following description of a dadaist publication: "On the same page, vertical and horizontal typographical arrangements were mixed. There are sometimes even diagonal arrangements" (Takahashi 1982, 4:181). As with Hirato, one senses that Takahashi was attracted to the formal aesthetic changes rather than to dada's potential for social revolution. He began writing dadaist poems in 1922 and the next year published a collection, *Dadaisto Shinkichi no shi* (Poems of dadaist Shinkichi), edited by the anarchist and nihilist critic Tsuji Jun (1884–1944). The book begins with a poem entitled "Dangen wa dadaisuto" (The assertion is dadaist). Here is an excerpt:

DADA asserts and denies all.
Infinity or nothingness or whatever, it sounds just like a cigarette or
 petticoat or word.
All that oozes up in imagination exists in actuality.
All the past is included in the future of fermented soybeans.
Things beyond human imagination can be imagined through a stone or
 a sardine's head—so imagine a ladle, a cat, and everyone else.
DADA recognizes ego in all.
It recognizes ego in vibrations of the air, in a germ's hatred, and in the
 smell of the word "ego."
All is one and the same. From Buddha's recognition there appears the
 remark "All is all."
All is seen in all.
Assertion is all.

The universe is soap. Soap is trousers.
Anything is possible.

To a Christ pasted on a fan, jelly wrote a love letter.
All this is true.
How could it be possible for nonsmoking MR. GOD to imagine
something that cannot be asserted?[14]

In 1923, the sixteen-year-old Nakahara Chūya (1907–37) was utterly captivated by Takahashi's book and a few years later wrote an essay on Takahashi and sent it to him. Nakahara, whose brief life left us with one of the most tragic, lyrical voices of modern Japan, experimented with dadaesque expressions for a while, but after studying Rimbaud, turned to more organized, lyrical forms of poetry. A few dada-inspired journals briefly came into being around that time: *GE • GJMGJGAM • PRRR • GYMGEM*, first published in 1924 with Kitasono Katsue (1902–78)[15] as its core member, and *Baichi shūbun* (Selling shame, ugly literature), also first published in 1924, with Yoshiyuki Eisuke (1906–40) and Tsuji Jun as its main contributors.[16] Dada in Japan, like everywhere else, was never thoroughly theorized or instituted as such, and was soon sublimated into more formal expressions, including surrealism.

ANARCHIST POETRY

In January 1923, the first issue of *Aka to kuro* appeared. Its coterie consisted of Hagiwara Kyōjirō (1899–1938), Okamoto Jun (1901–78), Kawasaki Chōtarō (b. 1901), and Tsuboi Shigeji (1897–1975). On the cover was a manifesto written by Tsuboi: "What is poetry? What is a poet? Abandoning all the concepts from the past, we boldly proclaim! 'Poetry is a bomb! A poet is a dark criminal who throws a bomb against the fortified walls and doors of a prison!'" (quoted in Nihon kindai shiron kenkyūkai 1974, 499). This proclamation was considered the first cry of the anarchist literary movement that peaked with the founding of the magazine *Bungei kaihō* (1927; Literary arts liberation)—which was intended to counter the overpowering Bolshevik movement—and ended with the last issue of *Shi kōdō* (Poetry action), which came out in October 1935. Though the manifesto was immature, it embodied a revolutionary radicalism. What was most significant about *Aka to kuro* was that the poets were aware of being at the bottom of the social scale and wrote poems that directly reflected their hunger and anger, and the insanity of city life. Though the manifestos printed in subsequent issues spoke of the liberation of the pro-

letariat, on the whole the group did not produce a coherent revolutionary theory. In the last issue, published in June 1924, after an interruption due to the great Kanto earthquake, we find the following
poem by Tsuboi:

> City
> DUST DUST DUST DUST DUST DUST DUST DUST DUST
>   MUD MUD MUD MUD MUD MUD MUD MUD MUD MUD
>   The burial of a grudge
> Expose everything
> You end up nowhere whipping a starving horse
>   A CRAnky horse-carriage
>   A SKeleton
>   Nothing seems dependable
> Anger wells up
> from the tip of my head ACHING
> The back of my head is full of holes
> No wonder my memory is gone
> Wave your arms! Wave your flag!
> Start a new riot at the chaotic crossroads!
>   (Quoted in Andō Yasuhiko 1978, 14)[17]

Hagiwara Kyōjirō was a central figure in the modernist poetry of
Japan. After *Aka to kuro* folded, he helped found both *Damudamu*,
another modernist, anarchist journal, published in November 1924,[18]
and *Mavo*, an avant-garde art magazine first published in July 1924,
edited by the artist and playwright Murayama Tomoyoshi (1901–
77).[19] His first collection of poems, *Shikei senkoku* (1925; Death sentence), is truly a monumental modernist work incorporating the tech-
niques of dada, constructivist art, and concrete poetry, framing texts
with thick black lines, and using a number of cubist and constructivist
art works. "Edible Frogs" is a typical poem.[20]

Anarchist, modernist literary movements gave birth to many *dōjin
shi* (coterie magazines) in the late 1920s. *Dora* (Gong) was founded
by one of the major poets of modern Japan, Kusano Shinpei (b.
1903),[21] in April 1925. Later issues included such important poets as
Takahashi Shinkichi, Takamura Kōtarō, and Miyazawa Kenji (1896–
1933).[22] The members of *Aka to kuro*, Ono Tōzaburō (b. 1903) and
Okamoto Jun, also began to contribute, offering a more anarchist out-
look to the journal. It was also the time when more organized Marxist
theories and groups were taking over anarchism, which had lost its

EDIBLE FROGS

A lady's basement●●●
We are edible frogs!
Klokke
Klokke
Cry! Scream!
"Love?"■■■ A heart exploded by a red lamp ■■■ "What an insult!"
That's human slaughter!
Lekkelo
Lekkelo
"Knock it down!" "Stab" ■■■■■ A red eyeball!
"That's ●●!"
"Shoot! Shoot!"............**Noise**.............An order!
"Oh, Fatherland"
"Oh, Fatherland"
Incessant fighting! Charge! A warship sinking in the dark night!
A fountain on a desk! A red lamp! A yellow circle—Encoffining!
"Banzai!" "Banzai!"
"Werraaa!"■■■■■■ A heap of corpses!

R•R•R•R

Ring! Shout! Sing! Leap!
The bell of life rings!
"Run!" "Assassination!" "Death itself!"
"I'll die! You coward! Before the life force!"
"Punish those who chase away to the hole! Punish! Slaughter them!"
●●●▲▲▲✖✖✖ ─ ─ ─ ■■■<<<
An officer exhaling the smoke of rose that bloomed in whisky!
A woman hitting the keys for the music of pain!
Men and gold coins! Millions of candlelights.....Love screaming to
the bottom of the graveyard!
"Oh my girl!" "Mother! My body is a machine!"
Cry! Scream!
Gold coins! The war that worships cowards!
This is human slaughter!
Lekkelo Lekkelo
We are edible frogs!

most important theorist, Ōsugi Sakae. In November 1926, at the second general meeting of Nihon puroretaria bungei renmei (Japan proletarian literary arts league),[23] the anarchist group was purged from the league. In the short-lived proletarian literature movement, the most notable poet was Nakano Shigeharu (1902–79).[24] Poems found in various proletarian literary journals and poetry anthologies—*Bungei sensen* (Literary arts front), *Senki* (Battle flag), and the two anthologies, *Nihon puroretaria shishū, 1927, 1928* (Japan proletarian poetry anthology, 1927 and 1928)—tended to be single-mindedly propagandistic, especially in contrast to the anarchist poetry that expressed human emotions with all their contradictions and weaknesses.

FORMALISM AND SURREALISM

The modernist journal *A* (亞) was founded by Anzai Fuyue (1898–1965), Kitagawa Fuyuhiko (b. 1900), and two others in 1924 in Ta-lien, Manchuria. Their poetry was more aesthetically oriented than that of anarchist poets, and thus it could be seen as a precursor to the aestheticism cultivated in the journal *Shi to shiron*, which they helped found. They both experimented with extremely short poems as well as with prose poems. From Anzai's first book of verse, *Gunkan mari* (1929; Warship Mari):[25]

Spring

A butterfly went across the Tartar Strait.[26]

Spring

A herring is about to be brought to the table, coming through a subway tunnel.[27]

Odalisque

The moon rose above the castle gate   a   pale   pale

woman was yielding her legs to a dog.[28]

From Kitagawa's book *Sensō* (1929; War):

Song of Despair

I am nursing a man on the cold concrete floor of an empty customs shed. Who is this man? I do not know the answer. My arm is creaking like an unoiled gear over one of his legs. The other leg has already fallen. From morning till midnight, from midnight till morning I have been caressing his preserved leg without a break. Why do I have to nurse this man? This stranger, this corpselike stranger? This stranger who cannot stop moaning, "Despair, despair, can't keep living unless we despair . . . ," partially exposing his eyeballs, which look like glass frosted by the moonlight flowing like phosphorus as the night deepens. I do not understand, do not understand, do not understand, do not understand, do not understand.[29]

Rush Hour

At the wicket a finger was cut along with a ticket.[30]

Camellia

Women's 800-meter relay. She fell, abruptly, at the final turn.

A fallen flower.[31]

Horse

Visceralizing a naval port.[32]

Compared with the outburst of raw emotion presented in anarchist poetry, these poems show the poets' conscious effort to construct an artificially aesthetic space, which is evocative of, but not a direct presentation of, emotion. Anzai's poetry tended to be hermetically sensual and dreamy, while Kitagawa wrote poems that incorporated possibilities for social criticism. Nonetheless, the aesthetic intellectualism seen in these poems was to be the emblem of *Shi to shiron*.

In November 1927, Kitasono Katsue, together with the Ueda brothers from the Keiō group, founded what is considered the first surrealist magazine in Japan, *Shōbi (or Bara)* • *majutsu* • *gakusetsu* (Rose • magic • theory). Kitasono had participated in the dadaist magazine *GE* • *GJMGJGAM* • *PRRR* • *GYMGEM* (1924), and had also contributed poems to avant-garde journals such as *Mavo* and *Bungei tanbi* (Literary aesthetics), which claimed the honor of being the first journal to publish "official" surrealist writings—translations of poems by French surrealists Paul Eluard and Louis Aragon in 1925. In the third issue of *Shōbi* • *majutsu* • *gakusetsu,* published in January 1928, a separate note was inserted:

A Note December 1927

A baptism was bestowed on us—we who have sung the praises to the progress of artistic desires and of senses in surrealism. We have mastered the technique of utilizing materials through the senses but without being limited by them. We construct a "Poetic Operation," which depends on a certain dispensation, in a condition separated from the human realm. This particular condition makes us feel a sense of indifference not unlike that of technology. In our attempt to establish the limits of objectivity, we feel as if we were "Poetic Scientists." We are neither melancholic nor happy. The human feeling that does not require the feeling subject to be human is suitably rigorous and sober. We sense an excitement appropriate to us as we construct our "Poetic Operation." We will continue *Surréalisme*. We sing a hymn of praise to the virtue of saturation.

Kitasono Katsue
Ueda Toshio
Ueda Tamotsu
(Quoted in Nakano 1975, 87–88)

The editorial in that issue claimed that a translation of this note was sent to "Communistes-Surréalistes, Louis Aragon, Paul Eluard, André Breton and Surréaliste non Communist Antonin Artaud" (ibid., 88). Commonly regarded as the first surrealist manifesto in Japan, it trailed Breton's "Surrealist Manifesto of 1924" by a few years, but it preceded Kitagawa Fuyuhiko's translation of Breton's manifesto published in *Shi to shiron* (nos. 4 and 5) in 1929. In November 1928, the members of *Fukuikutaru kafuyo* and *Shōbi • majutsu • gakusetsu* merged and founded another magazine, *Ishō no taiyō* (The costume's sun), on the cover of which were the words "L'ÉVOLUTION SURRÉALISTE."

The first issue of the journal *Shi to shiron* came out in March 1928 as a coterie magazine with eleven members: Anzai Fuyue, Ueda Toshio, Kanbara Tai, Kitagawa Fuyuhiko, Miyoshi Tatsuji, Kondō Azuma (b. 1904), Iijima Tadashi (b. 1902), Takiguchi Takeshi (1904–82), Takenaka Iku (1904–82), Toyama Usaburō (b. 1903), and general editor Haruyama Yukio (b. 1902). However, from the beginning it also solicited submissions from outside. Although not a *dōjin* (coterie member), Nishiwaki contributed a number of theoretical and academic writings as well as a few surrealist texts to the journal, and thus was acknowledged as a central figure in the venture. After publishing fourteen issues, the journal changed its name to *Bungaku* (Literature) in 1932 and folded in June 1933. Most of the young poets who did not belong to the proletarian literary movement contributed to *Shi to shiron*. Later Kitagawa recalled how the magazine began:

With Haruyama Yukio, whom I had met only once before, we began to look for members for a new magazine that would reform contemporary Jap-

anese poetry. That was early in 1928. I had begun writing poetry in the
early 1920s and since then I had always felt that neither the artless poetry of
the *minshūshi-ha* nor the lifeless poetry of the *shōchōshi-ha* (symbolists) was
any good. Haruyama had begun writing poetry before me. He too seemed
determined to sever himself from the old poetry establishment *(shidan)*,
being indeed quite indignant at it. . . .

I invited the imagist Anzai Fuyue, who belonged to a little magazine, *A,*
published in Ta-lien, Manchuria; Takiguchi Takeshi; Miyoshi Tatsuji, who
was writing new type of lyrical poetry in the coterie magazine *Aozora* (Blue
sky); Ueda Toshio, who was an ultra-strange surrealist at that time; Kanbara
Tai, who was once active in futurism; the fighter for *shin kankaku-ha* (new
sensationalist) Yokomitsu Riichi; and the film critic Iijima Tadashi, who
knew much about new poetry in France. . . .

Haruyama recommended the modernist Kondō Azuma, who just won
the first prize from the journal *Kaizō*, Sasazawa Yoshiaki, who was into the
neue Sachlichkeit, Takenaka Iku, who was under the wing of Horiguchi Daigaku, Yoshida Issui, who was writing anarchistic pure poetry, J. N. (Nishiwaki Junzaburō), who was a completely unknown supernaturalist, and Toyama Usaburō, who was known for his studies of poetic theory. (Quoted in
Harazaki 1980, 98)

As one can see from the list of the people invited to join the journal,
Shi to shiron was to be a stage where theoretical concerns shared the
forefront with the introduction of contemporary poetry and poetics
from abroad. Indeed, from the first issue Haruyama blasted the works
of the established Japanese poets, accusing them of belonging to the
mushigaku teki kyū shidan (the old poetry establishment with no poetic theory).

Central to Haruyama's poetics was the concept of *poejī* (poesy),
which he distinguished from *poemu* (poem). In "Poejī to wa nan de
aruka—kōsokudo shiron sono ichi" (What is poesy—a high speed poetics no.1) which appeared in the second issue of *Shi to shiron*, he
wrote: "To begin with, the problem with today's established Japanese
poets *(shidan)* arises from the imperfect understanding of the essence
of 'poesy.' They associate poetry immediately with 'vers' or with some
variations of verse. Thus their concept of poetry does not go beyond
the poem in which 'poesy' finds its expression. Or they simply do not
let the notion of poetry away from that of verse" (*Shi to shiron* 2:226).
The newness of Haruyama's argument can be found in his understanding of poesy as a certain essence of literature not limited to any particu-

lar genre. He contended that in order for the poesy to be realized, the expression must be guided by a methodology dictated by the implicit nature of poesy itself. For Haruyama, poetry was not something that naturally and automatically arose from the individual poet's interior, but something that had to be constructed with a lucid formalist methodology.[33] Therefore, in a sense, his use of the term *poesy* was close to what the latter half of the journal's title denoted: *shiron* (poetics, or theory of poetry).

Haruyama also actively solicited translations of and introductions to contemporary Western modernist writings for *Shi to shiron*. The first issue included theoretical essays by Louis Aragon and Henri Bremond. A special-issue format began with the fourth issue: "a review of contemporary poets of the world" in no. 4; "on Paul Valéry" in no. 5; "on André Gide" in no. 6; "works of Paul Valéry" in no. 7; "contemporary American literature" in no. 13; "issues on the novel" in no. 14.; and after it became *Bungaku*, "on James Joyce" in no. 2, and "T. S. Eliot" in no. 4. With Haruyama's two expressly stated policies, the emphasis on methodology and the introduction of contemporary poetics from abroad, the magazine performed a central role in creating what we now call *gendai shi* (contemporary poetry)—as opposed to *kindai shi* (modern poetry)—which continues its lineage in the poetry written today.

REALITY

The formalist aestheticism of *Shi to shiron* arose at a time when the proletarian literature movement was still going strong despite harassment by the authorities and its own factional infighting. In the year *Shi to shiron* came out, 1928, for example, Nihon musansha geijutsu renmei (All-Japan federation of proletarian arts) was organized and its journal *Senki* (Battle flag) was founded. Surprisingly, there arose few theoretical debates between the *Shi to shiron* group and the proletarian poets. Perhaps both camps knew too well that the chasm between them was too wide. However, criticism of formalist surrealism emerged from within the *Shi to shiron* group. In the essay "Shijin no me" (A poet's eye), published in the sixth issue of *Shi to shiron*, Kitagawa Fuyuhiko criticized Ueda Toshio's notion of surrealism: "Mr. Ueda Toshio hypothesizes a realm of art that does not relate to the human spirit. His could be a fictive world of surrealism. But it can never be surrealism's sun. His is merely a world landscape seen from a closed eye. Surrealism's sun is a world that relates to the human spirit. It is a fictive world that relates to the human spirit most directly" (*Shi to shiron* 6:34–35). Kitagawa's discontent with the methodologically oriented construction of poetry advocated by Haruyama and Ueda resulted in the secession of the five original members from *Shi to shiron*: Kitagawa, Kanbara, Miyoshi, Takiguchi, and Iijima. They went on to found another journal, *Shi • genjitsu* (Poetry • reality), in 1930. In its first issue, Kanbara wrote a scathing critique of surrealism, entitled "Chōgenjitsushugi no botsuraku" (The fall of surrealism), attacking the surrealists' lack of awareness of reality. Referring to Nishiwaki's stance on reality expressed in the first page of his *Chōgenjitsushugi shiron* (Surrealist poetics), he had this to say:

> Mr. Nishiwaki Junzaburō wrote:
>
> > Custom dulls the awareness of reality. Conventions let this awareness slip into hibernation. Thus our reality becomes banal. Then it follows that the break with custom makes reality exciting. For our awareness is refreshed. What we must note here, however, is that we are to break down the bonds of habits and conventions not for the sake of destruction itself but for the sake of poetic expression. In other words, this act of destruction, with its consequential process of making reality exciting, must be committed in order to fulfill the aim of poetry.
>
> What a reckless remark this is! We simply cannot allow any surrealists to say something so ridiculous. Not only does it show that Mr. Nishiwaki Junzaburō utterly lacks any awareness of reality that surrounds us now with an overwhelming power, any awareness of us contemporary people who must increasingly pay attention to reality, but also it covers up and beautifies the flight of those who lack sincerity, justice, power, and courage to face reality.[34]

Indeed, the social "reality" that surrounded those poets in 1930 was increasingly oppressive and demanded their committed responses. Yet, as history testifies, no Japanese poet had "sincerity, justice, power, and courage to face" fascism before and during World War II. Japanese fascism succeeded not only in silencing resistance from poets but also in having them actively participate in the war by writing patriotic war poetry. Most of the proletarian poets were captured at one time or another and eventually went through *tenkō* (apostasy) in prison, after the well-publicized *tenkō* of their leaders Nabeyama Sadachika and Sano Manabu on June 10, 1933. The collapse and the consequent reversal of the resistant spirit among the poets were almost eerie in their completeness. As if there had been no subjectivity, no identity, no belief, no spirit that would define one's existence as a continuous being, every poet began singing horrendous war-hymns praising Japan's "sacred" mission. One fiercely resistant poet who nonetheless went through a number of conversions was Tsuboi Shigeji. He began as an anarchist, modernist poet, but abandoned anarchism for communism in the late 1920s after he was badly injured in an attack by an anarchist terrorist group. He then became a central figure by publishing the proletarian journal *Senki*, for which he was thrown into jail a number of times. During his imprisonment in 1932, learning that the proletarian literature movement was totally wiped out, he recanted his communism and was released. After the war, he was elected to the executive committee of Shin nihon bungaku kai (Association of new Japanese literature). Apparently it was "only writers who did not collaborate with and resisted the Imperial War" who could qualify for the committee (Abe Takeshi 1980, 228). However, it was later discovered that Tsuboi had in fact written and published war-praising poems.[35]

The list of those who *actively* participated in writing prowar poems includes Takamura Kōtarō, Miyoshi Tatsuji, Kusano Shinpei, Noguchi Yonejirō (1875–1947), Maruyama Kaoru (1899–1974), Ozaki Kihachi (1892–1974), Murano Shirō (1901–75), Anzai Fuyue, Kondō Azuma, Takahashi Shinkichi, Satō Haruo (1892–1964), Horiguchi Daigaku, and Kitagawa Fuyuhiko. Takamura Kōtarō's severe self-criticism and consequent voluntary isolation from society after the war is well known. Most of the poets, however, attempted to ignore or even cover up their wartime activities. The cases of the perennial modernist Kitasono Katsue and the most celebrated resistant poet, Kaneko Mitsuharu (1895–1975), tragically fall into the latter category. Indeed, until recently Kaneko was thought to be one of the very few, if not the only one, who succeeded in publishing resistant poetry during the war.[36] But according to Sakuramoto Tomio, Kaneko revised his wartime poems when they were reprinted after the war in order to elude the accusation of writing propagandist poems. Sakuramoto contends that the poets were not coerced into writing propagandist poetry; they could have chosen to be silent (Sakuramoto 1983, 211–16). Nishiwaki was one of the few who chose to be silent.

What did the concept of "reality" mean for the poets who fervently engaged in discussions of this notion as the war approached?[37] I will later examine what position the notion of "reality" took in Nishiwaki's theoretical writings. Here I would simply like to look at some poems by the formalists Haruyama Yukio and Kitasono Katsue in order to contrast their surrealist formalism with the poetics on which Nishiwaki's work is founded. Here is a part of a representative poem by Haruyama published in *Shi to shiron* no. 2.

> It's a white promenade
> It's a white chair
> It's white perfume
> It's a white cat
> It's a white sock
> It's a white neck
> It's a white sky
> It's a white cloud
> It's a white girl
> doing a handstand
> It's my "Kodak"   (Murano et al. 1961, 7:124)

Here is an excerpt of a long poem from Kitasono's first book, *Shiro no arubamu* (1929; White album):

> *Semiotic Theory*
>
>   *
>
> white tableware
> flower
> spoon
> spring afternoon 3 o'clock
> white
> white
> red
>
>   *
>
> prism construction
> white animal
> space
>
>   *
>
> blue flag
> apple and lady
> white landscape
>
>   *
>
> flower and music instrument
> white window
> wind

*

blue sky
nothing visible
nothing visible
white house

*

white distant view
faint pink flag
despair   (Ibid., 7:59–60)

However much we may want to applaud their experimental spirit, these poems simply do not go beyond mere image-play. Compared with Nishiwaki's most experimental texts (for example, "A Fragrant Stoker"), their poems show none of Nishiwaki's vivacious boisterousness of images and words. It is not difficult to see why Kitagawa, Miyoshi, and others left *Shi to shiron* for more "reality." But during the war Kitagawa himself wrote:

The whole town
was completely filled with the Rising-Sun flags.
Its beauty was beyond words.
I heard later that
it was
the number-one town
in all of Malaysia
so much in love with Japan.[38]

As Singapore fell to Japan, Miyoshi wrote:

The warships are sunk everywhere.
A few surviving soldiers kneel and lower their heads beneath a white
    flag.
As the gun-smoke dissipates, the Rising-Sun flag stands here proudly.
Oh, truly, the government ordinance of the sly senile British Empire,
    along with their conspiracy and pillage,
are all finally kicked out beyond our realm
beyond this threshold for good.
Laugh, clap your hands, step on your mythical bellows![39]

Reality is overwhelming, as Kanbara's attack on Nishiwaki rightly observed. A reality that was thoroughly dictated by the monolithic discourse of war simply overpowered the poets. There is no way now to reconstruct exactly the reality that surrounded them. Through their texts (including their postwar texts) we merely glimpse the tattered bravado, the pathetic attempts at survival, the pestilent claustrophobia under the deified emperor system, the scared eyes, the guilty hearts. For us, who did not experience their reality, it is easy to condemn their cowardice and irresponsibility. Yet, however necessary, such condemnation remains hopelessly naive.

Under such an oppressive reality, formalist aestheticism was the first to die. There was no need for an aesthetic object divorced from the actual overwhelming insanity and sufferings that flooded reality. What happened to the concept of "poetry" during this period of an overwhelming reality? Did it have any other function except propagandistic expressionism? Nishiwaki fell silent. Through his silence, we can at least sense that he could not equate the concept of poetry with such expressionism. We also sense that "poetry" did not die with the war, as we witness in *No Traveller Returns*, which was published two years after the end of the war.

The relation between "reality" and "poetry (text)" is an essential one for both concepts. Nishiwaki's poetry survived because he pursued the relation between them more rigorously than any other Japanese poet at that time. While other Japanese modernist poets' fickle notions of "reality" came and went in many guises, Nishiwaki went on to found his entire poetics on a single notion of "reality": *tsumaranasa* (boredom, banality). One might wish to call him an escapist. Essentially, he was an escapist. Yet he encountered "reality" and "poetry" as no one else did. Nishiwaki is sometimes labeled a surrealist, other times a supernaturalist. In fact Nishiwaki never called himself a surrealist and was careful to keep his distance from surrealism.[40] Such literary historicist labeling of the poet, however, does not concern us here. What we must discern now is the relation between Nishiwaki's ideas of "poetry" and "reality." The next chapter opens with this inquiry.

CHAPTER TWO

Pure Poetry and Reality

> As he traveled alone, like a man lured on by a syllable without any
>
> meaning,
>
> A syllable of which he felt, with an appointed sureness,
>
> That it contained the meaning into which he wanted to enter,
>
> A meaning which, as he entered it, would shatter the boat and leave
>
> the oarsmen quiet
>
> As at a point of central arrival, an instant moment, much or little,
>
> Removed from any shore, from any man or woman, and needing
>
> none.
>
> —*Wallace Stevens, "Prologues to What Is Possible"*

> . . . the blasphemy to force God out of his silence.
>
> —*Maurice Blanchot, Lautréamont et Sade*

When poetic language, in a drive toward its own purity, loses external meaning, that is, the mediating function of language, silence falls. But then how can writing begin from the encased purity of silence, from the central, most immediate poetry, to which, paradoxically, Wallace Stevens's words yearn to return? Writing must come into being as a certain failure of this essential silence. And yet poetry itself seems to dwell within the originary silence. What follows is an attempt to trace this primordial struggle between silence and communicative writing—writing as a means to transport "reality" or "poetry."

In order to elucidate this issue, Nishiwaki's poetics of self-extinction expounded in *Surrealist Poetics* may be cautiously translated into the current critical terminology. For example, we may think of Roland Barthes's concept of text, especially that of the "writerly text" introduced in *S/Z*.[1] In the writerly text, Barthes argues, reading as a consumption of meaning becomes impossible. Writing, on the other hand, is posited as an act of pure production, an intransitive movement of text. We may also think of Georges Bataille's notion of poetry as a drive toward *non-savoir*, a sacrifice of knowledge, an absolute state he names "Sovereignty" by way of Hegel.[2] In this chapter, I would like to turn to Jacques Derrida's theory of *différance* or of supplementary traces in order to re-situate Nishiwaki's modernist discourse.

A central and most paradoxical problem concerning "writing" emerges here. Where does the notion of writing "pure poetry," or of writing the Barthesian "writerly text," stand in relation to the struggle between communication and silence, between reality and poetry? Both Nishiwaki and Derrida direct our attention to a certain negative movement inherent in language that (self-)transgresses the realm of meaning. While Nishiwaki's discourse traces the antimimetic movement of poetry, Derrida's deconstructive critique is directed at the language of metaphysics. We are repeatedly reminded through their writings that in the order of mimesis as well as of metaphysics, the recovery of "truth" and "meaning" (i.e., reading) plays a cardinal role. Derrida's grammatology attempts to open a field of writing that is free from the restricted economy of communication (reading). Similarly, Nishiwaki attempts to see the end of writing-as-reading (mimesis) where ultimately language (as a vehicle of representation) dies and so poetry dies of its own accord. (Pure) writing is thus released from the burden of closed communication and returns to a certain silence (reality), which is not an utter passivity of muteness, but a supplementary textual production that always precedes the silent origin, the "recovery" (reading) of the origin, beyond communication.

PROFANUS

In April 1926, in the pages of *Mita bungaku*, Nishiwaki broke his silence with these words: "To discourse upon poetry is as dangerous as to discourse upon God" (*NJZ* 4:8). At the end of the essay thus began, we are again reminded of the danger: "It is dangerous to discuss poetry. I have already fallen off the cliff" (*NJZ* 4:26). Nishiwaki's first published writing on poetry was thus appropriately entitled "Profanus." What danger does poetry contain? What danger does God contain? Perhaps we could call this danger either "Sovereignty" or "Purity." For Nishiwaki, "poetry" signified a textual movement toward an absolute state of signification (or of nonsignification). The metalanguage of poetics in which he had to engage was a "profane," that is, essentially blasphemous, language doomed to failure (failure of poetry, failure of silence) from the start. The metalanguage may speak of poetry, but it cannot speak poetry. (But again, what danger, what blasphemy?) Nishiwaki was about to describe not the murder of God but the suicide, the self-extinction of poetry.

In "Profanus," however, Nishiwaki was yet to push his notion of poetry to its limits. Through his more or less historical charting of "what poetry is," Nishiwaki reiterates a Romantic thesis that poetry is an ever-renewing method of cognizing reality. As for the method of poetic creation, Nishiwaki endorses the surrealist technique of conjoining two distant elements to create a new "reality." Yet Nishiwaki's intention in "Profanus" seems not merely to define this method as one peculiar to the surrealist strategy but rather to regard it as the historically developed, and thus universally acceptable, essence of poetry. Commenting on Pierre Reverdy's notion of image—"It cannot be born from a comparison but from a juxtaposition of two more or less distant realities" (quoted in Breton 1969, 20)—Nishiwaki writes: "In short, this idea of supernaturalist poetry has always been present in the works of great poets since antiquity and in fact is not particularly a new mode of poetry" (*NJZ* 4:13).

Nishiwaki celebrates Francis Bacon as the first critic to discover this modernist method of poetic creation. In "The Tvvo Bookes of the Proficience and Advancement of Learning, Divine and Hvmane" (1605), Bacon offers the following definition of poetry: "Poesie is a part of Learning in measure of words for the most part restrained, but in all other points extreamely licensed, and doth truly referre to the Imagination, which, beeing not tyed to the Lawes of Matter, may at pleasure ioyne that which Nature hath seuered, & seuer that which Nature hath ioyned, and so make vnlawfull Matches & divorses of things" (Bacon 1908, 1:5). Nishiwaki was intrigued to find that this insight into the nature of poetry displayed by a seventeenth-century thinker was actualized by contemporary dadaists and surrealists in Europe. Throughout his life Nishiwaki maintained that the most fundamental method of generating poetry is to juxtapose two distant elements—indeed, to "make unlawful matches and divorces of things." At that time, the French surrealists, led by André Breton, were seeking new relationships between those "distant elements." For Breton, the juxtaposition could not end up in a mere comparison; it had to generate a poetic energy. Distance was needed. In his first *Manifesto of Surrealism* (1924), Breton writes:

In my opinion, it is erroneous to claim that "the mind has grasped the relationship" of two realities in the presence of each other. First of all, it has seized nothing consciously. It is, as it were, from the fortuitous juxtaposition of the two terms that a particular light has sprung, *the light of the image*, to which we are infinitely sensitive. The value of the image depends upon the beauty of the spark obtained; it is, consequently, a function of the difference of potential between the two conductors. When the difference exists only slightly, as in a comparison, the spark is lacking. (Breton 1969, 37)

TSUMARANASA

Nishiwaki, however, criticizes surrealist poetry for being solely concerned with the transformation of reality and consequently for "forgetting reality." For Nishiwaki, poetry must not and cannot forgo what he calls the *tsumaranasa* (banality) of reality. Thus, he claims, "Poetry must be founded in reality" (*NJZ* 4:21). Also, at the beginning of "Profanus," he writes: "The reality of human existence itself is banal [*tsumaranai*]. To sense this fundamental yet supreme banality [*tsumaranasa*] constitutes the motivation for poetry" (*NJZ* 4:8). *Tsumaranai* can be translated as trifling, insignificant, worthless, silly, dull, or common, but is usually used in the much lighter sense of "boring." What we see here is a unique transplanting of a key term employed in Romantic poetics into Japanese soil. The key term is "familiarity," used by both Coleridge and Shelley. Nishiwaki in fact translates Shelley's famous sentence, "[Poetry] makes familiar objects be as if they were not familiar" (Adams 1971, 503), using the word *tsumaranai* for "familiar" (*NJZ* 4:12). Also, once juxtaposed to certain passages of Coleridge and Shelley, the following assertion by Nishiwaki seems a more or less faithful translation of their ideas: "Custom dulls the awareness of reality. Conventions let this awareness slip into hibernation. Thus our reality becomes banal. Then it follows that the break with custom makes reality exciting, for our awareness is refreshed."[3] In the *Biographia Literaria*, Coleridge notes: "[The purposes of poetry are] to give the charm of novelty to things of every day, and to excite a feeling analogous to the supernatural, by awakening the mind's attention from the lethargy of custom, and directing it to the loveliness and the wonders of the world before us; an inexhaustible treasure, but for which in consequence of the film of familiarity and selfish solicitude we have eyes, yet see not, ears that hear not, and hearts that neither feel nor understand" (Coleridge 1983, chap. 14, p. 7). And Shelley, who was evidently influenced by Coleridge, writes in his "Defense of Poetry": "[Poetry] reproduces the common universe of which we are portions and percipients, and it purges from our inward sight the film of familiarity which obscures from us the wonder of our being. It compels us to feel that which we perceive, and to imagine that which we know. It creates anew the universe, after it has been annihilated in our minds by the recurrence of impressions blunted by reiteration" (Adams 1971, 512).

Yet the significance of *tsumaranasa* cannot simply be contained by "familiarity." In fact in Nishiwaki's poetry *tsumaranasa* begins to take a central position, often carrying a feeling of timeless weariness hovering around a forgotten object. In poem 82 of *Tabibito kaerazu* (No traveller returns), we read:

> In an old garden
> where tiger lilies bloom
> a forgotten
> broken watering can
> lying . . . (*ZS*, 207)

In *Eterunitasu* this *tsumaranasa* becomes articulated as the nonsymbolic that the poet ultimately seeks:

> A teacup abandoned in a puddle,
> a trace of children's play,
> a crest imprinted upon the back of a loach,
> a madman crossing a bridge,
> the nervous flurry of a stone thrown into a bamboo thicket,
> the scream of a meteorite struck by a plow,
> a louse left on a traveller's hat,
> the movement of Pound's Adam's apple,
> a man
> on the run
> chewing
> a soil-crusted bitter root
> of nipplewort—
> these things do not symbolize.
> Things that do not symbolize
> attract us more. (*ZS*, 621–22)

The nonsymbolic, something that does not symbolize anything, is literally *insignificant*, meaning-less.[4] An object stripped of meaning, of its own name, of its function, cannot register itself in our consciousness except as a tear in the fabric of our "meaningful" language. The forgotten, broken watering can lying on the ground has lost its function (to water plants) and has returned to its own mute being. In a sense, it has gained the weight of its own presence by asserting its pure object-ness. But at the same time, it signifies a certain absence, a gap in the exquisite order of the ancient garden. The broken watering can has no formal place in the garden. It is a negative-code of the garden. It must be buried and forgotten; otherwise it will erode the whole garden with its "absence" (negative-code). But perhaps the garden is already ruined, devoid of human voice, ancient, and forgotten. In such a strange silent vividness, how regally the tiger lilies survive the ruins!

Nishiwaki's blasphemy is thus directed against the world of codified functions and meanings. Once deprived of its code, the object manifests the "supreme banality" (*idai na tsumaranasa*) of its being. Despite his endorsement of defamiliarization as the primary function of poetry, Nishiwaki repeatedly warned against losing sight of what is familiar, that is, reality itself. When the most familiar is defamiliarized, the resulting effect becomes, poetically speaking, strongest. But also, for Nishiwaki poetry provided a method of returning to the fundamental *tsumaranasa,* the loss of meaning, which *is* the primal reality. Here we can sense a fundamental difference between the formalist surrealism practiced by such poets as Haruyama Yukio and Kitasono Katsue and the poetics of Nishiwaki. Haruyama and Kitasono may have produced texts that defy an ordinary assignment of "meaning," yet their texts utterly lack the sense of "reality" that Nishiwaki talks about—reality that is from the beginning "meaning-less," always anterior to language. The paradox here is evident. It is this irreversible, inevitable anteriority of reality to language that produces *tsumaranasa* in a text that is nonetheless fated to employ language. It is apparent that, unlike the proletarian poets, Nishiwaki was not much interested in "social reality"—a reality that has already been soaked with "meanings." Rather, he wanted to find his topos vis-à-vis insignificant beings that defy language's manipulation.

ANTIEXPRESSION

If we take "Profanus" as Nishiwaki's attempt to delineate a poetics of the past, the next chapter of *Surrealist Poetics,* "The Extinction of Poetry" (*Shi no shōmetsu*), can be regarded as his bold hypothesis about the poetics of the future. Nishiwaki begins with the following postulate: "The realm of poetry expands infinitely and finally disappears. As a corollary (ipso facto) of this hypothesis the following rule is set forth: 'The most expanded, the most advanced mode of poetry is that which is closest to its own extinction.'" (*NJZ* 4:27).

This hypothesis about the self-extinction of poetry can be seen as a logical extension of the antimimetic theory of poetry traced back to Bacon in "Profanus." In "Profanus," Nishiwaki divided the poetic modality into two distinct categories: (1) poetry that is closely related to human emotions, and (2) poetry that breaks away from common sense, emotion, custom, and so forth. In "The Extinction of Poetry" this schema is further elaborated in terms of expression (*hyōgen*). First, nature and art are clearly distinguished. Nishiwaki claims that any expression (or "textual manifestation") that pertains to nature cannot legitimately be art. What Nishiwaki means by "nature" includes natural phenomena as well as human expressions of emotions, of dreams, and the like. In other words, a "natural expression" is inescapably confined to the order of mimesis. In the mimetic order, a writer attempts to represent an extralingual truth of presence through the ideal transparency of language. Nishiwaki presents his point in his characteristically witty manner: "Moreover, just as conscientious objectors are sometimes exonerated from the usual legal obligations, in the poetic legal system, when an author believes that what he has thought or felt is true, he will be exonerated from the obligations of art. In other words, his work will not be considered art" (*NJZ* 4:23). If a writer believes he or she is faithfully representing "true" feelings or thoughts, then that writer's mimetic work cannot gain the status of art. This indeed shows Nishiwaki's radical rejection of the mimetic order in art.

In Nishiwaki's view, artistic expression must be absolutely deliberate, artificial, non-natural—that is, essentially ironic. In this light, for Nishiwaki, Baudelaire becomes the first and primary exponent of what he calls the "legal" (legitimate) artist. In "Esthétique Foraine" Nishiwaki quotes Baudelaire: "Two fundamental literary qualities: supernaturalism and irony" (*NJZ* 4:42). This dictum constitutes the principal law of poetry. A poem, then, must be an intentionally artificial expression, disrupting the "natural" flow of feelings and thoughts, which constantly seeks to be represented most "truthfully." This type of poetry thus carries within it a movement against what Derrida calls "logocentrism"—the monolith of "Truth." The negative movement of poetry, when developed to its fullest, will lead itself to its own extinction. What is excluded from this negative order of poetry then constitutes the world of positivity—nature, reality, truth, identity—in other words, any objects of mimetic expression. What is left to be expressed?

Nishiwaki further divides the second mode of poetry ("legal" poetry) into three periods. The first period is called "the era of expression," the second, "the era of antiexpression," the last, simply "extinction." To the first period belongs most of modern poetry from Baudelaire to dadaist and surrealist poetry. Nishiwaki claims that even the radical antiart movement of dadaism failed to reach the second period, though it predicted the arrival of a new mode of poetry. On the antiexpressive era, he writes: "In this period, the poet manifests a will that shows his deliberate wish *not to express*. In the First Period, poetry was still an effort to express, whereas in the Second Period it is to *make an effort not to express*" (*NJZ* 4:32). Such an antiexpressive effort certainly marks the limit of poetry as a mode of expression. For Nishiwaki, this antiexpressive mode becomes "the most advanced mode of poetry."

When logic is pushed to its limits, only an absurd end is possible. In the final hypothetical stage of poetry, even the act of refusal to express is erased. What remains then? A prose poem by Hagiwara Sakutarō depicts a starving octopus in an aquarium eating away its own body little by little until it completely disappears.[5] Yet something still remains in the dark, forgotten aquarium. A trace of being? A trace of hunger?

THE IMPOSSIBLE OBJECT OF EXPRESSION

In the second section of "The Extinction of Poetry," "The Limits of the Object of Expression," Nishiwaki attempts to illustrate the limits of poetry in terms of the object of expression, that is, what is to be expressed. After rejecting anything that relates to humanity, subjectivity, or reality as a legitimate object of expression, Nishiwaki develops a certain negative dialectic employing the Kantian notion of "objective will." According to Nishiwaki, the a priori objective will itself becomes the object of expression in the "legally" expressive period. The objective will comes into being as the result of a purifying process that the human will undergoes by transgressing the bounds of individual subjectivity. It is, in a sense, a self-hypostatization of the will to express. The will to express finally becomes itself (and thus *kanzen*, perfect) by eliminating all the other elements that may be the object of expression (*NJZ* 4:36).

Nishiwaki goes on to connect this self-referential movement of the will to express with our will to live. For Nishiwaki, the will to live marks a movement that is uncontrollable, something beyond mere subjectivity. This fierce movement of the will to live also attempts to reach its own pure hypostatization by transgressing the bounds of reality. According to Nishiwaki, it defines the poetry of surrealism. Against this self-objectifying movement of the will to live, the final rebellion of the subject takes place. Nishiwaki writes:

> The will to live is the will of a creator. Man is helpless to deal with this blind will. This absolutely unmanageable will exists objectively in man. The mere existence of such a will, which is so utterly beneath contempt, is the subject of helpless rage. At times one may feel physically throughout one's brain the startling jolt of an esprit that attempts to resist this blind will. This is a strange phenomenon in which an attempt to rebel against a will that created the human race is manifested. It is a rebellion against the creator's will. Or it can be said that in fact the real creator holds a will that seeks to oppose his own creative will. A creator is a self-deceiver. The poetry that attempts to present the energy of an esprit rebelling against the very effort to live, that is, the effort to break down reality, creates the next poetic region. (*NJZ* 4:37)

The "antisurreal" mode thus predicted is based on its denial of the will to live, or of the will to express. Moreover, it is based on the denial of the transgressive, that is, essentially exclusive, purifying movement of the will toward itself. What this final mode of poetry accomplishes is the relentless and absolute deconstruction of the a priori, including such stabilizing notions as man, reality, self, and life, as well as the self-purification of the will. At this point poetry as expression commits suicide, and mankind perishes. What remains now? A grotesque laughter? A trace of spent *jouissance*? Nishiwaki's words turn tragicomic: "Poetry dies as mankind dies. The lamp is turned off. But things like kangaroos or cactuses may be still trying to survive, fidgeting here and there. How pitiful" (*NJZ* 4:37). What survives after the death of poetry and mankind are *insignificant* things like "kangaroos or cactuses." Nishiwaki in these essays has delineated an immanent movement within what we can only name "poetry." It is a movement toward pure poetry divorced from nature, yet at the end, it moves beyond its self-encased purity. It reaches for a reality anterior to language, but first poetry must die in order to return to this "insignificant" reality. In order to clarify this peculiar notion of poetic movement as well as that of the anterior reality, I will now examine them in terms of Derrida's deconstruction of presence. A thorough critique of the notion of presence should illuminate the notion of the insignificant reality in direct relation to the movement of poetry.

DERRIDA'S TRACE

As if to echo Nishiwaki's ideas about the self-extinction of poetry, Susan Sontag remarks on the self-sacrificial tendency of modern literature in her preface to Barthes's *Writing Degree Zero:* "As modern literature is the history of alienated 'writing' or personal utterance, literature aims inexorably at its own self-transcendence—at the abolition of literature" (Sontag 1967, xvii). Indeed, this negative movement of literature/poetry finds its common ground in a theory of writing (grammatology) proposed by Derrida. Derrida's field of investigation is the language of metaphysics imbued with logocentrism. What he champions in his criticism is "writing" (as opposed to "speech"), which, he claims, forces a rupture within the closure of metaphysics. Rigorously, Derrida makes any trace of logocentrism manifest and resituates it in the field of what he calls *différance*,[6] or the "chain of supplements." In a sense, Nishiwaki's notion of poetry as a negative movement can be said, according to Derrida's grammatology, to have existed from the very beginning of any movement of signification, provided we are aware that in the Derridian universe there is no "very beginning" as such.

What can then be thought of as being at the very beginning of representation, of appearance? What is at the origin of a text, or "writing"? Derrida's answer is a trace, an "arche-trace," though he takes great pains not to reestablish this *archē*, this beginning, as a theological, originary point of departure:

> The trace is not only the disappearance of origin—within the discourse that we sustain and according to the path that we follow it means that the origin did not even disappear, that it was never constituted except reciprocally by a nonorigin, the trace, which thus becomes the origin of the origin. From then on, to wrench the concept of the trace from the classical scheme, which would derive it from a presence or from an originary nontrace and

which would make of it an empirical mark, one must indeed speak of an originary trace or arche-trace. Yet we know that that concept destroys its name and that, if all begins with the trace, there is above all no originary trace.[7] (*DG*, 61)

This paralogical replacement of "origin" with "trace" must be considered an extension of a thesis concerning the arbitrariness of the sign posited by Ferdinand de Saussure in his *Course in General Linguistics*. Saussure states, as the first linguistic principle, "The link between signal [signifier] and signification [signified] is arbitrary" [*Le lien unissant le signifiant au signifié est arbitraire*] (Saussure 1986, 67). That is, there is no natural connection between the "sound-image" of a word and the concept signified by it. This arbitrary nature of the sign does not, however, mean that the regulation of a sign-system is utterly capricious. In order to clarify this point, Saussure replaces the word "arbitrary" with "unmotivated": "The word *arbitrary* also calls for comment. It must not be taken to imply that a signal depends on the free choice of the speaker. . . . The term implies simply that the signal is *unmotivated:* that is to say arbitrary in relation to its signification, with which it has no natural connexion in reality" (ibid., 68–69). When there is no "natural" link between the signifier and signified, then what determines the link? It is not "nature" but "institution" that makes the sign possible. Every sign is thus "instituted." And this "institution" is grounded on a system of differences and not of identities-as-plenitudes. Saussure writes: "Everything we have said so far comes down to this. *In the language itself* [*langue*], *there are only differences.* Even more important than that is the fact that, although in general a difference presupposes positive terms between which the difference holds, in a language there are only differences, *and no positive terms.*" (ibid., 118).

Derrida's description of the "trace" can be thought of as a rewriting of this Saussurian notion of sign in a system of difference. Though Derrida endorses the notion of "instituted sign," he warns that the very idea of institution must not be uncritically derived from the classical oppositional scheme of nature versus institution, in which he sees Saussure still being caught. The notion of "naturalness" must be deconstructed. Now the instituted sign, the "immotivation" of the sign, must be seen, rigorously and relentlessly, from the perspective of "difference," which Saussure himself indicates is the very foundation of language. Derrida replaces the Saussurian sign, the synthesis of signifier and signified, with the words "instituted trace," in which the synthesis appears as that of a trace and a difference, where an indefinite play of absence is enacted:

> The instituted trace cannot be thought without thinking the retention of difference within a structure of reference where difference appears *as such* and thus permits a certain liberty of variations among the full terms. The absence of *another* here-and-now, of another transcendental present, of *another* origin of the world appearing as such, presenting itself as irreducible absence within the presence of the trace, is not a metaphysical formula substituted for a scientific concept of writing. . . . The "unmotivatedness" of the sign requires a synthesis in which the completely other is announced as such—without any simplicity, any identity, any resemblance or continuity— within what is not it. (*DG*, 46–47)

The structure (or better, the movement) of the trace is the indefinite announcing of the completely other within what is not it. This announcing of alterity cannot stop at a determined point that would establish itself as a "theological" presence/origin. Thus the notion of "institution" itself cannot be thought of as a solid, permanent "structure" as seen in the notion of *langue* proposed by Saussure. Rather, it must be thought of as already permeated with the originary movement of trace.

In this Derridian formula, the "trace" resembles what Saussure calls the "signifier," and the "other" seems to parallel the "signified." But Derrida's logic of trace takes us beyond (or before) the clarity of the tripartite structure of the Saussurian sign in that on both levels (signifier and signified) of the sign, the movement of *différance* is always already at work. The trace/signifier "produces itself as self-occultation" and the other/signified "presents itself in the dissimulation of itself":

> The trace, where the relationship with the other is marked, articulates its possibility in the entire field of the entity, which metaphysics has defined as the being-present starting from the occulted movement of the trace. The trace must be thought before the entity. But the movement of the trace is necessarily occulted, it produces itself as self-occultation. When the other announces itself as such, it presents itself in the dissimulation of itself. . . . The presentation of the other as such, that is to say the dissimulation of its "as such," has always already begun and no structure of the entity escapes it. (Ibid., 47)

Thus the notion of "unmotivatedness" itself must be deconstructed: "Without referring back to a 'nature,' the immotivation of the trace has always *become*. In fact, there is no unmotivated trace: the trace is indefinitely its own becoming-unmotivated" (ibid.). Not only at the site of the origin but at the site of a seemingly unmotivated sign, a certain movement of slippage from itself, a subtle dissimulation of "as such" is at work. For Derrida, this general movement of trace is none other than "writing."

This peculiar notion of "writing" emerges out of the hierarchical interplay between writing and speech that Derrida finds dominating Western philosophical discourse, including that of Saussure. Derrida points out a pervasive privileging of speech over writing. For example, in Plato's *Phaedrus*, writing is condemned because, in the absence of the speaker (the signifying intention), it can give rise to various misunderstandings. Also, in Saussure's otherwise fundamentally deconstructive discourse on language, Derrida finds a logocentric privileging of speech over writing. Saussure attempts to reinstate the principal status he sees as "usurped" by writing to its true inheritor, speech.[8]

Derrida links this privileging of speech to the logocentric notion of truth, which in turn derives from the sense of proximity. A vocal sign is more "natural" than a written one. A written sign is merely a representation of a vocal sign, which is "closer" to the origin, the meaning present in the speaker's consciousness (intention). But Derrida argues again that the notion of "naturalness" must be first called into question. Nature is after all a structure of proximity to itself. The perfect understanding that the speaker is supposed to possess over what he or she speaks reveals a structure of auto-affection. The French phrase *s'entendre parler* effectively fuses the acts of hearing oneself and understanding oneself. In the system of *s'entendre parler* the signifier effaces itself before the signified, while the silent ruin of the written remains foreign and exterior to the living speech. But as we have seen in Derrida's discourse on trace, the derivative status to which writing has been relegated must be thought of as already inherent in *any* sign, be it vocal or written, or, for that matter, of any origin. The proximity to itself can never become equivalent to itself. Proximity already contains within it a sense of separation, of distance.

Nishiwaki's notion of poetry discussed in *Surrealist Poetics* can be seen as similar to the notion of "writing" that Derrida proposes here. Poetry, for Nishiwaki, is a textual movement that throughout its history has continually moved away from the origin (object) of its representation (expression), be it "nature" or "reality." Nishiwaki also insists that the essential constituent of poetry is "distance." By following this textual movement of distance (difference) to its limit, Nishiwaki arrives at a dead end: poetry distancing itself from itself into its own extinction. Poetry, like Derrida's "writing," is a (non-)concept that can never coincide with itself. It is a movement that forever deconstructs itself. One cannot overlook the danger implicit in such poetry/writing—"I have fallen off the cliff."

DANGEROUS SUPPLEMENTS

Derrida finds a similar privileging of speech in Rousseau, who writes: "Languages are made to be spoken, writing serves only as a supplement to speech. . . . Speech represents thought by conventional signs, and writing represents the same with regard to speech. Thus the art of writing is nothing but a mediated representation of thought (quoted in *DG*, 144). By according the status of "supplement" to writing, Rousseau provides Derrida with an effective tool of deconstruction. Derrida deploys this notion of supplement in order to reveal an originary lack in the seemingly *complete* plenitude of the origin. A supplement is added in order to compensate for a lack in what was supposed to be complete in itself. If this logic of supplement is applied to the argument of Rousseau quoted above, we must conclude that there is a lack in speech that calls for writing, and, similarly, there is a lack in the originary thought/meaning. Thus what inaugurates "meaning" and language is not presence but rather a certain "absence" (lack) that calls for a chain of supplements—that is, writing.

From the standpoint of logocentrism, this operation of supplements is not merely an extension that is foreign to the essential nature. *It is a dangerous operation.* Writing is a parasite that eats away at the origin. It "usurps" the throne of living speech. It threatens the notion of nature where ultimate goodness should reside. The supplement not only (innocently) adds to the origin; it also *replaces* it. Hence the danger. It is the case in which an image overtakes the place of the "real" thing. For example, Rousseau talks of masturbation as a dangerous supplement. In onanism the image of a woman *replaces* the "actual" woman. Moreover, onanism threatens a young man with the punishment of castration and death. It replaces a "natural" order of sexuality with an "artificial," imaginary order even at the risk of death. Why? The answer must be definite: because the secondary order of imagery (writing) is intensely seductive. Derrida quotes a famous passage from *The Confessions* in which Rousseau describes the seductive power of the secondary order:

> I should never have done, if I were to enter into the details of all the follies which the remembrance of this dear mamma caused me to commit when I was no longer in her presence. How often have I kissed my bed, since she had slept in it; my curtains, all the furniture of my room, since they belonged to her, and her beautiful hand had touched them; even the floor, on which I prostrated myself, since she had walked upon it! Sometimes, even in her presence, I was guilty of extravagances, which only the most violent love seemed capable of inspiring. At table one day, just when she had put a piece of food into her mouth, I exclaimed that I saw a hair in it; she put back the morsel on her plate, and I eagerly seized and swallowed it. In a word, between myself and the most passionate lover there was only one, but that an essential, point of distinction, which makes my condition almost unintelligible and inconceivable. . . . [A little above, we read] I only felt the full strength of my attachment when I no longer saw her. (Ibid., 152)

What this structure of fetishism discloses is that not only the prior term, "Mother/Nature," is usurped by its supplements but also the secondary order, the imaginary, has gained the status and force of "presence." And only through this illusory presence does pleasure (*jouissance*) appear. But this pleasure is not a simple one of possessing the desired object. Rather, in it, desire and fear are fused. Pleasure becomes possible only through a certain distance between the image and the actual. And this distance nurtures desire as well as fear. But what happens if this distance of illusion collapses, if the primary and the secondary orders merge into each other, if "pure presence" appears? Derrida remarks: "Thus, the supplement is dangerous in that it threatens us with death, but Rousseau thinks that it is not at all as dangerous as 'cohabitation with women.' Pleasure *itself*, without symbol or suppletory, that which would accord us (to) pure presence itself, if such a thing were possible, would be only another name for death. Rousseau says it." Derrida quotes Rousseau: "Enjoyment [*Jouir*]! Is such a thing made for man? Ah! If I had ever in my life tasted the delights of love even once in their plenitude, I do not imagine that my frail existence would have been sufficient for them, I would have been dead in the act" (*Confessions*, Book VIII; (quoted in *DG*, 155). What was most "seductive" to Nishiwaki in his theoretical writings is obvious: poetry.

The first sentence of "Profanus" tells all: "To discourse upon poetry is as dangerous as to discourse upon God." In this "dangerous" equation (supplement) of poetry and God, a sovereignty is declared—the negative sovereignty of pure poetry.

TOWARD A NEGATIVE PARADISE

From this moment of "pure presence" we may thus return to the notion of pure poetry or sovereignty. In Derrida's language of *différance,* sovereignty appears as that which cancels the movement of *différance* with absolute authority. Indeed sovereignty is, as Derrida puts it, "presence, and the delight [*jouissance*] in presence" (*DG,* 296). The sovereign presence in its absolute completeness does not require any supplement, does not reveal any originary lack within. It is "the inalienable immediacy of self-possession [*jouissance de soi*] . . . the moment of the impossible representation" (ibid., 297). The sovereign presence cannot be determined merely by "what it is not" as a sign is so defined. It must be something absolutely not (like) anything in the world. It must be the absolutely unknown, absolutely new, that is, pure poetry. Moreover, it must escape the order of representation (*hyōgen*). Indeed, sovereignty signifies the death of signification, that is, the absolute independence from the other. Derrida links the sovereign state to his (and Mallarmé's) notion of game—*un coup de dés:*

> Far from suppressing the dialectical synthesis, it inscribes this synthesis and makes it function within the sacrifice of meaning. It does not suffice to risk death if the putting at stake is not permitted to take off, as chance or accident, but is rather invested as the work of the negative. Sovereignty must still sacrifice lordship and, thus, the *presentation* of the meaning of death. . . . The poetic or the ecstatic is that *in every discourse* which can open itself up to the absolute loss of its sense, to the (non-)base of the sacred, of nonmeaning, of un-knowledge or of play, to the swoon from which it is reawakened by a throw of the dice. (Derrida 1978, 261)

If we are to follow Nishiwaki's negative poetics to its limits, we must go further into the abyss of signification, even to the negation of the "presentation of the meaning of death." If sovereignty still *signified* even the loss of signification, it would still be subordinate to the supplementary system. We may follow the agonizing footsteps of Sade. He sought sovereignty to the extent that it would become a pure destructive force, a pure *dépense* (in Georges Bataille's terminology), which would even free itself from its dependence on the preexistence of what it destroys. Maurice Blanchot observes: "The originality of Sade seems to reside in his extremely resolute claim to found man's sovereignty on the transcendental power of negation—a power that does not depend on the objects it destroys, a power that, in order to destroy its objects, does not even presuppose their anterior existence, for at the moment of their destruction, it already and beforehand regards them as nothing" (Blanchot 1963, 36).

If we remain in the restricted logic of positivity, the impossibility of absolute sovereignty is evident. We could only name this impossibility "the impossible." How can a master be a master without depending on the existence of a slave? But in the sovereign moment even naming must disappear. In the negative theology of sovereignty, one must suspend the movement of Hegelian dialectics, and must affirm one's presence by an immense negation. And this negation must be pushed to its limits, or beyond them, to its own death. Blanchot writes on Sade's negative heroes: "All these great libertines who live only for pleasure are great only because they have annihilated in themselves all the capacity for pleasure" (ibid., 45). How can we name the consequence of this absolute negation? Does the death of negation signify a new positivity? Pure poetry? *Jouissance*? The Sovereign Moment? Nishiwaki compared the danger of discoursing upon (or naming) poetry to that of discoursing upon God. We remember that the Jews fear to pronounce the name of their ineffable God. It is a bright silence. Language fails by definition. Yet kangaroos and cactuses so pitifully attempt to survive. A Nietzschean laughter begins. The Nishiwaki-text begins to laugh.

Nishiwaki's impulse toward the Derridian "supplement" is evident in his insistence on the artificial mode of expression, which consequently negates "nature" within a poetic text. But what Nishiwaki's method of pure poetry shows is that the chain of supplements called "writing" must transgress its own *mise en abyme*, must return to the deathly pure presence. Poetry is thus an effort to reenter the realm of the lost presence. Of course this must be realized after the classical presence has been deconstructed and effaced from the field of language. What remains may be merely the ruins of things, allegories of meanings. Susan Sontag remarks that for Walter Benjamin ideas and experiences appear as ruins: "Benjamin's recurrent themes are, characteristically, means of spatializing the world: for example, his notion of ideas and experiences as ruins. To understand something is to understand its topography, to know how to chart it. And to know how to get lost" (Sontag 1981, 116).

Indeed, Derrida has charted the territory, but poetry invites us to get lost in it. The world, the real, is this map of fictionality (supplementarity) where the infinite movement of *différance* operates. Literature, as opposed to philosophy or science, from the beginning, has signified itself as the fundamental fictionality of the world. (Everything is slipping from itself everywhere.) Classical literature (in Barthes's terminology) with its faith in the transparency of language may not have fully manifested this fictionality. Modernist literature (the writerly text), however, has begun to reveal its own inevitable destiny by crystallizing the fictionality of the world and has begun moving forward with its inherent negativity. Nishiwaki writes: "The adage *Ars longa* is merely a children's song. It only appears on the surface that art creates. In fact, art is an effort at self-extinction" (*NJZ* 4:37–38).

Through this negative movement, paradoxically, poetry strives to transgress the boundaries of fictionality and regain presence, its sovereignty, its absolute loss of meaning. Representation serves only the perpetuation of fictionality. Poetry must move, instead, through a gap, an interruption within the field of representation, a difference, created by the confusion of distant elements which appear on the white page. Words serve as positive nodes, as a guide (Vergil) into the Inferno, as the walls of a fathomless abyss of signification into which we fall. But why do we step into the abyss in the first place? Because we are seduced? Are we seduced by the striptease of dissimulation, by the play of presence and absence on the surface of a text? So we fall, like blind lovers. This must be a reversed fall into the Garden of Eden. We fall losing our identity and exteriority, reversed as if in a photographic negative. When the last positivity of a poem disappears, when the walls of language crumble, only the movement of the fall in its absolute negativity remains. And this is the state/movement of pure poetry.

Yet no one exists in pure poetry. Only when pure poetry begins to translate itself do we begin to encounter poetry. In the next chapter, we will go through a detour—a detour to the paradise of language—in order to arrive at Nishiwaki's poetic language: a language of translation.

CHAPTER THREE

The Detour of Translation

How would you translate a signature? And how would you refrain, whether it be Yahweh, Babel, Benjamin when he signs right next to his last word?—*Jacques Derrida*

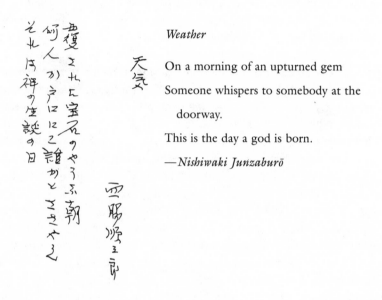

Weather

On a morning of an upturned gem
Someone whispers to somebody at the
  doorway.
This is the day a god is born.
—*Nishiwaki Junzaburō*

A poem is placed at the gate of this chapter. To be more precise, a copy of the original, handwritten text with Nishiwaki's signature is juxtaposed with its translation. This is the poem that opens *Ambarvalia,* which in turn opened a new era of modernist poetry in Japan. This chapter presents an alternative textual practice to what we usually call "reading a poem." My reading here does not overtly take the mode of commentary or of interpretation, nor does it aim at what we usually call "understanding a poem." My reading is rather presented as a detour, a meandering journey aided by the current of a textual movement that I name "translation." The poem is paradisal. In order to reach this paradise, I must take a long detour—the detour of translation, the detour of writing (in Derrida's sense). Translation traces a certain paradise. Yet, as we will see, the origin (paradise) already speaks of translation, is a translation, is translating. The present writing traces such a paradise translating.

WRITING/READING

In *S/Z* Roland Barthes delineates the notions of reading and writing in terms of an evaluative schema in which two opposing textual values are introduced: *le lisible* (the readerly) and *le scriptible* (the writerly). Barthes regards reading essentially as an activity of capturing the meaning of the text—in other words, as consumption. But writing (even about an anterior text, as in a critique) remains as pure productivity. No doubt Barthes's classifications of the readerly and the writerly point to certain absolute states at both poles. Actually, certain texts may simply appear more or less readerly or writerly than others. The more readerly text, then, invites reading—a search for the stabilized meaning of the text. The more writerly text, on the contrary, invites writing—the production of "the infinity of language." Barthes explains: "The writerly text is a perpetual present, upon which no *consequent* language (which would inevitably make it past) can be superimposed; the writerly text is *ourselves writing,* before the infinite play of the world (the world as function) is traversed, intersected, stopped, plasticized by some singular system (Ideology, Genus, Criticism) which reduces the plurality of entrances, the opening of networks, the infinity of languages" (Barthes 1974, 5). The writerly text is thus more like an "arche-movement" of production itself without any referential or representative limit imposed by illusory unifying principles such as "Ideology, Genus, Criticism." We may say that it is a monstrous production of infinite meanings (or nonmeaning), a construction of an utterly heterogeneous paradise. It simply invites more writing, more dissemination of language in difference.

As opposed to this prodigious movement of pure production of difference, the readerly text invites reading, which in turn attempts to delimit (to close the gate on) the violent current of writing in the name of meaning, motivated and sanctified by certain (illusory) systems. Reading thus reveals itself as an essentially theological operation searching for the final and securely singular ground where the signifier and the signified coincide in a perfect enclosure of the same—the homogeneous paradise.

Where does translation itself figure in this polarized schema of reading and writing? Let us go back to the beginning. The poem is paradisal. The poem seduces and calls forth my writing's coming-into-being. It prompts my writing to approach it, to approximate it, to appropriate it. The ideal language to carry out such an ambition (to capture the anterior, original text) must employ something close to a perfect tautology: the poem is the poem. Indeed, translation, more than any other mode of secondary writing (literary criticism, commentary), "literally" strives for this ideal tautological state.

Since translation attempts to transfer an anterior text into a different material, that is, into a foreign language, it resembles more the process of simulation than that of commentary. In a story recounted by Jorge Luis Borges, we meet the image of an ideal simulacrum and its consequent decline. It is a story of an ideal map, which covers the whole empire exactly point by point, then is abandoned by succeeding generations as useless. Exposed to natural elements, its ruins were to be seen only in the deserts inhabited by beasts and beggars (Borges 1964, 90). Is the ideal translation also doomed from the start precisely by the glory of the empire, of the original text?

THE EMPIRE OF THE ORIGINAL

Even in this age of mechanical reproduction, there seems to be no other language-movement that so emphatically brings out the notion of the *original* text than translation. A translation is always designated as secondary to the original in its "truthfulness." The ideal tautology of "Nishiwaki is Nishiwaki" is never possible in translation. Translation emerges only as a simulacrum destined to decay. " 西脇 is Nishiwaki." The copula, the virtual translator, the ferry, *unnaturally* strains beneath the weight of such an alien invasion.

As the readerly value of the text shows its theological linkage to what Barthes calls "the closure of Western discourse" (Barthes 1974, 7), translation also reveals a ghost of theology in its subordinate relation to the original. Reading a translation, we are assailed by a strange anxiety of *not facing the original directly*. The uncertainty created by the detour of translation in turn intensifies our longing for the original, for the certainty of meaning that is the predetermined goal of reading. We could say that the original text gains the status of inhabiting the house of truth *by way of* a translation. Does the original then require translation so as to gain the very status of origin? Is a translation merely a readerly reading of the anterior text? Or, on the contrary, does it participate in the dissemination of the original text in an infinite field of the writerly text ("arche-writing")? Is translation reading or writing? Is it a faithful transmitter or a covert deconstructor of an origin?

The ending of the story by Borges is suggestive. The frayed ruins of the map return to dust; they become indistinguishable from the desert to which perhaps the empire itself will return. The simulacrum and the original are both transformed into the desert—the ever-shifting movement of sand.

The Latin root of the verb "translate," *trans latus,* suggests the meaning "carried across." The original text thus is carried across a certain space, a difference. What is this space of difference? The obvious answer is the difference between the language of the original text and that of the translation. But it also seems possible to detect this essential operation of translation in the fundamental movement of language itself, that is, in the process of figural transposition within language, in the process of "troping," of "turning" an origin, a presence. As we have seen, in his critique of "origin," Derrida has introduced the term *différance* to designate an endless supplementary movement at the site of origin. It not only marks the spatial difference but also the temporal detour of deferral. Thus according to Derrida, origin (or presence) is always already differed and deferred. Is it possible, then, to regard the "carrying-across" operation of translation as something similar to the originary activity named *différance?* Perhaps translation can be regarded as a site where the movement of *différance* becomes most visible, most emphatically enacted. It is a site where a certain slippage from the origin occurs. But the origin is already slipping from its throne.

I began this book with the sentence "Nishiwaki is paradisal." This sentence is thus already traversed by a movement of translation, albeit in complex ways. Carried across by the copula, Nishiwaki (a name) is transposed into a quality. But even before this transposition, the status and the definition of Nishiwaki are already in flux. Of course "Nishiwaki" is the transliteration of a Japanese name. Moreover, within the intended context, "Nishiwaki" functions as a kind of synecdoche, representing a larger unit, namely the Nishiwaki-text (Nishiwaki as a text; texts written by Nishiwaki). Translation is also already involved in the "paradisal." Carried across from the Greek *paradisos,* carried across from the parent-noun "paradise," and furthermore transferred from the literal (pure) paradise to this earthly language, across its unbridgeable distance from the pure paradise, from the pure tongue, but at the same time revealing itself as a mark of seduction, the paradisal induces our desire for the literal paradise, causing the coming-into-being of this writing-flow, carrying across the distance posited by the paradise itself, weaving a new text, renaming Nishiwaki, translating 西脇 , transplanting Nishiwaki in the most foreign of gardens: paradise.

SUPRAHUMAN LANGUAGE

In his "Die Aufgabe des Übersetzers (1923)" (The task of the translator), Walter Benjamin posits a type of paradise as a messianic destination of languages, intimated by the operation of translation. He calls this paradise "pure language." Benjamin's text deserves special attention here because it addresses the issue of the very nature and function of language, which I have been outlining with the notions of reading, writing, and translation. However, like many other texts by Benjamin, this text on translation shows a peculiarly elusive textual density that makes it difficult for readers simply to understand.[1] The text borders on being scandalous in terms of its style as well as its content. It singlehandedly abandons the common notion of translation as the transferring of the content from the original language to another one. Instead, it promotes an absolutely literal (word-for-word) translation. In a strange sense, the text seems to advocate a pure meaning-less text, of which the text itself attempts to be an example by making two contradictory statements at once: translation is and is not possible.[2]

Benjamin begins his essay with this premise: "No poem is intended for the reader, no picture for the beholder, no symphony for the listener" (*BJ*, 69).[3] The reader is thus radically expelled from the text. With the banishment of the reader comes the abolition of communicable meaning, or of the semantically oriented relationship between languages. Even the figure of the author barely surfaces in this text. There are only the doomed translator[4] and the sacred anterior text—either Holy Writ or poetry. What is this suprahuman, suprameaning movement of language here called "translatability"? Let us follow Benjamin's text closely.

We have seen that according to Benjamin the anterior text (art) ignores reception. Benjamin reasons that since the original text is not written for the reader, neither should translation attempt to serve the reader. Here Benjamin is not even concerned with the transmission of a so-called poetic effect ("the unfathomable, the mysterious, the poetic") in translation. He simply dismisses such an attempt as "the inaccurate transmission of an inessential content" (*BJ*, 70). Then what are the function and nature of a poem, of a translation, if we are so thoroughly excluded from their realm? What place does poetry inhabit, for what purpose? Simply put, both poetry and its translations inhabit the realm of language. And this realm is suprahuman. We remember that for Nishiwaki also poetry manifests itself as its own return journey to the fundamental meaninglessness called "reality." People as creatures fatefully attached to meaning do not figure in the self-extinguishing movement of poetry Nishiwaki envisioned.

Benjamin delimits translation succinctly: "Translation is a mode," and poses a question with regard to the original: "Does its nature lend itself to translation and, therefore, in view of the significance of the mode, call for it?" (ibid., 70). In order to explain this strange calling forth of translation by the original, Benjamin introduces a suprahuman realm, "God's remembrance":

> It should be pointed out that certain correlative concepts retain their meaning, and possibly their foremost significance, if they are referred exclusively to man.[5] One might, for example, speak of an unforgettable life or moment even if all men had forgotten it. If the nature of such a life or moment required that it be unforgotten, that predicate would not imply a falsehood but merely a claim not fulfilled by men, and probably also a reference to a realm in which it *is* fulfilled: God's remembrance. Analogously, the translatability of linguistic creations ought to be considered even if men should prove unable to translate them. (Ibid.)

BABEL

Derrida sees in the above passage a fundamental "sur-vival" force inherent in language, or in the constitutive structure of the original, which first appears as a suprahuman demand for translation. According to Derrida, this survival force, which surfaces through the relationship between the original and the translation, deploys a strategy involving a contractual indebting of the translator as well as of the original itself: "For if the structure of the original is marked by the requirement to be translated, it is that in laying down the law the original begins by in-debting itself *as well* with regard to the translator. The original is the first debtor, the first petitioner; it begins by lacking and by pleading for translation" (*DD,* 184).[6]

How should we mark this originary lack within the original? Derrida now recalls the story of the Tower of Babel where the original need for translation is inscribed. First he points out that this myth is involved with the problem of naming. The story tells us that the people wanted to make a name for themselves. But they ended up receiving a name from God: Babel. The name "Babel" given to this site has two dimen-sions, one a common noun, the other a proper noun: confusion and the name of God.[7] This double signature of God initiates the contrac-tual movement of language, the calling forth of translation. Derrida continues:

> This demand is not only on the side of the constructors of the tower who want to make a name for themselves and to found a universal tongue trans-lating itself by itself; it also constrains the deconstructor of the tower: in giving his name, God also appealed to translation, not only between the tongues that had suddenly become multiple and confused, but first of *his name,* of the name he had proclaimed, given, and which should be trans-lated as confusion to be understood, hence to let it be understood that it is difficult to translate and so to understand. At the moment when he imposes and opposes his law to that of the tribe, he is also a petitioner for transla-tion. He is also indebted. He has not finished pleading for the translation of his name even though he forbids it. For Babel is untranslatable. God weeps over his name. (Ibid.)

What Derrida attempts to describe here is the complex situation of "the very beginning" where, in an absolutely paradoxical way, God (the origin) separates "his name" (language) from himself, gives it an absolute status by inscribing "confusion" (that is, incomprehensibility, for God must remain aloof) on it, but in so doing, creates the first demand for "translation" because of the very "confusion of tongues" now inscribed within "his name," Babel. God must be kept "incom-prehensible." But in order for "his name" (language) to "sur-vive," it must be transported in a certain movement of transference, namely translation. Babel reveals a demand for "confusion" and at the same time an originary want of translation. The desire for an absolute sepa-ration and that for transportation/transference/translation collide at this "very beginning." What is meant by "translatability of the original" in Benjamin is thus linked to this paradoxical "weeping of God over his name." From the moment the "untranslatable Babel" demands its own translation, language begins its hidden life, drawing in languages through the gate of translation to itself.

SUR-VIVAL (*ÜBERLEBEN*) AND TRANSLATION (*ÜBERSETZEN*)

Benjamin calls this survival movement the "hallowed growth of language" (*BJ*, 74), with its destination in the seemingly messianic end of "pure language." This pure language, according to Benjamin, is the ultimate "harmony" or "reconciliation" of different languages attained through the operation of translation. Is the survival movement of language, then, instead of heading toward "confusion"—the Babelian dissemination of difference—growing in the direction of the promised land of the same, toward the pre-Babelian name of God?[8]

Let us follow Benjamin's text again. First, Benjamin points to a "natural" or "vital" connection between the original and the translation:

> It is plausible that no translation, however good it may be, can have any significance as regards the original. Yet, by virtue of its translatability the original is closely connected with the translation; in fact, this connection is all the closer since it is no longer of importance to the original. We may call this connection a natural one, or, more precisely, a vital connection. Just as the manifestations of life are intimately connected with the phenomenon of life without being of importance to it, a translation issues from the original—not so much from its life as from its afterlife [*Überleben*]. (ibid., 71)

What does this "sur-vival/after-life" (*Überleben*) of the original reveal here?[9] Benjamin says that a translation issues from it. Both are connected "vitally." But strangely enough, he also says that the translation does not hold any importance or significance for the original. Why? Benjamin seems to answer, "precisely because the bond between them is *natural*." There is no room for "significance" in the "sur-vival" within nature. Or we may put more emphasis on the "afterlife" of the original, as does Paul de Man in his interpretation of this passage (de Man 1986, 85). That is, the original does not see any significance in the translation *because the original itself is already dead*. A translation issues from the original's "afterlife." Translation announces the death of the original. The survival movement of language from the original to a translation, therefore, does not mean that the original itself survives through the translation. The translation attends the wake of the original.

Yet Benjamin says: "The life of the originals attains in them [translations] to its ever-renewed latest and most abundant flowering" (*BJ*, 72). Then what survives through translation? It is not the original itself but its "life" that survives. What is this "life"? Benjamin literally "translates" this "life" as a certain purposiveness:

> Being a special and high form of life, this flowering is governed by a special, high purposiveness. The relationship between life and purposefulness, seemingly obvious yet almost beyond the grasp of the intellect, reveals itself only if the ultimate purpose toward which all single functions tend is sought not in its own sphere but in a higher one. All purposeful manifestations of life, including their very purposiveness, in the final analysis have their end not in life, but in the expression of its nature, in the representation of its significance. Translation thus ultimately serves the purpose of expressing the central reciprocal relationship between languages. (Ibid.)

The purposiveness of life becomes visible only when a transcendental state, toward which every purposeful manifestation of life moves, is considered. This transcendental state is situated *after life*. The *Überleben* of the original appears only when this transcendental final goal is taken into account. But the goal's very transcendence requires an incommensurable distance from mere "life." What survives then is not the "life" of the original but the "purposiveness," or the drive toward the final expression of the purpose of language. Benjamin names this transcendental goal of languages "pure language": "Wherein resides the relatedness of two languages, apart from historical considerations? Certainly not in the similarity between works of literature or words. Rather, all suprahistorical kinship of languages rests in the intention underlying each language as a whole—an intention, however, which no single language can attain by itself but which is realized only by the totality of their intentions supplementing each other: pure language" (ibid., 74). Here we must note that the "origin" of the kinship of languages does not rest with the originary being, the author, who intends a certain meaning. Rather, this "intention" belongs to pure language—a totality in which the unfulfilled intentions of actual languages supplement each other.[10] And this supplementary movement toward pure language is instigated only by the workings of translation. Benjamin envisions this linguistic paradise as follows: "Although translation, unlike art, cannot claim permanence for its products, its goal is undeniably a final, conclusive, decisive stage of all linguistic creation.

In translation the original rises into a higher and purer linguistic air, as it were. It cannot live there permanently, to be sure, and it certainly does not reach it in its entirety. Yet, in a singularly impressive manner, at least it points the way to this region: the predestined, hitherto inaccessible realm of reconciliation and fulfillment of languages" (*BJ,* 75).

THE UNTRANSLATABLE

What, then, specifically reaches this paradise? Benjamin reiterates that it is not the semantic dimensions (the signifieds) transmitted through a translation that reach there. Rather, it is, ironically yet precisely, that which remains as untranslatable in a translation: "The transfer can never be total, but what reaches this region is that element in a translation which goes beyond transmittal of subject matter. This nucleus is best defined as the element that does not lend itself to translation. Even when all the surface content has been extracted and transmitted, the primary concern of the genuine translator remains elusive" (ibid., 75). This is a particularly perplexing passage. Is Benjamin saying that though the task of the translator has nothing to do with the transmittal of content, nonetheless the ("surface") content is transmitted through translation; but at the same time, strangely enough, the untranslatable appears not in the original but rather in a translation? In this sense, translation becomes a doubly negative, impossible operation. It does what is not its primary task: transmission of content. And it announces its profound failure by somehow manifesting that which cannot be translated. Indeed, at this point, translation becomes impossible *and* possible—possible only in announcing its ultimate failure, namely, the untranslatable. By now we begin to understand what the untranslatable is. It must be the linguistic being of language itself.

Derrida offers another astute reading of the untranslatable. By manifesting this nucleus as the untranslatable in a translation, the nucleus becomes an injunction against further operations of translation upon itself. In other words, it forbids the translation of translation. Derrida reads this nucleus as "the original as such" and brings out a dialectical relationship between the original and the translation: "One recognizes a core (the original as such) by the fact that it can bear further translating and retranslating. A translation, *as such,* cannot. Only a core, because it resists the translation it attracts, can offer itself to further translating operations without letting itself be exhausted" (*DD,* 192). This indicates a latent power-structure sustaining the relationship between the original and the translation. The nucleus as the original as such (not the original text itself but its very status of being original) bears a fundamentally paradoxical relationship to the translation. At once it attracts and resists translation. This is because the nucleus, the untranslatable, requires translation to protect its ineffable status. It needs translation to declare that it is untranslatable. In other words, unless "translated" the untranslatable cannot exist as such.

Benjamin speaks of this essential dilemma of translation in similes: "Unlike the words of the original, it [the nucleus] is not translatable, because the relationship between content and language is quite different in the original and the translation. While content and language form a certain unity in the original, like a fruit and its skin, the language of the translation envelops its content like a royal robe with ample folds. For it signifies a more exalted language than its own and thus remains unsuited to its content, overpowering and alien. This disjunction prevents translation and at the same time makes it superfluous" (*BJ*, 75). The nucleus, therefore, is the Sovereign, the untouchable. It is neither the fruit (content) nor the skin (language). Derrida sees this nucleus as the space between the tenor and the language. And for him this space, this Saussurian difference, is adhesive: "The essential core, that which in the translation is not translatable again, is not the tenor, but this adherence between the tenor and the language, between the fruit and the skin" (*DD*, 193). This adhesive difference itself, uniting the skin to the fruit, mobilizes the operation of guaranteeing the status of the original to itself by demanding a "royal robe"—the language of translation. We notice that this royal robe does not cling tightly to the naked body of the Sovereign. By the luxury of this superfluousness of "ample folds" the Sovereign comes to be signified *as such*.

The nucleus, the attachment between the skin and the fruit, the status of the original, the untranslatable in a translation, that which reaches the messianic end of all languages, is the true language. It is, however, as Carol Jacobs points out, not "the apotheosis of an ultimate language, but rather that which is purely language—nothing but language" (Jacobs 1975, 761). In the true language, the word becomes truth instantaneously. Within the true language there is no opening where meaning can appear. Neither is there space nor time in it. It is the eternal present. It is both the absolutely readerly and writerly text at once. And the possibility of this language is glimpsed only through translations. According to Benjamin, "If there is such a thing as a language of truth, the tensionless and even silent depository of the ultimate truth which all thought strives for, then this language of truth is—the true language. And this very language, whose divination and description is the only perfection a philosopher can hope for, is concealed in concentrated fashion in translations" (*BJ, 77*). We must note here the qualification of "if" that Benjamin attaches to the concept of the true language. We must also note that it can be found only in a *secondary* text called translation. Furthermore, it appears as the *failure* of translation in the name of "the untranslatable." What is indicated through the series of "inferior" qualifications (secondary, failure) is the utmost difficulty in glorifying and hypostatizing the concept of pure language. Without the reification and glorification, pure language remains merely a directional marker toward the messianic paradise. It cannot constitute an essence or a "prison house." It is not God. It is the Name of God.

LOSS OF MEANING

The truth of language is the purity of language itself devoid of its referential or representative function. Translation thus aids in purifying the original text of its meaning. Benjamin writes:

> And that which seeks to represent, to produce itself in the evolving of languages, is the very nucleus of pure language. Though concealed and fragmentary, it is an active force in life as the symbolized thing itself, whereas it inhabits linguistic creations only in symbolized form. While that ultimate essence, pure language, in the various tongues is tied only to linguistic elements and their changes, in linguistic creations it is weighted with a heavy, alien meaning. To relieve it of this, to turn the symbolizing into the symbolized, to regain pure language fully formed in the linguistic flux, is the tremendous and only capacity of translation. In this pure language—which no longer means or expresses anything but is, as expressionless and creative Word, that which is meant in all languages—all information, all sense, and all intention finally encounter a stratum in which they are destined to be extinguished. (Ibid., 79–80)

Thus, what a poem says is merely a "heavy, alien meaning." Meaning is essentially alien to language. A translation can get rid of the alien meaning because it is not facing the extralingual realm from which "meaning" is supposed to derive. A translation is only facing another language of the original text, while the original text must form a relationship to the outside in order to construct a structure of meaning (the readerly text). Thus being a step further away from the burden of meaning, from the world of referents, a translation approaches the core of language, language as is.

The only possible method of translation to achieve this end can be seen in the absolutely literal rendering of syntax, word by word, which Hölderlin performs in his "monstrous" translations of Sophocles. The result is of course beyond comprehension. What we see in them is the violent intrusion of a foreign syntax into Hölderlin's mother tongue. Translation thus radically destabilizes our own tongue, as it deprives the "alien meaning" of the original text. The meaning is alien not to the original text itself but to this suprahuman movement of language, the sur-vival of language, pure language. The symbolizing (the literary effecting of meaning—the poetic, the mysterious) has its end not in the alien meaning but in the final symbolized—pure language.

But the enormous danger the translator encounters through this teratogenesis of language cannot be forgotten. Benjamin writes: "For this very reason Hölderlin's translations in particular are subject to the enormous danger inherent in all translations: the gates of a language thus expanded and modified may slam shut and enclose the translator with silence. Hölderlin's translations from Sophocles were his last work: in them meaning plunges from abyss to abyss until it threatens to become lost in the bottomless depths of language" (ibid., 81–82).

We are definable only through meaning, that is, through reading. When we cease reading and thus lose meaning, there is only one thing left to do. We begin to translate language itself. Pure writerly production does not belong to us but to language itself. Language writes itself. We only translate. We ourselves are silent. At the moment when this overcoming of people by language becomes manifest, the translator (Zohn) attempts to stop the threatening current of language. Zohn translates: "There is, however, a stop [Halten]. It is vouchsafed to Holy Writ alone, in which meaning has ceased to be the watershed for the flow of language and the flow of revelation."[11] Jacobs points out that the crucial word here is Halten—which can mean "holding" or "retaining" as well as "halt"—and asks whether the precipitous loss of meaning (and thus of ourselves) is "stopped" in the sacred text or "retained" in the true language of Holy Writ, or poetry (Jacobs 1975, 765). Does the Holy Writ save us from the abyss of meaninglessness, or does it retain from the start the function of relieving us of meaning, erasing us in its process? The tension of this ambiguity concerning the disappearance of meaning along with ourselves, as we have seen, is sustained throughout the writings of Nishiwaki. There is no definite answer to Jacobs's question. We only see the longing of the poet, the longing of language, and their longing to merge.

Benjamin concludes his essay: "Where a text is identical with truth or dogma, where it is supposed to be 'the true language' in all its literalness and without the mediation of meaning, this text is unconditionally translatable. In such case translations are called for only because of the plurality of languages. For to some degree all great texts contain their potential translation between the lines; this is true to the highest degree of sacred writings. The interlinear version of the Scriptures is the prototype or ideal of all translation" (*BJ*, 82). This is the longing of translation. It longs for the Holy Writ or poetry where meaning is silent. The Holy Writ is the absolute foreign text. Nishiwaki's search for poetry also led him toward the foreign. Poetry does not reside in the native tongue. It must be translated.

BABEL REVISITED

The sacred text's calling forth of translation "because of the plurality of languages" again reminds us of the story of Babel. The Tower of Babel marks a certain originary loss of communicable meaning. But did the pre-Babelian language "retain" the germ of such a loss? The sacred text, being the absolutely literal text, does not lose its meaning (its literality itself) through a literal translation. In a sense, it says nothing to us. It simply is. Was the pre-Babelian language this literality itself also?

We know only that after Babel translation became necessary. But at Babel, God's ostensible aim was to "confuse" our tongue, to pluralize the pre-Babelian language, to force the loss of meaning within language and between languages. The result was the emergence of translation as a remedy for the loss of meaning, to fill the gap between languages. But again, God's command was explicitly directed at the loss of meaning. What was God jealous of? Let us look at the story as recounted in Genesis:

> Then they said, "Come, let us build ourselves a city, with a tower that reaches to the heavens, so that we may make a name for ourselves and not be scattered over the face of the whole earth." But the Lord came down to see the city and the tower that the men were building. The Lord said, "If as

one people speaking the same language they have begun to do this, then nothing they plan to do will be impossible for them. Come, let us go down and confuse their language so they will not understand each other." So the Lord scattered them from there over all the earth, and they stopped building the city. That is why it was called Babel—because there the Lord confused the language of the whole world. (Gen. 11:3–9)

In the motivation for building the tower, we see a curious causal connection between the self-naming of the people (the Sem) and the prevention of their dissemination. Why is the erecting of the self-name equated with the raising of the tower? And how do the self-naming and the building of the tower prevent dissemination of the people? God sees that the sameness of the people and their language, and consequently their "understanding" proper, will grant them the status of omnipotent gods. In the sameness the tower grows higher. The very presence of the tower itself was to become the name of the people. The ever-increasing "presence" in the perfect sameness was to become our name. God deconstructs this presence, disseminates the Sem and its language, and then gives a name to the ruins of the "presence": Babel. The *Oxford English Dictionary* gives the following etymological information: "Babel: Heb. *bābel*. Babylon. Associated in Genesis with the idea of "confusion," but not referable to any known Semitic root; according to Prof. Sayce, for Assyrian *bāb-ilu* gate of God, or *bāb-ili* gate of the gods."

God translates the self-name, the tower, and opens the gate that has been enclosing the Same. Meaning is always a nostalgic return to the tower of the Same. Thus the loss of meaning that God willed manifests itself as the original deconstruction of the self-name and of the self-presence within the order of the Same. The loss of meaning within translation, to use Benjamin's simile, can be located in the empty space between the naked body of the Sovereign and the royal robe that covers it with ample folds. Translation thus performs two contradictory operations with regard to meaning. Translation attempts to restore the pre-Babelian Sameness by bridging the difference between languages. At the same time, it preserves the loss of meaning within its ample folds. Moreover, it protects the naked body of the Sovereign and proclaims his originary status with the space of the loss of meaning (ample folds).

God requires the loss of meaning. God is the loss of meaning. God is jealous of any other presence. For he must be the only presence. And presence in the Same has no meaning. It becomes the absolute proper name (the self-name) without any etymon. A proper name is untranslatable but can be transliterated. What about a signature, then? Derrida asks: "How would you translate a signature? And how would you refrain, whether it be Yahweh, Babel, Benjamin when he signs right next to his last word?" (*DD*, 205). We may recall how Barthes defined literature in *S/Z*: "(Literature is an intentional cacography)" (Barthes 1974, 9). Translation may be a worse, more dangerous handwriting that unknowingly attempts to trace exactly, turn by turn (*des tours de Babel*), the lost signature, the absolute untranslatable, pure language, presence. We are contracted, we are signed, to be translators.

WEATHER

天気

覆された宝石のやうな朝
何人か戸口にて誰かとささやく
それは神の生誕の日

Tenki

Kutsugaesareta hōseki no yōna asa
Nanpito ka toguchi nite dareka to sasayaku
Sore wa kami no seitan no hi

On a morning of an upturned gem[12]
Someone whispers to somebody at the doorway.
This is the day a god is born.

This is literally the morning of translation. Nishiwaki has borrowed the phrase "like an upturn'd gem" from Keats and translated it into Japanese.[13] *Nanpito* ("Someone," an archaic, literary expression) is whispering to *dareka* ("somebody," a colloquial expression). There is a translation occurring between these two synonyms. We cannot hear their whispered words. They are meaning-less. This is a poem of arrival. At the origin (the original Japanese text, the origin of a modernism) someone, something, has arrived, or is perhaps perpetually arriving. Who is whispering to whom at the gate of God? Can we say, at the risk of anthropomorphism, that Translation has arrived, is arriving, is translating at the gate of God—that is, Babel?

CHAPTER FOUR

Ambarvalia to Eternity

Des meubles luisants,

Polis par les ans,

Décoreraient notre chambre;

Les plus rares fleurs

Mêlant leurs odeurs

Aux vagues senteurs de l'ambre,

Les riches plafonds,

Les miroirs profonds,

La splendeurs orientale,

Tout y parlerait

À l'âme en secret

Sa douce langue natale.

—*Baudelaire, "L'invitation au voyage"*

VIOLATION OF THE MOTHER TONGUE

Baudelaire evokes our nostalgia for a poetic (and thus necessarily an Oriental?) paradise where only the sweetest language of all, our "mother tongue," is spoken. We could well assume that Nishiwaki, who was considered one of the best readers of Baudelaire in Japan,[1] was well aware of the homesickness for a purer, more authentic language that would afflict any poet. Yet Nishiwaki's effort at creating his own poetic voice took a direction totally opposite from the search for a more authentic, "Oriental" mother tongue. Indeed, his first book of poetry written in Japanese, *Ambarvalia,* presents itself as a surrendering of the mother tongue to the invasions of foreign tongues.

For anyone attempting to translate such a text as *Ambarvalia,* a series of questions will arise. What if the text to be translated is already a translation? What if the "sweet mother tongue" of the original text is already violated by the invasions of foreign tongues? How can a translation of such an "original" text begin? Must we, then, "untranslate" such a text, uncovering the invasions and the tattered ruins of the mother tongue? Especially when we, as Occidental translators, dream of the "sweet mother tongue of the Orient" and face such a translatory text as Nishiwaki's, the suspicion of not having the authentically original language in the original text troubles our motivation for translation. As translators, we long for the stability and the purity of the original text. Why should we deal with such an "inauthentic" text that seems already a translation of Western texts? Should we not rather deal with more authentically "Japanese" texts, such as haiku and *waka*? This anxiety may well explain the long neglect of Japanese modernism by the Western scholars of Japan.

It is true that modern Japanese poetry in general began by translating Western poetry. In order for Japanese poetry to become "modern," it had to free itself from the restrictions of traditional forms (of *waka* and haiku) and adopt freer expressive imagery and styles from Western poetry. Soon after the Meiji restoration in 1868, pioneering collections of translations began to appear in succession: *Shintaishi shō* (A selection of new style verse) in 1882, *Omokage* (Vestiges) in 1889, *Kaichōon* (Sound of ocean tides) in 1905.[2] The language of these translations remained, however, markedly Japanese, for the translators were mainly concerned with rendering Western poetry into the elegant literary style of the Japanese language.

Nonetheless, these pioneering translations did nurture the growth of original modern Japanese poetry during *kindai* (the modern period, arguably from the mid-nineteenth century to the end of World War II). Especially prominent among *kindai* poets was Hagiwara Sakutarō, whose *Tsuki ni hoeru* (Howling at the moon), published in 1917, displayed his unprecedented skill and originality in using the modern vernacular language as well as the style of the so-called *jiyūshi* (free verse). It was Hagiwara's new poetic language that allowed Nishiwaki to envision the possibility of writing poetry in Japanese for the first time. Before encountering Hagiwara's experimental poetic language, Nishiwaki simply refused to associate the notion of modern poetry with the classically defined, elegant literary language that other *kindai* poets employed.

The transition, however, from the elegant literary language to the vernacular as the vehicle of poetry was by no means easy. Even Hagiwara, abandoning the flexible vernacular language of *Tsuki ni hoeru,* had to resort to the classical literary language in his last poetic work, *Hyōtō* (Ice island), published in 1934. Hagiwara acknowledges his failure: "After desperate attempts to discover a new language for Japanese poetry, I ended up returning to the age-old literary language. In doing so, I abandoned my cultural mission as a poet. I have aged. May new poets emerge and open a new road, a road I failed to build in my time" (quoted in M. Ueda 1983, 179–80).

The anxiety one senses in Hagiwara may be called the anxiety of translation, or the anxiety of the language of modernity. I suggest here that the anxiety of translation lies at the nucleus of modernism in Japan; one may even claim that this anxiety single-handedly constitutes and defines the modernist text in Japan. If we are to define "modernity" as the anxiety of the past and the impulse toward the patricide of history, we should be able to extend the idea that the anxiety of translation is essential to the constitution of Japanese modernism to modernism in general. The anxiety of translation projects the image of the father onto the original foreign text. It faces the father with fear, admiration, and abomination. Similarly, the patricidal impulse of modernism stems from the anxiety that the present (or the location of the present self) does not coincide with the father, the origin, the past, and history. In the case of translation, the origin may appear to be the object of love; in the case of modernism, it may appear to be the object of hatred. In both cases, however, the authentic origin remains a powerful source of seduction, the final paradise, waiting for our naked entry—we, moderns, who may one day finally discard the robes of translation. Yet we remain alien to foreign tongues; we remain alien to the past. We cannot comprehend the sweet native language that everyone speaks in the Baudelairean Oriental chamber. Thus we begin to speak a language of translation.

We should also note that the idea of the paradisal "authenticity" of the original text arose because the original text had to be a distant, foreign text. In the origin called a foreign text that is located far away from us, we dream of "authenticity." This is what Baudelaire's Oriental dream-chamber tells us. Only distant people, foreigners, speak the "sweet mother tongue." We are secondary. We are dislocated from the origin. We are merely translators. In Japan also, poets dreamed of the "authenticity" of modernity in faraway lands. Consider a poem by Hagiwara Sakutarō:

On a Trip

Though I think I'd like to go to France,
France is too far away;
I would at least put on a new jacket
and go on a carefree trip.
When the train takes a mountain path
I would lean on an aquamarine window
and think, alone, of happy things
on a May morning when eastern clouds gather
leaving myself to my heart with fresh young grass glaring.

(Sato and Watson 1981, 475)

Written in 1913, this was Hagiwara's first poem to be published, marking the beginning of the "modern" poetry that he instituted in Japan. In this beginning of modern Japanese poetry, France is thus evoked as a distant, unreachable, foreign origin of modern poetry. In this conflation of "origin" and "foreign," we must seek the beginning of modernism, or even the essential constitution of Japanese modernism. Japanese modern poetry thus begins from an aporia, an impasse, or the anxiety of being unable to reach its origin, though longing to return to it. The point here is that this anxiety that engendered modernism in Japan is analogous to the anxiety of translation. Both Japanese modern poetry and translation exhibit a similar anxiety vis-à-vis their origins. They are seduced by their origins, but cannot return. At this impasse, violence must occur. It is the violence of translation, transference, transportation, transplanting of "the origin as the foreign" to the sweet mother tongue.

A collection of poems with an unfamiliar foreign title, *Ambarvalia* was published in 1933, a year before the publication of Hagiwara's *Hyōtō*. With *Ambarvalia*, an utterly new poetic language was introduced in Japan. Its newness, however, did not reside simply in the innovative employment of the existing Japanese language, whether colloquial or literary, but more importantly in Nishiwaki's idiosyncratic use of translation, effecting a radical deformation and foreignization of the Japanese language. There was no longer Hagiwara's sentimental longing for France, for the language of *Ambarvalia* was, in a sense, already foreign. If it were, however, absolutely "foreign," it could have established itself as the unreachable origin. But no; it was rather a translatory language invaded by foreign tongues. In *Ambarvalia* the anxieties of translation and of modernity—of being "secondary" to the original text; of being "secondary" to the past or to the foreign origin—*perfectly* coincided. And this perfection was such that it erased any trace of anxiety. The resulting text now boldly and confidently proclaimed its modernity in its translatory language, which translated even the language of antiquity, as seen in the section called "Le Monde Ancien."

Ambarvalia was Nishiwaki's first collection of poems written in Japanese. Prior to *Ambarvalia*, he had published a collection of English poems, *Spectrum*, in London in 1925, privately published another collection of English poems, *Poems Barbarous*, in Tokyo in 1930, attempted to publish a volume of French poems, *Une montre sentimentale*, in Paris, and also had an unpublished collection of English poems, entitled *Exclamations: Music of the Soul*.[3] It is now evident that some of the poems included in *Ambarvalia* are more or less direct translations of poems originally written in foreign languages by Nishiwaki himself. Consequently the text reveals a peculiar Japanese language, one willfully affected by Nishiwaki's sometimes extremely "literal" translations. In fact, the language of *Ambarvalia* shows some typically awkward expressions and mistakes commonly found in the literal translations by foreign students who have just begun studying Japanese with a dictionary. Such problems include the overuse of Chinese expressions where simpler Japanese expressions would suffice, the incorrect use of counters, and the use of grammatical constructions that are not "natural" in Japanese but possible in foreign languages.

For example, there is a line in a poem entitled "Shitsurakuen": "Ikko no taripotto no ki ga onkyō o hassuru koto naku seichō shite iru" (*ZS*, 46). Its "original" version is found in a French poem written by Nishiwaki entitled "Paradis Perdu." The French simply reads, "Un palmier se grandit sans bruit" (*NJZ* 9:688). The first word in the Japanese line "Ikko no" must be the translation of the French article *Un*. But "ikko no" is not the correct counter to use for a tree. It should rather be "ippon no." "Onkyō o hassuru" is also awkward. It displays a somewhat forced use of Chinese words where the simpler Japanese words "oto o dasu" would have sufficed.

As an example of foreign grammar invading the Japanese language, the following should be illuminating: "Ore no yūjin no hitori ga kekkon shitsutsu aru" (*ZS*, 50). Literally translated into English, it becomes "One of my friends is getting married." This sounds natural enough. In fact, the original French simply reads: "Un de mes amis va se marier" (*NJZ* 9:690). But Nishiwaki willfully takes advantage of the ambiguous English construction—the copula followed by a present participle, indicating an action either in the present progressive or in the near future—and translates the English sentence in the sense of the present progressive into, again, a very "unnatural" Japanese sentence.

Nishiwaki's experiment with this peculiar style of literal translation can be seen in his translations of European poems quoted in *Chōgenji-tsushugi shiron* (Surrealist poetics). His eccentric style can be best illustrated when we compare his translations with the elegantly "Japanized" renditions collected in *Kaichōon* by Ueda Bin, or in *Gekka no ichigun* (A moonlit gathering) by Horiguchi Daigaku. In the traditional 7–5, 7–5 syllabic rhythm, Horiguchi translates Jean Cocteau's lines, "Mon oreille est un coquillage / Qui aime le bruit de la mer" (Cocteau 1925, 259), as "Watashi no mimi wa kai no kara / Umi no hibiki o natsukashimu" (Horiguchi 1981, 2:51). Nishiwaki's version is more literal, more *kanbun chō* (Chinese style): "Ore no mimi wa hitotsu no kaigara de aru / Umi no onkyō o aisu" (*NJZ* 4:13).

Paul Verlaine's "Chanson d'automne" may be considered the best-known foreign poem in Japan thanks to the beautiful translation by Ueda Bin:

> Les sanglots longs
> Des violons
> De l'automne
> Blessent mon coeur
> D'une langueur
> Monotone   (Verlaine [1890] 1973, 58)

Ueda's translation uses five-syllable lines:

秋の日の	*Aki no hi no*
ギョロンの	*Vioron no*
ためいきの	*Tameiki no*
身にしみて	*Mi ni shimite*
ひたぶるに	*Hitaburuni*
うら悲し	*Uraganashi* (*Yakushishū* 1969, 33)

(A rough literal translation into English: "The sighs of a violin of an autumn day seeping into my body; and I am infinitely sad.")

Nishiwaki's translation:

> 秋のヴィオロンの長いシャクリナキは
> おれの魂を一つの単調なダルサをもって傷つける

Aki no vioron no nagai shakurinaki wa
Ore no tamashii o hitotsu no tanchō na darusa o motte kizutsukeru

(*NJZ* 4:29)

(A rough literal translation into English: "The long convulsive sobs of an autumnal violin injure my soul with a certain monotonous languor.")

Compared with the sentimental, lyrical tonality of Ueda's rendition, the violence of Nishiwaki's literal translation may appear simply grotesque at first. For a moment we seem to lose our long-cherished faculty of judgment—we do not know whether to grimace or to burst out laughing. Yet the vitality of this new "poetic" language, freed from the established Japanese literary styles and sensitivities, would greatly influence new generations of *gendai* (contemporary) poets.

DISAPPEARANCE OF THE AUTHOR

Ambarvalia is invaded not only by literal translations of his own works but also by another kind of unannounced translation by Nishiwaki. We now know that some poems in *Ambarvalia* are Nishiwaki's translations of poems written by other poets.[4] But the book itself does not reveal any indication that these poems are in fact not Nishiwaki's originals. Such translations include all the poems except one in the "Raten aika" (Latin elegies) section as well as "Renka" (Love song) in the "Le monde moderne" section. "Latin elegies" consists of four poems: "Catullus," "Ambarvalia," "Vīnasu sai no zenban" (Eve of the Venus festival), and "Aika" (Elegy). "Catullus" is a translation of a poem by the Roman poet Catullus. "Ambarvalia" is a translation of an elegy written by a Roman poet of the Augustan Age, most likely Tibullus. "Vīnasu sai no zenban" is a translation of a Latin poem presumably written by several anonymous poets around the second or third century A.D. "Aika" is composed of a "free" translation of Nishiwaki's own poem originally written in Latin, followed by the original Latin text, and concluded by a "literal" translation of the Latin text. "Renka" is Nishiwaki's translation of "Poèmes d'amour" by the French-German poet Yvan Goll.

These translations were well hidden in *Ambarvalia*.[5] Perhaps Nishiwaki did not feel it was important to note the authorial sources, for, after all, *Ambarvalia* was meant to be a small publication. Only three hundred copies were printed. Many readers discovered the existence of

Ambarvalia only after the war, by reading the revised version, *Amu-baruwaria* (the Latin title transliterated into *hiragana*).[6] Nonetheless, just as Ezra Pound's translations are highly regarded on their own, Nishiwaki's translations are greatly esteemed by critics. In fact, when the editors of *Gendaishi tokuhon* (Contemporary poetry reader)— Kagiya Yukinobu, Shinoda Hajime, and one of the most important poets since Nishiwaki, Tamura Ryūichi (b. 1923)—were put to the task of selecting thirty poems out of Nishiwaki's enormous corpus,[7] they selected three translations from *Ambarvalia:* "Vīnasu sai no zen-ban," "Aika," and "Renka."

If Nishiwaki was not concerned with authorship as much as "conscientious" modern scholars concern themselves with the issues of copyright and plagiarism, then possibly something else was at work behind these "authorless" translations. Here we must shift our critical attention from Nishiwaki's personal reason for not revealing the authors to a more strictly textual question: what made the authors disappear from the text? Let us here follow the path Michel Foucault and Roland Barthes, among others, audaciously opened up for us with regard to the modern text. *It is the modern text itself that demands the author disappear. Ambarvalia,* then, could be regarded as an exemplary text in which the disappearance of the author is clearly enacted. Foucault in his essay "What Is an Author?" aptly describes the situation: "The writing of our day has freed itself from the necessity of 'expression'; it only refers to itself. . . . [T]he essential basis of this writing is not the exalted emotions related to the act of composition or the insertion of the subject into language. Rather, it is primarily concerned with creating an opening where the writing subject endlessly disappears" (Foucault 1977, 116).[8] Accordingly, Nishiwaki's writing of *Ambarvalia* can be seen as an effort to lose his authorial self as well as others' authorship by staging a radical violation of the mother tongue by means of his translatory textual strategies.

Nishiwaki, in his autobiographical note "Nōzui no nikki" (Journal of a brain), comments on his attitude toward the Japanese language:

> The reason I did not write poems in Japanese was that I was convinced that, in order to write poems in Japanese, one had to employ such an outdated "literary" language (*bungakugo*) or "elegant" style (*gabuntai*). By writing poems in English, I could evade this problem. It was Hagiwara Sakutarō who taught me that we did not necessarily have to use an elegant style to write poetry. I totally supported not only his use of language but also his

naturalism. Before Hagiwara, Japanese poetry had been steeped in sentimental romanticism. Maybe my enthusiasm for Hagiwara came from my
reaction against such poetry. Since I was in middle school, I had felt embar-
rassed about such poetry. . . . I was already over thirty when I finally began
writing poems in Japanese for the periodical *Mita bungaku*. But that was
also accompanied by a feeling of embarrassment. (*ZS*, 1240)[9]

Nishiwaki's shyness with regard to the mother tongue reveals an essentially elusive subject. The subject refuses to use the mother tongue. By
doing so, the subject eludes the risk of being constituted solely by the
mother tongue. The subject must resist the sweet mother tongue that
has always already nestled at its core. Nishiwaki, the author-subject,
recoiled from the mother tongue, from his center. The text he was to
produce was not to be a vehicle of the expression of the subject. Here
we may recall that both Nishiwaki (in *Surrealist Poetics*) and Foucault
strongly asserted this aspect of the modern text. Rather, as Foucault's
statement suggests, *Ambarvalia* becomes the text into which "the
writing subject endlessly disappears." The textual openings Foucault
talks about are, in the case of *Ambarvalia,* seen in the gaps created by
translation, between the invisible originals and Nishiwaki's translations, between the foreign tongues and the mother tongue. By employing translation as the primary means of deconstructing the established language of poetry, Nishiwaki thus succeeds not only in creating
a new "poetic" language but also in making the author-subject disappear into the "porous" text. Catullus disappears, Tibullus disappears,
Goll disappears, and essentially so does 西脇 .

Consider a section of "Shitsurakuen" (Paradis Perdu):

貧弱な窓を開けば
おれの廊下の如く細い一個の庭が見える
養鶏場からたれるシアボンの水が
おれの想像したサボテンの花を暗殺する
そこに噴水もなし
ミソサザイも弁護士も葉巻もなし
ルカデルロビアの若き唱歌隊のウキボリもなく
天空には何人もゐない

Hinjaku na mado o hirakeba
Ore no rōka no gotoku hosoi ikko no niwa ga mieru
Yōkeijō kara tareru shabon no mizu ga
Ore no sōzō shita saboten no hana o ansatsu suru

Soko ni funsui mo nashi
Misosazai mo bengoshi mo shigā mo nashi
Rukaderarobia no wakaki shōkatai no ukibori mo naku
Tenkū ni wa nanpito mo inai

When I open a shabby window,
I see a singular garden as narrow as my hallway.
The soapy water dripping from the chicken coop
assassinates my imagined cactus flowers.
No fountains exist there.
No wrens, no lawyers, no cigars.
Neither are there the reliefs of choirboys by Luca della Robbia.
There is nobody in the heavens.   (*ZS,* 48–49)

What remains, therefore, is this subjectless textual surface "hardened"
by the invasions of foreign languages. The expressions of the self, "the
cactus flowers of my imagination," are "assassinated." The garden is
unnaturally objectified and solidified by its strange modifiers: "ore no
rōka no gotoku hosoi ikko no" (as narrow as my hallway, a singular
object). *Ikko* (a singular object) is a grammatically incorrect counter
for "garden." It should rather be *hitotsu. Ikko* is originally a Chinese
word with a Sino-Japanese pronunciation, which sounds "harder"
than the Japanese word *hitotsu.* Thus by putting *ikko* in place of *hitotsu,* the garden acquires an unnatural sense of solidification. The
word *niwa* (garden) no longer refers to a garden in reality. It becomes
a purely linguistically constructed new image, a piece of a solidified
and objectified "garden." In this linguistically unnatural garden no
presence is allowed. "No fountains exist there. / No wrens, no lawyers, no cigars. / Neither are there the reliefs of choir boys by Luca
della Robbia. / There is nobody in the heavens."

KATAKANA

Instances of the violation of the mother tongue can be seen on the
orthographic level as well. The Japanese writing system involves three
kinds of writing symbols: two *kana* phonetic syllabaries (*hiragana* and
katakana) and semantically functioning *kanji* (Chinese characters). In
modern Japanese, *katakana* is mainly used for writing transliterations
of foreign words, as well as for instances of onomatopoeia. Therefore,

whenever one sees a word in *katakana,* the instant impression one receives is that of "foreignness." Nishiwaki exploits this peculiar function of *katakana* to an extreme degree. Not only does he use transliterated foreign words often, but he even uses *katakana* for Japanese words commonly written in *hiragana* or *kanji.* For example (*katakana* underlined in the transliteration):

わが魂の毛皮はクスグッたいマントを着た

Waga tamashii no kegawa wa <u>kusuguttai</u> <u>manto</u> *o kita*

My spirit's fur wore a cloak that was really ticklish　　　　(*ZS,* 53)

柔らかにねむるまで自分の家にゐるやうにスコヤカに眠る

Yawaraka ni nemuru made jibun no <u>uchi</u> *ni iru yōni* <u>sukoyaka</u> *ni nemuru*

Sleeps soundly as if being at home until he slips into a soft sleep
　　　　　　　　　　　　　　　　　　　　　　　　　　　(*ZS,* 53)

The effect of such a contrived use of *katakana* is twofold: the foreignization of the word and the rendering of the word into a kind of onomatopoeia of *its own sound.* In the first example, one adjective, *kusuguttai* (ticklish), is separated into two orthographical components—*kusugut* written in *katakana* and *tai* in *hiragana;* thus the "skipping" sound (double consonant) *gutt* becomes emphasized and then is released into the softer sound and letters of *tai* in *hiragana.* An ordinary word is thus made into an onomatopoeia *of its own sound.* In the second example, the word *sukoyaka* is written in *katakana,* when it should be written in *hiragana* or *kanji.* The resulting effect is that suddenly the *sound* of the word rather than its "meaning" comes to the foreground. The text thus announces itself as a field of signifiers (sounds) rather than one of signifieds (meanings).

Other instances of Nishiwaki's peculiar use of *katakana* can be seen in the following poem from the "Girisha teki jojōshi" (Greek lyrics) section in *Ambarvalia* (*katakana* underlined in the transliteration):

太陽

カルモヂインの田舎は大理石の産地で
某処で私は夏をすごしたことがあった 。
ヒバリもゐないし 、蛇も出ない

ただ青いスモモの藪から太陽が出て
またスモモの藪へ沈む 。
少年は小川でドルフィンを捉えて笑った 。

Taiyō

Karumojiin no inaka wa dairiseki no sanchi de
Soko de watashi wa natsu o sugoshita koto ga atta.
Hibari mo inaishi, hebi mo denai.
Tada aoi sumomo no yabu kara taiyō ga dete
mata sumomo no yabu e shizumu.
Shōnen wa ogawa de dorufin o toraete waratta.

The Sun

The countryside of Karumojin produces marble.
Once I spent a summer there.
There are no skylarks and no snakes come out.
Only the sun comes up from bushes of blue damson
And goes down into bushes of damson.
The boy laughed as he seized a dolphin in a brook.   (ZS, 9)

Karumojiin written in *katakana* receives our first attention. Because of
its context and because it is written in *katakana,* we infer that it is the
name of a foreign location. Since the poem is in the section called
"Greek Lyrics," the location is very likely in Greece or its surrounding areas. The mentioning of "marble" confirms this inference. But
"Karumojiin" was actually Nishiwaki's pure fabrication. There is no
actual place named "Karumojiin." Reportedly, Nishiwaki coined the
name by association, from the brand name of a then-popular sleeping
medication from Germany called "Calmotin."[10] Of course, this fact is
not provided with the text. What we see, therefore, is the *katakana*
and the "sound" of Karumojiin. There we fall into a beautiful vessel of
fictionality induced by a proper name without "property," without a
real referent.

    The *katakana* for *hibari* (skylarks) may not seem so unnatural, for
often names of animals and birds are written in *katakana*. But at the
same time, *hibari* is not a foreign bird such as, for example, a flamingo.
Nishiwaki could have used either *hiragana* or *kanji* for it. In fact,
in the revised version of the same poem published in 1947, *hibari* is

written in *hiragana*. What the *katakana* does here, however, is to make the bird foreign.

The images of skylarks and snakes are negatively presented, as absences: "There are no skylarks, and no snakes come out." This presentation of absence must be difficult to make in the visual arts. Only language seems capable of such paradoxical image-production. Then, *hibari* in *katakana* is many times removed from the real referent, the real bird. First, it is made foreign by the *katakana*. Second, it does not exist in Karumojiin. Third, Karumojiin does not actually exist. What exactly do we have left here? A ghostly trace of a trace of a trace?

Hibari is a common bird in Japan, and both skylarks and snakes are heavily allegorized, familiar figures in Western literature. Again we have a paradoxical situation in which a familiar object is presented as an absence, which is already made foreign (defamiliarized) *before* it is even announced as an absence.[11] The absence of skylarks is not simply the absence of a familiar presence. The presence of *hibari* has already been turned into an orthographically induced "trace." Here we may witness a case of Derridian *différance* at work, producing Nishiwaki's peculiar poetic effects.

We see a similarly unusual employment of *katakana* for the word *sumomo* (a type of damson). *Sumomo* is a specifically Oriental plant, imported to Japan from China in ancient times. Therefore, it is usually written in *hiragana* or *kanji*. In the revised version in *Amubaruwaria*, Nishiwaki uses the *kanji* for it. In any case, to find this Oriental plant in this putatively Mediterranean scene seems most unusual. On the other hand, since it is made foreign by the use of *katakana*, one may say that the plant somehow fits into the scene. A gap thus opens up between the "Japaneseness" of the plant (the signified of the word) and the foreignness of the *katakana* (the signified of the script). What appears is a certain negative space of fictionality on the surface of the text.

"Only the sun comes up from bushes of blue damson / And goes down into bushes of damson." A slow cyclic movement of the cosmos is suggested. There are no animals. A hard landscape of marble is established. Then suddenly, "Shōnen wa ogawa de dorufin o toraete waratta" (The boy laughed as he seized a dolphin in a brook). "*A* boy" instead of "*The* boy" seems more natural in English because he has not been introduced. But in the original, his sudden appearance and the apparent shift in the narrative perspective make us feel that we have

known him all along, that he has been the main character of this little
story. For example, if the author were to keep the first-person narrative
with which he began ("Once I spent a summer there"), the last sentence could be "Hitori no shōnen ga ogawa de dorufin toraete wa-
ratte ita" (A boy was laughing as he seized a dolphin in a brook). This
gives a sense of observation by the speaker. But from the original line
we sense that suddenly the center of the perspective has shifted from
the first-person narrator to the boy. The narration is now performed
by the omnipresent third person for whom the boy is (has been) the
main character. This effect must be due to the use of the particle *wa*
instead of *ga. Wa* is generally considered the topic-marker, as opposed
to *ga*, which is the subject-marker. As the topic-marker, *wa* can be
rendered something like "as for." Literally, then, the line can be translated as "As for the boy, he laughed as he seized a dolphin in a brook."

There are more elements in this line that make us feel strangely dis-
oriented. First of all, dolphins cannot inhabit a small brook! And
"dolphin" is presented by the transliteration of the English word "dolphin" in *katakana*. The usual Japanese word for dolphin is *iruka*. Elsewhere (in "Sara [Platter]") Nishiwaki uses the *kanji* 海豚 (literally,
"sea-pig").

As a whole, "The Sun" presents itself as an exemplary space of literature that is formed by the strata of various fictionalizing strategies.
After the "real" referential sphere is disrupted by various purely linguistic displacements, what remains is a beautifully concerted movement of evocative images, traces, and signifiers that refuse to be mere
transparent carriers of meanings but rather fasten themselves to the
surface and movement of "pure language" (in Benjamin's sense).

But what is this space of literature, the fictionality proper, toward
which the modernist language itself seems inevitably to be drawn?
Away from the real, away from the proper, away from the signified,
Nishiwaki's language seems to direct itself to a tenuous epidermis that
we can only call "poetic text," where depth is no longer possible; yet
paradoxically, the surface is already a trace of a trace of a trace. . . . This
space of literature is the field of signifiers where language begins to
speak of itself, to play its own games. In this self-referentiality of language, a strange survival movement of language itself can be detected.
In his essay "Language to Infinity," Foucault brings out the image of
language's own survival force discovering its self-referentiality, its *mise
en abyme:* "Before the imminence of death, language rushes forth, but
it also starts again, tells of itself, discovers the story of the story and the

possibility that this interpenetration might never end. Headed toward death, language turns back upon itself; it encounters something like a mirror; and to stop this death which would stop it, it possesses but a single power: that of giving birth to its own image in a play of mirrors that has no limits" (Foucault 1977, 54).

The fictionality (as opposed to the mimetic referentiality) of Nishiwaki's text is enhanced by various workings of translation. How does translation function in relation to the self-referential movement of language Foucault talks about? In the previous chapter I discussed how Walter Benjamin's kabbalistic theory of translation leads this inquiry in the direction of "pure language" where "meaning" becomes unmediatedly and instantly truth. According to Benjamin, this absolute state of language can be intimated only by means of a violently literal translation, which allows a radical violation of the mother tongue by foreign tongues. Benjamin quotes Rudolf Pannwitz advocating this violation of the mother tongue: "Our translations, even the best ones, proceed from a wrong premise. They want to turn Hindi, Greek, English into German instead of turning German into Hindi, Greek, English. . . . The basic error of the translator is that he preserves the state in which his own language happens to be instead of allowing his language to be powerfully affected by the foreign tongue. He must expand and deepen his language by means of the foreign language" (quoted in *BJ*, 80–81). It is astonishing to see how faithfully Pannwitz's proposal is enacted in the text of *Ambarvalia*.

Benjamin goes further. All languages strive to become one in pure language, in the paradisal state of nonmeaning. For Benjamin, a translation is not merely a way to transmit the meaning of the original text. On the contrary, it purifies the original of its "meaning." The paradisal state of nonmeaning, pure language, is already in the original text, in a poem. Recall Benjamin: "No poem is intended for the reader, no picture for the beholder, no symphony for the listener" (*BJ*, 69). Thus poetry and pure language become synonymous in their refusal of the reader, that is, of meaning.

The "new" poetic language that Nishiwaki devised in *Ambarvalia* may be seen as a gateway to this pure language. It is a porous text. Many gaps are opened by the force of translation. Into these openings the author-subject falls, along with "sa douce langue natale" (Baudelaire). This writing-subject's surrender to the flow of the translatory writing marked the birth of a Japanese modernist text. Yet being always already a translation, it transcends the boundaries of merely "Japanese" poetry. Along with Foucault and Benjamin, we may say that it is rather a manifestation of language's own movement to infinity, to poetry.

RETURN OR NO RETURN: A POSTMODERN TEXT

The year *Ambarvalia* came out, 1933, was the year the leading proletarian writer Kobayashi Takiji (1903–33) was tortured and murdered by the police.[12] As Fascist oppression increased, Nishiwaki's interest in writing poetry waned. Being the editor in chief of the journal *Mita bungaku,* he was often questioned by the police about the contents of the journal. It does not, however, seem that he was seriously harassed. When his fellow surrealist Takiguchi Shūzō was arrested for being a surrealist, Takiguchi reportedly told the police that Nishiwaki had nothing to do with surrealism (Kagiya 1983, 62). Throughout his life Nishiwaki felt indebted to Takiguchi for that. Unlike most of his fellow poets, Nishiwaki did not participate in writing propagandistic poetry. During this period he was mostly immersed in his academic work, writing his doctoral dissertation *Kodaibungaku josetsu* (An introduction to ancient literature) among other things. In 1944, he returned to his hometown, Ojiya, to escape the bombing of Tokyo. There he began to read classical Japanese literature, which eventually inspired him to write more poetry.

In 1947, Nishiwaki published *Tabibito kaerazu* (No traveller returns), along with *Amubaruwaria,* a revised version of the original *Ambarvalia.* There is now a consensus among critics that *Amubaruwaria* is an inferior revision that took away the raw edges and surprising "unnaturalness" from the original version. In the epilogue of *Amubaruwaria* Nishiwaki wrote: "As I reread the poems [of *Ambarvalia*], now I understand how my mental state has changed" (*ZS,* 168). *Tabibito kaerazu* also appeared as a product of this change in Nishiwaki.

Reviewing the book, the avant-garde poet Kitasono Katsue sharply criticized Nishiwaki's loss of modernist energy and his decline into a weakened, decadent poetic sensibility.[13] Indeed, *Tabibito kaerazu* was a shock to those who had been familiar with Nishiwaki's prewar penchant for radical modernism. Another prominent poet, Miyoshi Tatsuji, observed: "In *Tabibito kaerazu* the previous incomprehensibility of Nishiwaki's poetic language has almost vanished. And his surrealist ideas have become nothing but ruins" (quoted in Kitagawa 1971,

138). What bewildered readers at the time was Nishiwaki's seemingly complete return to the East, to its "philosophy" of *mujō* or *hakanasa* (transience),[14] and to the traditions of Japanese classical literature.

Nishiwaki's insistence on *mujō*, however, can be traced back to "Profanus," in which he stressed the *tsumaranasa* (banality) of reality. In *Tabibito kaerazu*, however, the refreshingly colloquial expression *tsumaranasa* is replaced by more classically coded literary expressions, such as *sabishiki* (lonely, desolate), *nagekawashiki* (pitiful, lamentable), *koishiki* (longing for something, someone), and so on. The word *sabishiki* (including its variants *sabishi* and *sabishisa*) appears especially often—over forty times throughout the work. The resulting textual matrix clearly manifests a strong link to the traditional Japanese literature of *hakanasa, mujō*, and *sabi*.[15]

Not only the tone set by the repetition of *sabishiki*, but also the form of the poem, suggests a return to tradition. *Tabibito kaerazu* is divided into one hundred sixty-eight sections, whose lengths vary from a single word to over forty lines. There is no apparent linear development or narrative progression from one section to the next. Thus each section can be considered an independent poem, though it is far more intriguing to regard each section as part of a more or less loosely orchestrated whole, which somehow reminds us of a *renga* sequence.[16] In some shorter sections, the trace of haiku is undeniable, though Nishiwaki does not conform to the metrical restriction of a 5-7-5 syllabic format. For example:

14

暮れるともなく暮れる
心の春

Dusk falling
    as if not falling . . .
Spring is in my heart.

15

行く道のかすかなる
鶯の音

Faint,
    this road,
    a sound   of
    a warbler.

16

ひすいの情念
女の世のかすむ

The passion of jade
    the world of women fading . . .   (*ZS*, 179–80)

200

Can the text of *Tabibito kaerazu*, then, be summed up as the result of Nishiwaki's nostalgia for the past and his exhausted modernist voice? A closer reading reveals a far more complex and unstable textual structure that defies such a simplistic conclusion. The key to this structure is the intertextuality of *Tabibito kaerazu*. A recent study by Nii-kura Toshikazu uncovers the astonishing array of allusions that Nishi-waki employed in constructing the text.[17] First, the title, *Tabibito kaerazu*, is very likely a translation of the phrase "no traveller returns," uttered by Hamlet.[18] At the same time, however, it points to the Japanese (and Chinese) tradition of *hyōhaku no bungaku* (literature of vagabondage) whose most prominent spokesman was Matsuo Bashō, the famous *haikai* poet of the seventeenth century.[19] In the opening section of *Tabibito kaerazu*, we may hear an echo of *Oku no hosomichi* (The narrow road to the deep north) by Bashō: "Days and months are travellers of eternity. So are the years that pass by. Those who steer a boat across the sea, or drive a horse over the earth till they succumb to the weight of years, spend every minute of their lives travelling. There are a great number of ancients, too, who died on the road. I myself have been tempted for a long time by the cloud-moving wind—filled with a strong desire to wander" (Matsuo 1966, 97).[20]

If this ostensibly "Japanese" text's citational practice were limited to Eastern literary sources, Nishiwaki's "return to the East" would have been indisputable. After all, within the tradition of classical Japanese literature, various methods of artful citation (such as *honmondori*, *honkadori*, *honzetsu*, and *hikiuta*) were firmly established conventions. What is intriguing about *Tabibito kaerazu*, however, is the sheer number of hidden allusions to Western literary sources. In fact, the range of Western as well as Eastern allusions is so extensive that the uncovering of sources begins to resemble a game of literary trivia.

Allusions to Japanese sources may be easier to detect. For example, the last line of section 13 reads: "Sabishiki mono wa wagami narikeri" (What is lonely is my life). Anyone familiar with classical Japanese literature would notice that the line is a slight modification of the last line of a famous *waka* by Fujiwara no Kintsune collected in *Hyakunin isshu*:

Hana sasou	It is not snow
Arashi no niwa no	In the garden where the storm
Yuki narade	Entices the blossoms
Furiyuku mono wa	What drifts by
Waga mi narikeri	Is my life[21]

By contrast, Western sources are far more difficult to uncover, for they are buried under Nishiwaki's unique pseudoclassical Japanese diction and imagery. For example, what is the buried pre-text of the following?

131

衣裳哲学こそ	The philosophy of clothes
女の哲学なれ	*is* the philosophy of women.
女のまる帯の	How sorrowful,
うらがなしき	a woman's one-piece sash . . . (*ZS*, 231)

Reading this section, who would have thought of *Sartor Resartus* by Thomas Carlyle, in which Carlyle's "clothes philosophy" is expounded? Another humorous example can be seen in the following passage, the beginning of section 156:

ふところにパン粉を入れ	Putting breadcrumbs in my bosom,
瓢箪に茶を入れ	tea in my gourd,
柿の木の杖をつき	I was walking up a hill
坂をのぼって行く	with a persimmon cane. (*ZS*, 241)

This is a parody of a passage in *La culture des idées* by Remy de Gourmont: "Despite his tendency to lie, man has a great respect for what is called 'truth,' for truth is his stick to aid his journey through life, for commonplaces are the bread in his beggar's pouch and the wine in his gourd" (Gourmont [1900] 1964, 66). What we witness here is a decisive shift from the destructive, antitraditional language of *Ambarvalia* to a more frivolous parodic mode of writing, in which the past traditions become the object not of destruction but of appropriation, of recycling by way of parody. Here, in this parodic mode, the modernist impulse toward "purity," toward its autonomous status (that is, to be the object of its own referent) is replaced by a postmodernist strategy that problematizes the very activity of reference by revealing a referential *mise en abyme*, as it were, or to quote Douglas Crimp, "strata of representation" (Crimp 1979, 87).

APORIA AND THE INCESSANT VOICE

In *Tabibito kaerazu* the parodic mode does not limit itself to passages where traditional pre-texts are hidden. The ostensible seriousness of the elegiac tone that seems to pervade the text is jolted by sudden appearances of the frivolous. In the same vein, the repetition of *sabishiki* begins to appear self-parodying. Does the text not achieve, through its overrepetition of *sabishiki,* a parody of its own voice, its own dominant message? Does the text not deconstruct its most apparent feature, that is, its "return to the East / return to the classical past," by a subtle strategy of fictionalizing its own ontological status, its own historicity and topos? Let us analyze a section that seems to reveal this postmodernist impulse toward self-deconstruction, toward self-fictionalization:

39

九月の始め	Early September
街道の岩片から	from a rock by the avenue
青いどんぐりのさがる	a green acorn hanging . . .
窓の淋しき	Desolate is the window.
中から人の声がする	Inside there is someone's voice.
人間の話す音の淋しき	How desolate, the sound of human speech,
「だんな　このたびは金毘羅詣り	"Hey, mistah, dis time I hear you goin' a pilgrimage
に出かけるてぇことだが	to Konpira, eh? Please take dis wid ya.
これはつまんねーものだが	No, no, it's nothin' mistah, just a partin' token.
せんべつだ　とってくんねー」	Take it, take it."
「もはや詩が書けない	"I can no longer write poetry.
詩のないところに詩がある	Poetry exists where there is no poetry.
うつつの断片のみ詩となる	Only a shred of reality becomes poetry.
うつつは淋しい	Reality is loneliness.
淋しく感ずるが故に我あり	I feel loneliness, therefore I am.
淋しみは存在の根本	Loneliness is the root of existence.
淋しみは美の本願なり	Loneliness is the ultimate desire for Beauty.
美は永劫の象徴」	Beauty is the symbol of eternity."

Kugatsu no hajime
Kaidō no iwakake kara
Aoi donguri no sagaru

Mado no sabishiki
Naka kara hito no koe ga suru
Ningen no hanasu oto no sabishiki
"Danna konotabiwa Konpira mairi
Ni dekakeruttē kotodaga

Kore wa tsumaranē monodaga senbetsuda
Totte kunnē"

"Mohaya shi ga kakenai
Shi no nai tokoro ni shi ga aru
Utsutsu no danpen nomi shi to naru
Utsutsu wa sabishii
Sabishiku kanzuru ga yue ni ware ari
Sabishimi wa sonzai no konpon
Sabishimi wa bi no hongan nari
Bi wa eigō no shōchō"   (ZS, 189–90)

The abrupt leaps of imagery seen in *Ambarvalia* have not entirely disappeared in *Tabibito kaerazu*, though what "leaps" here is not imagery but voice. The sudden intrusion of direct speech, made more vibrant, more "real" by the use of a rural dialect, disrupts the *sabishisa* (desolation / loneliness) established in the previous lines. The speaker seems to be what Nishiwaki often calls a *dojin* (native; literally translated, man of soil), whose voice contrasts sharply with the abstractions of the intellectual voice in the following lines—the voice of aporia, an internal soliloquy on loneliness and beauty. The stark contrast between the two voices is stunning. Their relation seems to be exactly that of "nonrelation" (*kankei ga nai*), which Nishiwaki promoted in his theoretical writings as the essence of the surrealist text.[22] At the same time, however, there is a certain incessant movement that traverses the whole section.

The first stanza is not a complete sentence. The last line, "Aoi donguri no sagaru" (A green acorn hanging) may be considered to be modifying the first line, "Kugatsu no hajime" (The beginning of September), though belatedly.[23] Or it may even be modifying the first word of the second stanza, *mado* (window). (This fluidity is reinforced by the elimination of punctuation from the entire text of *Tabibito kaerazu*.) Or again, it may be modifying a certain vacuum created by the elimination of the possible final modified word—for example, it could be *hi* (day), thus, "Aoi donguri no sagaru hi" (A day when a green acorn hangs). The overall effect of the syntax of the first stanza is a sense of slight instability. On the one hand, the haikulike completed image of early autumn is clearly stressed by the cyclic movement of the syntax (the last line of the stanza returning to the first line). On the other, the elimination of the expected modified word brings out a certain empty space in the text. We do *read* this otherwise unmarked sign of vacuum. (Is the blank space of the stanza break the sign of this vacuum?) Finally, there is a sense of continuation, the imagery of the first stanza spreading out to the next. As a result of all these different syntactical movements within the stanza, the text begins to "quaver," as it were, in its incompleteness. Perhaps this is where we may begin to hear the incessant murmuring of language that Foucault calls "literature," which attempts to break the constraining shell of human speech, to supersede man, to transcend his aporia of poetry.[24] Now a certain autonomous movement of language begins to flow, almost imperceptibly.

In the next stanza, *sabishiki* is used twice, modifying first *mado* and then *ningen no hanasu oto* (the sound of humans speaking). *Sabishiki* is the central sign of *Tabibito kaerazu*, establishing itself by its excessive repetition. What is the function of such excess? No doubt it creates a dominant mood. But we begin to suspect that this excessive repetition may be a device to "exhaust" the repeated sign so that the signified (the sentiment of desolation) becomes "insignificant," like a cliché, too familiar, like the sight of a window. The signifier, however, remains an empty shell on the surface of the language. It becomes, in turn, the sign of this loss of meaning from the signified. Various subjects of the repeated modifier *sabishi* also begin to lose their sentimental attachment to the signified of *sabishi*.

So "window" is modified by an empty modifier, the nonsignificant signifier *sabishi*. But we are going around in a circle. Does not *sabishi* signify from the beginning this state and feeling of loss, of insignificance? According to the *Kōjien* dictionary, *sabishi* means: (1) a sense of lacking the object of desire, not being content; (2) sad, not merry; (3) quiet and forlorn, not lively. We remember that in his theoretical writings Nishiwaki endorsed the notion of defamiliarization as the aim of poetry. The line *Mado no sabishiki* in a sense achieves this defamiliarization because not too many people would customarily associate *sabishiki* (note also that it is in *bungotai*, classical literary style) with such a familiar object as a window. But now, because of the excessive repetition, *sabishiki* has become as familiar and as *tsumaranai* as the window. At this point, therefore, the subject (window), the signifier (*sabishiki*), and the signified (feeling of lack, desolation, loneliness) become curiously identical. They all become one in "familiarity," in *tsumaranasa*.

The subject of the next *sabishiki* is *ningen no hanasu oto* (the sound of humans speaking). We must note here that what is *sabishiki* is not the *hito no koe* (human voice) of the preceding line, but *oto* (sound).

The transition that occurs between these two lines is that from the human-centered "voice" to the neutral "sound," which is, as Saussure indicated, a signifier par excellence. Thus what is to come as a quoted speech is defined not as a "voice" but as a signifier—a "sound" (*oto*) yet to be attached to any signified.

The sound comes abruptly, carrying an irrelevant content: "Hey, mistah, dis time I hear you goin' a pilgrimage to Konpira, eh? Please take dis wid ya. No, no, it's nothin' mistah, just a partin' token. Take it, take it." It has to be irrelevant because, dictated by the preceding transition from voice to sound, the arbitrary relation between the signifier (the sound of the speech) and the signified (the content of the speech) is clearly underlined. Here the sign (the speech) itself seems cut off from the rest of the poem, floating. The content could have been anything, a slice of any human speech; the signifier (the sound) could have been anything, incomprehensible gibberish in a foreign tongue. But here, appropriate to both concepts, "sound" and "human speech," a dialect is used. By presenting the speech in a dialect, the distance from the "normal" speech, that is, its "sound," is emphasized. At the same time, using the naturalist technique of presenting a slice of human life, with the dialect adding a sense of specificity, the speech effectively exhibits itself as a "real" human speech. This is where, so cunningly again, *sabishiki* sneaks in: "ningen no hanasu oto no sabi-shiki." However pitifully, this noise (*oto*) nonetheless has to carry a content. What is indeed *sabishi* (lonely) is both the arbitrariness of the sign (the speech) and the linguistic fact that, however arbitrarily, a signifier (a mere noise) is inescapably tied to a content. If the sound did not carry any meaning at all, then it might reach the region of absolute *tsumaranasa*, absolute unnameable reality.

Then the poet reaches his poetic aporia, trapped in this *sabishisa*, in the meaninglessness of sound and speech: "I can no longer write poetry / Poetry exists where there is no poetry." How can we name this empty space gaping within the semiosis of language, this ultimate aporia of poetry? What kind of poetry can exist where there is no poetry? It is the impossible space of poetry, a gap between the signifier and signified, the limit of fictionality, nonmeaning, *tsumaranasa*. Yet it is from this aporia that the text of *Tabibito kaerazu* is woven. Aided by the incessant murmuring of language, a collage of scattered pre-texts, the text achieves an allegory of itself, that is, an allegory of fictionality/poetry. The fictive by definition differs from and defers the ultimate transparent revelation of the actual. By appropriating literary history, Eastern and Western, into its translatory citational strategy, the text of

Tabibito kaerazu deconstructs its own originality. It is a fictive text citing and translating other fictive discourses of the past. It is, essentially, a story of its own fictiveness as well as of the limits of that abysmal fictionality. Poetic defamiliarization must eventually return to the "familiar"—*tumaranai/sabishii*—reality (*utsutsu*).[25] For there, and there only, one finds the true loss of "meaning," the sudden departure of the signified. The ultimate poetry keeps translating itself—from "September" to "a green acorn" to "a window" to "a human voice" to "the sound" to the paradoxical nonpoetry to *utsutsu* (reality/dream) to "Beauty" to "eternity." This is the incessant murmur of language flowing out of the gap opened between signifier and signified. It carries so much *sabishisa* (desolation) that we burst out laughing.

PROPER NAMES

An unusually great number of proper names, especially names of plants, stud the text of *Tabibito kaerazu*. No doubt the plant names contribute to the establishment of a clear link with traditional Japanese literature, in which seasonal changes manifested in nature and the strong bond between the poet and nature are cardinal motifs. Although some of the plants mentioned in the poem seem "classically coded" (such as *yūgao, ominaeshi,* and *tsuyukusa*), the majority of plants are little-known nonliterary names (such as *akanomanma, enokorogusa,* and *yabukōji*). The specificity Nishiwaki brings forth by employing such nonliterary names seems to point to the *tsumaranasa,* the insignificance of the plants thus referred to. For example:

56

Green acorns of an oak tree.
Loneliness . . .   (*ZS,* 197)

A more peculiar emptiness can be seen in the following one-word section:

5

やぶがらし

Yabugarashi (sorrel).   (*ZS,* 175)

What is behind *yabugarashi*? *Yabugarashi* only refers to a species of plant, nothing more, nothing less. It does not refer to a specific object at a particular time and place. It is merely a name. Yet it is a proper name, more specific than, say, "grass." Again, it is not literarily coded enough to be symbolic or allegorical. What is the semiotic status of this text, save the emptiness of the sign, save the peculiar specificity of the signifier whose destination (signified) is after all not grounded in "real" specificity? *Yabugarashi* appears only as a certain negative code, which "floats" over the field of signifiers. It is simply and purely language: a name. It is an insignificant noise that paradoxically poses as a specificity. We touch the being of language here, albeit bewilderingly.

The inclusion of proper names also brings an autobiographical specificity to the text. Certainly Niikura's study suggests that the people and events described in some sections are based on actuality. For example, section 41:

高等師範の先生と一緒に	I went for a hike to Koma Mountain
こまの山へ遊山に行った	with a teacher from a higher teacher's school.
街道の鍛治屋の庭先に	In a blacksmith's garden by the road,
ほこりにまみれた梅もどき	we saw a dusty holly.
その実を二三摘みとって	Taking a few berries from the tree
喰べた	we ate them.
「子供の時によくたべた」	"I used to eat these when I was a child,"
といって無口の先生が初めて	said this taciturn teacher.
その日しゃべった	For the first time that day
	he spoke.

Kōtōshihan no sensei to isshoni
Koma no yama e yūzan ni itta
Kaidō no kajiya no niwasaki ni
Hokori ni mamireta umemodoki
Sono mi o nisan tsumitotte
Tabeta
"Kodomo no toki ni yoku tabeta"
To itte mukuchi no sensei ga hajimete
Sono hi shabetta (ZS, 190–91)

This section can certainly be taken as an autobiographical sketch. Specificities established in this text include *kōtōshihan no sensei* (a teacher at a higher teacher's school) (as opposed to simply saying *sensei*),[26] the proper name *koma no yama* (Koma Mountain), which is not a famous mountain (thus yet to be "coded"), and another proper name, *umemodoki* (a type of holly) curiously specified by its introductory modifying phrase "kaidō no kajiya no niwasaki ni hokori ni mamireta" (in a blacksmith's garden by the road, a dusty). What is peculiar in this modifying phrase for *umemodoki* is the mention of "blacksmith," whose specificity (as opposed to saying "someone") seems utterly irrelevant in relation to the holly, except that its fortuitous irrelevance itself, in a strange way, enhances the specificity of what it modifies: the holly. The sentence involving the holly is not complete; it ends with the proper name, *umemodoki,* without a verb following to complete the sentence. The reader's attention stops at this proper name, *umemodoki.* There seems to be a subtle stratagem of fictionalization (away from the autobiographical, that is, nonfictional mode) hidden in it.

Umemodoki means, literally translated, "something that is like *ume* (Japanese plum)." *Modoki,* a suffix, functions as a simile-maker (like). Thus *umemodoki* is a tree that looks like the famous (heavily coded) *ume* but is not really it (the origin). Something extraordinary (though well hidden) happens after this strange proper name is specified and put in focus. Someone (presumably "we," though in the Japanese text the subject is omitted) eats the berries of the *umemodoki.* Anyone who is familiar with this tree knows that its berries are inedible. *Umemodoki*'s leaves look like those of *ume,* but its fruit is a far cry from the *ume*-fruit (not edible fresh but treasured for pickling). Nonetheless, the teacher's childhood memory is evoked. The teacher speaks for the first time. But he speaks "fiction," for he could not have eaten these inedible berries when he was a child. Language is born for the first time when he eats this inedible fruit of *umemodoki,* which in turn is a mere verisimilitude of the classically coded *ume* (classical Japanese literature). But at the same time, this verisimilitude is well hidden under the cover of its "proper name." And this "proper name" has gained more specificity (sense of presence) from its introductory modifying phrase. In order to deconstruct this specificity, a violent operation (the eating of the inedible) is required. The specificity, the absolute uniqueness, indicated by the proper name thus opens itself up to the invasions of otherness. The *umemodoki* is eaten despite its defense of being inedible, of not being *ume,* thus being specific, unique, proper, and "insignificant" (not coded). From this violence against the proper, the text suggests, language is born, fiction is born, and the incessant movement of *différance* begins to flow.

Throughout the text of *Tabibito kaerazu,* through the reflecting (citational) strata of its intertextuality, the figure of a phantasmal traveller is evoked. He wanders around the fictive landscape of hidden citations and translations. He collects the ruins of language, the ruins of literary history. Where is he returning, if he ever is returning? Consider the last section of *Tabibito kaerazu:*

168

Touching the roots of eternity,
passing the field's end
where the heart's quails cry,
where wild roses burst into bloom,
passing a village where fulling blocks echo,
passing a country where a woodsman's path crosses,
passing a town where whitewashed walls crumble,
visiting a temple by the road,
viewing a mandala tapestry with reverence,
walking over crumbled mountains of dead twigs,
crossing a ferry where reed stalks are reflected in long shadows,
passing a bush where seeds hang from grass leaves,
the phantasmal man departs.
The eternal traveller never returns.   (*ZS*, 255)

The traveller is the figure of what Barthes calls *écriture*.[27] He moves intransitively, toward the nondestination, taking detours (*michi kusa*), picking forgotten roadside weeds, reflecting and refracting voices from the past, writing again, writing again in translation of history. This may well be the destiny of postmodernist writing.

AETERNITAS

Eterunitasu was published in 1962 as one of three poems included in a volume of the same title. In its epilogue, Nishiwaki wrote: "I hear that Murō Saisei eliminated the word 'eternity' from his *Collected Poems*. In dedication to his spirit, I wrote this text, picking up what he had discarded, using the word 'eternity' as many times as possible" (*ZS*, 640). For Murō, the word *eien* (eternity) must have appeared poetically exhausted, whereas Nishiwaki, just as he overcoded the word *sabishiki* in *Tabibito kaerazu*, uses the very exhaustion of the sign "eternity" to poetic advantage.

conversations I hear in the streets,
a stone on which the shadows of grass are cast,

the weight of a fish,
the shape and color of corn,
the thickness of a column.
I would prefer things that do not symbolize.
Upon the banal existence
infinite loneliness
is reflected.
Loneliness is the last symbol
of eternity.
I want to abandon even this symbol.
Not to think of eternity
is to think of eternity.
Not to think is the symbol
of eternity.
I want to abandon even this symbol.
To want to abandon it
is the ultimate symbol of eternity.   (*ZS*, 629–30)

"Eternity" is here conceived of as an impossible concept that cannot even be thought of with our symbolic language. The putative poetic exhaustion of the sign "eternity" comes about because its signified (however distant) becomes too familiar within the poetry-code. What Nishiwaki does in *Eterunitasu* is to exhibit this overcoded sign so many times that the familiar signified is shaken off the sign, so that only the signifier remains as the sign of its own emptiness. The negative dialectic inherent in the above lines again directs the language of *Eterunitasu* to its own limits, to nonmeaning.

Georges Bataille also connects the notion of poetry to that of eternity. He cites Rimbaud:

Elle est retrouvée.
Quoi? L'éternité.
C'est la mer allée
Avec le soleil.

Bataille continues: "[La poésie] nous mène à l'éternité, elle nous mène à la mort, et par la mort, à la continuité: la poesie est l'*éternité*."[28] For Nishiwaki, "poetry is eternity." His language takes us to a death, the death of "meaning," and through this nonmeaning (*tsumaranasa*) to the continuity within the sign—the signifier and the signified linked by the loss of meaning. Eternity is this state of pure language.

Toward this paradise of "nonmeaning," the traveller walks on meandering paths. His walk is always essentially a detour (*michikusa*), to defer the final destination. Gazing into eternity, he stumbles over "boring" things. His twists and turns of language thus come into being as repeated failures to reach the final paradisal state of language. But "boring" things are always already there, defying and at the same time inviting the incessant flow of writing.

> Again I stumbled over a stone.
> Again half of the dream
> was severed.
> Oh, Cynara!
> I recalled something about sesame and lilies.
> Like Ruskin,
> like Hopkins
> I must begin to study clouds again,
> I must begin to love stones again:
> that stone jutting out from a tea plantation,
> that stone I found under a Japanese pepper tree by the Tama River,
> that milestone
> buried in a bamboo thicket,
> and that stone of Venus in the waning light . . .
> Ah, again I stumble over a stone.
> Ah, again
> without knowing
> I am using the deluxe words
> of man . . .   (ZS, 637–38)

How should we begin an eternity, the eternity of language, the eternity of writing? First, we must hear a murmuring, an incessant flow of language, the movement of "arche-writing" translating itself, translating itself into an abyss. Our actual writing, be it a poem or a critique, appears only as a result of some "turning"—displacement, slippage, supplementation—of the origin. Inevitably our writing confesses its failure to be the origin of itself.

What a poem attempts to convey is not the "meaning" of the origin of the poem, but the "nonmeaning" of the origin, that is, the *origin itself* before the movement of supplements begins to operate. We have called this origin of a poem "reality." In fact, reality escapes the domain of text. It is a puncture in the text. It is beyond our earthly languages.

Our nostalgia for the origin (what we ultimately want to communicate through writing) is always intense. Nishiwaki's notion of poetry, which was tirelessly reiterated in his essays on poetics as well as in his poems, reveals our intense nostalgia for the origin/nonmeaning. The intensity is such that the actual existence of language itself is threatened.

Yet instead of returning to the originary silence, to the aporia of poetry, Nishiwaki's poetic language never ceased to expand. After *Tabibito kaerazu,* in 1953, he published what many critics regard as his most satisfying collection of poems, *Kindai no gūwa* (Modern fables). Then, much inspired by James Joyce's *Finnegans Wake,* Nishiwaki began to write increasingly longer poems. Nine more collections of poems were to follow: *Dai san no shinwa* (1956; The third myth), *Ushinawareta toki* (1960; Lost time), *Hōjō no megami* (1962; The goddess of fertility), *Eterunitasu* in 1962, *Hōseki no nemuri* (1963; A gemstone's sleep), *Raiki* (1967; Book of rites), his longest (two thousand lines), which was *Jōka* (1969, Earth song), *Rokumon* (1970; Lu-men), and his final collection, *Jinrui* (1979; Mankind).[29] What does this colossal expansion of language signify? Eternity invites writing. Poetry is language, though it may be the final mode of language on the verge of disappearance. At the moment of this paradox, Nishiwaki's language touches, not the mute, but the incessant.

Nishiwaki died at his birthplace in Ojiya, on June 5, 1982. He was eighty-eight years old.

Notes

INTRODUCTION

1. Quotations from Nishiwaki Junzaburō's works are cited using the following abbreviations:

NJZ   *Nishiwaki Junzaburō zenshū*, ed. Kagiya Yukinobu et al., 12 vols. (Tokyo: Chikuma shobō, 1982–83)

ZS   *Teihon, Nishiwaki Junzaburō zenshishū* (Tokyo: Chikuma shobō, 1981)

2. Nishiwaki was again a candidate for the prize in 1962 and 1963, along with Kawabata and Tanizaki Jun'ichirō (1886–1965).

3. See Kagiya 1983, 9. Although Nishiwaki never met or corresponded with Eliot, his interest in Eliot went much deeper than the rivalry Nishiwaki often jokingly expressed. Nishiwaki translated *The Waste Land* and *Four Quartets* and wrote a number of essays on Eliot, which made Nishiwaki an authority on Eliot in Japan. His rather idiosyncratic (poetic) essays on Eliot are, however, far from what the academy would expect. One senses that Nishiwaki was writing about his own ideas on poetry through Eliot.

4. There is no biography of Nishiwaki except the detailed chronicle of his public life written by his most dedicated disciple and scholar, Kagiya Yukinobu. The chronicle is in the form of the *nenpu* (chronology) that one finds attached to the collected works of every canonized writer in Japan. This section is based on the *nenpu* in the eleventh volume of *NJZ*.

5. Reportedly, his uncle had been to Cambridge, England, to study. See Fukuda, Murano, and Kagiya 1971, 503.

6. See "Esthétique Foraine" in *Surrealist Poetics*, translated below.

7. Actually, he never gave up his paint brush. In November 1981, the eighty-seven-year-old Nishiwaki held an art exhibition at the Sōgetsu Art Museum in Akasaka, Tokyo. The exhibition included thirty-six oil paintings, twenty-nine watercolor pieces, and one India-ink drawing that he produced during the period from 1923 to 1981. His style shows a touch of Cézanne.

8. See Andō Ichirō 1971, 11.

9. Hagiwara was the most innovative modern poet before Nishiwaki. For the English translation of his poetry, see *Howling at the Moon* (Hagiwara 1978). On the poet and his work, see M. Ueda 1983, 137–83. At first Hagiwara was wary of Nishiwaki's intellectualism and criticized his poetics for its neglect of the emotional aspects of poetry. However, the two men became intimate friends in the end.

10. *Kaigyaku* (wit, humor) is one of the most important words in Nishiwaki's poetic universe. It is a bizarre sense of dry humor born of the *tsumaranasa* (banality) of reality, but at the same time it carries the reader to

Nishiwaki's unique sense of the sublime. All his literary criticism after *Chōgen-jitsushugi shiron* was based on his notion of *kaigyaku*. Nishiwaki called his theory "Critique d'omoshiroi" (*omoshiroi* meaning "funny, interesting"). A poem Nishiwaki wrote as a monody for T. S. Eliot exemplifies his special sense of *kaigyaku:*

> You were truly *L'homme d'esprit*
> But no one understands the *kaigyaku* of your wit
> Only those who eat loaches in the old dear Kanda
> Truly lament your death
> You were the poet of *kaigyaku* like Donne
> But I wanted you to shake hands
> in this old homeland with Furuta's Chikuma
> and with Aida no Arei
> In this capital of Changan, *kaigyaku* has weakened
> One cannot succeed in the world unless one becomes sentimental
> But I, roaming through old books,
> am not particularly thinking of you.
>
> (From "Tengoku no natsu" in *Raiki, ZS,* 739)

11. See Naka 1979, 172–78.

12. Along with T. S. Eliot, Joyce was one of the few modern writers to whom Nishiwaki paid serious attention. He translated and published a collection of Joyce's poems in 1933, which included a partial translation of *Finnegans Wake.* His interest in Joyce heated up again in the 1960s, resulting in his writing a number of essays on Joyce.

13. Nishiwaki and Marjorie Biddle were divorced in 1932. That same year, Nishiwaki married Kuwayama Saeko. As far as I know, the circumstances surrounding Nishiwaki's marriage to and divorce from Marjorie are not documented anywhere.

14. Both reviews are quoted in Nenpu, *NJZ* 11:647. *Spectrum* is now included in *NJZ* 3:548–485.

15. Natsume Sōseki spent two years in England (1900–1902) as a student of English literature. His alienated existence in England, however, left him on the brink of a nervous breakdown with a permanent sense of bitterness toward England.

16. Takamura Kōtarō was a major poet of modern Japan. For English translations of his poetry, see *Chieko and Other Poems* (1988) and *Chieko's Sky* (1978). On the poet, see M. Ueda 1983, 232–83. He seemed to have suffered from a racial inferiority complex during his visits to America and France, which eventually took expression in his feverishly patriotic poems published during World War II.

17. Anyone who studies cultural conflicts and politics knows that there is no such innocent "neutrality" possible at the crossroads of East and West. Thus one may argue that Nishiwaki was unwittingly assuming an auto-Orientalist position by so thoroughly transforming himself into a Westerner. However, determining Nishiwaki's political and personal relationship to the West as well as to the East is a difficult task, largely because of the lack of biographical documentation. At least we know that, unlike Natsume and Takamura,

Nishiwaki did not leave any document revealing his disdain for or exaltation of one culture, or his shame about being Japanese. Nishiwaki's texts mainly refer to his relationship to the notion of poetry. Since poetry is a linguistic construct, Nishiwaki's relationship to it was first and foremost a linguistic one. Nishiwaki's subject was elusive; it perpetually escaped the alluring yet tyrannical grasp of the mother tongue. His subject was thus "translatory." The word *neutral* should here be understood in this translatory mode. One critique of such an ironic neutrality of subject can be seen in Karatani Kōjin's discussion of the transcendental, ironic self found in Kunikida Doppo as well as in Murakami Haruki. Karatani warns that such an ironic self fails to recognize the irreplaceable singularity (i.e., historicity) of the self. See Karatani 1990.

18. A modernist he may be, but his scholarship showed a wide range of interests. His scholarly publications include *William Langland* (1933), *Yōroppa bungaku* (1933; European literature), *Gendai igirisu bungaku* (1934; Contemporary English literature), *Kodai eigo bunpō* (1935; Old English grammar), *Kōgo to bungo* (1936; Colloquialism and literary language), *Eibei shisōshi* (1941; An intellectual history of Britain and America), *Kinsei eibungakushi* (1948; A history of modern English literature), his doctoral dissertation, *Kodai bungaku josetsu* (1948; An introduction to ancient literature), *Fūshi to kigeki* (1948; Satire and comedy), and a translation of Chaucer's *Canterbury Tales* (1949).

19. A surrealist poet until the end of his life, Ueda Toshio was well known as a theorist and poet of the avant-garde movement in early Showa. He wrote the first surrealist manifesto in Japan, which was published in *Shōbi, majutsu, gakusetsu*, no. 3 (January, 1928).

20. As a poet, artist, and art critic, Takiguchi Shūzō was the most authentic and orthodox surrealist in Japan. The noted literary critic Kobayashi Hideo (1902–83) had this to say: "Contemporary French surrealism was imported to Japan and mainly due to its name was miserably misunderstood to the point that one can no longer laugh about it. Among all the Japanese surrealist poets who appeared one after another, within my knowledge, the only one I feel isn't a fake is Mr. Takiguchi Shūzō" ("Bungei jihyō: Bungaku wa esoragoto ka," *Bungei shunjū* [January 1930]).

21. A scholar of French literature, Satō Saku taught at Keiō from 1930 to 1972. He is known for his work on Baudelaire and French modernist poetry as well as on Sartre and Camus.

22. Ueda Tamotsu was a critic and translator. He was the younger brother of Ueda Toshio. A professor at Keiō, he was well known for his translations of the works of T. S. Eliot.

23. Miura Kōnosuke was a poet and professor of English at Keiō.

SURREALIST POETICS

Chōgenjitsushugi shiron consists of five essays: "Profanus," "Shi no shōmetsu" (The extinction of poetry), "Esthétique Foraine," "Chōshizenshugi" (Supernaturalism), and "Chōshizenshi no kachi" (The value of supernatural poetry). The first four essays were previously published in *Mita bungaku* (April

1926, January 1927, May 1927, and February 1928, respectively), and the last one in the first issue of *Shi to shiron* (September 1928) under the title "Chōshizenshi gakuha." I have omitted the last two, "Chōshizenshugi" and "Chōshizenshi no kachi," from my translation, for they seem to contain much that is already stated in the first three essays. The language of *Chōgenjitsu-shugi shiron* is a far cry from common scholarly discourse, which is supposed to display seriousness and clarity. Nishiwaki's language is often highly playful, and does not hesitate to bring in "nonserious" discourse. To the dismay of any translator, Nishiwaki's style is often extremely elliptical, and thus demands much interpretation. Although my aim was to translate as literally as possible so as to preserve the flavor of the original text, often I was forced to supplement its frugality with interpreted "meanings" for the sake of clarity. There are some notes provided by Nishiwaki in the original text, identifying the sources of quotations. I have added more specific bibliographical information to them. I enclose the text of all my own notes in square brackets to distinguish them from Nishiwaki's notes. In the notes, I provide the original versions of French passages that Nishiwaki quotes in translation. The passages Nishiwaki quotes directly from foreign texts without translation are left in their original languages.

Profanus

1. [Mallarmé gave a lecture at Oxford on March 1, 1894. See "La musique et les lettres," in Mallarmé 1945, 635.]

2. See Janko Larvin, *Nietzsche and Modern Consciousness.*

3. Charles Baudelaire, "La chevelure" [from *Les fleurs du mal,* in Baudelaire 1975, 1:27.

> Je m'enivre ardemment des senteurs confondues
> De l'huile de coco, du musc et du goudron].

4. Baudelaire, "Journaux intimes, Fusées, I" [1975, 1:649.

> Dieu est le seul être qui, pour régner, n'ait même pas besoin d'exister].

5. Baudelaire, "Notes nouvelles sur Edgar Poe" [1975, 2:334. "Ainsi le principe de la poésie est, strictement et simplement, l'aspiration humaine vers une beauté supérieure, et la manifestation de ce principe est dans un enthousiasme, une excitation de l'âme"].

6. [Baudelaire 1975, 1:649. "L'amour, c'est le goût de la prostitution."]

7. Baudelaire [1975, 2:334. "Car la passion est *naturelle*, trop naturelle pour ne pas introduire un ton blessant, discordant, dans le domaine de la beauté pure, trop familière et trop violente pour ne pas scandaliser les purs Désirs, les gracieuses Mélancolies et les nobles Désespoirs qui habitent les régions surnaturelles de la poésie"].

8. Baudelaire, "Enivrez-vous" [from *Le spleen de Paris,* in Baudelaire 1975, 1:337. "Il faut être toujours ivre. Tout est là: c'est l'unique question. . . . Mais de quoi? De vin, de poésie ou de vertu, à votre guise"].

9. Quoted in Otto Jespersen, *Progress in Language* [(1894) 1909, 361].

10. [See Garrod 1924, in which we read: "I say that the race of long-haired poets is dead" (6). "Poetry seems ill-paid, indeed, but easy. Yet never, I fancy, was it harder. Easy, no doubt, it was, once upon a time. Once upon a time, the world was fresh, to speak was to be a poet, to name objects an inspiration; and metaphor dropped from the inventive mouths of men like some natural exudation of the vivified senses" (8).]

11. [Baudelaire, "Richard Wagner et *Tannhäuser* à Paris," in Baudelaire 1975, 2:793. "(T)ous les grands poètes deviennent naturellement, fatalement, critiques. Je plains les poètes que guide le seul instinct."]

12. See F. G. Selby, *The Criterion* [1925].

13. See J. E. Spingarn, ed., *Critical Essays of the Seventeenth Century* [1908, 1:x].

14. Max Jacob, *Art poétique* [N.d., 34. "L'imagination n'est pas autre chose que l'association des idées"].

15. Samuel Johnson, "Cowley" [(1783) 1890, 1:25].

16. Garrod [1924, 16].

17. [Shelley 1971.]

18. "Clorinda and Damon," in *Poems of Andrew Marvell* [Marvell 1898, 41].

19. Jean Cocteau, "Cannes" [1925, 259.

> Mon oreille est un coquillage
> Qui aime le bruit de la mer].

20. [Reverdy 1975, 73. Nishiwaki quotes from André Breton, "Manifeste du Surréalisme (1924)" in *Manifestes du Surréalisme,* ed. Jean-Jacques Pauvert (Montreuil: Editions J.-J. Pauvert, 1962), 37. I quote the translation by Richard Seaver and Helen R. Lane in Breton 1969, 20. "L'Image est une création pure de l'esprit. Elle ne peut naître d'une comparaison mais du rapprochement de deux réalités plus ou moins éloignées. Plus les rapports des deux réalités rapprochées seront lointains et justes, plus l'image sera forte— plus elle aura de puissance émotive et de réalité poétique."]

21. See Théodore de Banville, *Petit traité de poésie française* [1872, 3].

22. Bacon, "Advancement of Learning," in *Critical Essays of the Seventeenth Century* [1908, 1:6].

23. [Ibid.]

24. Spingarn [1908, 1:xi].

25. See Bernard Fay, *Panorama de la littérature contemporaine.*

26. [Quoted in German by Nishiwaki. Source not indicated.]

27. See *Surréalisme I* (Paris: October 1924) [edited by Yvan Goll, in Goll 1968, 1:87–88, in which we read: "Le premier poéte au monde constata: 'Le ciel est bleu.' Plus tard, un autre trouva: 'Tes yeux sont bleus comme le ciel.' Long temps après, on se hasarda à dire: 'Tu as du ciel dans les yeux.' Un moderne s'écriera: 'Tes yeux de ciel!'"].

28. [Source not indicated by Nishiwaki.]

29. See Osbert Sitwell, *Who Killed Cock Robin?* [1921].

30. [Quoted in Garrod 1924, in which we read: "As to prosaicalness in general, it is sometimes indulged in by young writers on the plea of its being

natural; but this is a mere confusion of triviality with propriety; and is sometimes the result of indolence" (6).]

31. Tristan Tzara ["Sur une ride du soleil" from *De nos oiseaux* (Paris: Editions kra, 1929), in Tzara 1975, 238.

> le monde
> une bague faite pour une fleur
> une fleur fleur pour le bouquet de fleurs fleurs
> un porte-cigarette rempli de fleurs
> une petite locomotive aux yeux de fleurs
> une paire de gants pour des fleurs
> en peau de fleurs comme nos fleurs fleurs fleurs de fleurs
> et un oeuf].

32. [Quoted in Breton 1969, 36.]
33. [Ibid.]
34. Arthur Rimbaud, "Oraison du Soir" [1972, 39.

> Doux comme le Seigneur du cèdre et des hysopes,
> Je pisse vers les cieux bruns, très haut et très loin,
> Avec l'assentiment des grands héliotropes].

35. "The Old Vicarage, Grantchester" [Brooke 1918, 53].
36. [Poe does not cite "The Raven" in "The Poetic Principle" but does so
extensively in "The Philosophy of Composition." Also, Poe does not mention
"mysticism" specifically in either of the above essays.]
37. *Menschheitsdämmerung*.
38. [See May Sinclair, introduction to Bosschère 1917, 2.]
39. Bosschère, "Doutes" [1917, 72, 74. In his translation, Nishiwaki
brings the first section, "J'étais un enfant vert," to the end. Also, he seems to
mistranslate "La rosée froide" as "tsumetai tsuyu" (cold dew).

> J'étais un enfant vert
> Et aigre comme du brou.
>   .   .   .   .
> Le chapeau du père était sacré.
> Certes il y avait d'autres pères
> Mais celui-ci était le seul
> Qui fut tel et tel.
> Il fumait sa pipe avec intégrité.
> On se collait près de lui
> Pour tirer par le nez son odeur d'homme.
>   .   .   .   .
> Et la mère était le pain et le beurre
> La rosée froide de six heures et la cerise].

40. T. S. Eliot, *The Waste Land* [1971, 46].
41. See Jules Romains and G. Chennevière, *Petit traité de versification*
[1924, 23].

42. [Goll 1968, 1:87–88. "Jusqu'au début du XXe siècle, c'était l'OREILLE qui décidait de la qualité d'une poésie: rythme, sonorité, cadence, allitération, rime: tout pour l'oreille. Depuis une vingtaine d'années, l'OEIL prend sa revanche."]

43. [See Bahr 1925.]

The Extinction of Poetry

1. [Paul Verlaine, "Chanson d'Automne," in Verlaine (1890) 1973, 58. For a discussion of Nishiwaki's idiosyncratic translation of this poem, crudely retranslated from Japanese into English here, see chapter 4 below, "Violation of the Mother Tongue."

Les sanglots longs
Des violons
De l'automne
Blessent mon coeur
D'une langueur
Monotone.]

2. [Baudelaire, "L'âme du vin," from *Les fleurs du mal*, in Baudelaire 1975, 1:105.

Un soir, l'âme du vin chantait dans les bouteilles:
"Homme, vers toi je pousse, o cher déshérité,
Sous ma prison de verre et mes cires vermeilles,
Un chant plein de lumière et de fraternité

"Je sais combien il faut, sur la colline en flamme,
De peine, de sueur et de soleil cuisant
Pour engendrer ma vie et pour me donner l'âme;
Mais je ne serai point ingrat ni malfaisant,

"Car j'éprove une joie immense quand je tombe
Dans le gosier d'un homme usé par ses travaux,
Et sa chaude poitrine est une douce tombe
Où je me plais bien mieux que dans mes froids caveaux."]

3. [The original title as published in *Le magasin des familles*.]

4. "A Russian Song," by Igor Severyanin [in Deutsch and Yarmolinsky 1927, 160].

5. Philippe Soupault, "Souffrance" [1973, 28.

Si tu savais si tu savais
Les murs se resserrent
Ma tête devient énorme
Où sont donc parties les lignes de mon papier

Je voudrais allonger mes bras pour
secouer la tour Eiffel et le Sacré-Coeur de Montmartre

Mes idées comme des microbes dansent sur mes méninges
au rhythme de l'exaspérante pendule
Un coup de revolver serait une si douce mélodie].

6. Paul Valéry, "La soirée avec Monsieur Teste" [1960, 2:17. "Teste avait peut-être quarante ans. Sa parole était extraordinairement rapide, et sa voix sourde. Tout s'effaçait en lui, les yeux, les mains. Il avait pourtant les épaules militaires, et le pas d'une régularité qui étonnait. Quand il parlait, il ne levait jamais un bras ni un doigt: il avait *tué la marionnette.* Il ne souriait pas, ne disait ni bonjour ni bonsoir; il semblait ne pas entendre le 'Comment allez-vous?' "].

7. [In 1919, in Paris, Goll published a volume of poems entitled *Die Unterwelt.*]

8. Pierre Reverdy ["Pointe" in *Les ardoises du toit* (Paris: Chez Paul Brirault, 1918), reprinted in Reverdy 1969, 1:190.

Adieu je tomb
Dans l'angle doux des bras qui me reçoivent
Du coin de l'oeil je vois tous ceux qui boivent
    Je n'ose pas bouger
Ils sont assis
        La table est ronde
Et ma mémoire aussi
Je me souviens de tout le monde
Même de ceux qui sont partis].

9. Reverdy, "Tard dans la nuit . . ." [1969, 1:174.

Au coin du bois
Quelqu'un se cache
On pourrait approcher sans bruit
Vers le vide ou vers l'ennemi].

Esthétique Foraine

1. [See Kant 1929, 202. Also see Coleridge 1983, 1:289, in which we read:

I take this occasion to observe, that here and elsewhere Kant uses the term intuition, and the verb active (Intueri [*sic*], *germanice* Anschauen [*sic*]) for which we have unfortunately no correspondent word, exclusively for that which can be represented in space and time. He therefore consistently and rightly denies the possibility of intellectual intuitions. But as I see no adequate reason for this exclusive sense of the term, I have reverted to its wider signification authorized by our elder theologians and metaphysicians, according to whom the term comprehends all truths known to us without a medium.

Nishiwaki uses the German verb *anschauen,* transliterated into Japanese in the text.]

2. "Histoire des Fleurs du mal et des Epaves" by M. J. Crepet.

3. See Edgar Allan Poe, *Eureka* [(1902) 1965, 16:314, in which we read "What you call The Universe is but his present expansive existence. He now feels his life through an infinity of imperfect pleasures—the partial and pain-intertangled pleasures of those inconceivable numerous things which you designate as his creatures, but which are really but infinite individualizations of Himself"].

4. [Ibid.]

5. [See Baudelaire 1975, 1:668–75.]

6. [Source not indicated by Nishiwaki.]

7. [Source not indicated by Nishiwaki.]

8. [Source not indicated by Nishiwaki.]

9. "Of Adversity" [Bacon (1908) 1936, 16–17].

10. [See Coleridge 1983, 2:16–17, in which we read that the poet

diffuses a tone, and spirit of unity, that blends, and (as it were) *fuses*, each into each, by that synthetic and magical power, to which we have exclusively appropriated the name of imagination. This power, first put in action by the will and understanding, and retained under their irremissive, though gentle and unnoticed, controul (*laxis effertur habenis*) reveals itself in the balance or reconciliation of opposite or discordant qualities: of sameness, with difference; of the general, with the concrete; the idea, with the image; the individual, with the representative; the sense of novelty and freshness, with old and familiar objects; a more than usual state of emotion, with more than usual order; judgement ever awake and steady self-possession, with enthusiasm and feeling profound or vehement; and while it blends and harmonizes the natural and the artificial, still subordinates art to nature; the manner to the matter; and our admiration of the poet to our sympathy with the poetry.]

11. Paul Claudel, *Art poétique* [1929, 64. "Vraiment le bleu connaît la couleur d'orange, . . . vraiment et réellement l'angle d'un triangle connaît les deux autres au même sens qu'Isaac a connu Rébecca"].

12. Poe, "Marginalia" [(1902) 1965, 16:155–56].

13. [Ibid., 14:198.]

14. [Ibid., 14:201.]

15. "On Beauty" [Bacon (1908) 1936, 134].

16. [Baudelaire 1975, 1:661. "Le mélange du grotesque et du tragique est agréable à l'esprit."]

17. [Ibid., 1:658. "Deux qualités littéraires fondamentales: surnaturalisme et ironie."]

18. [Ibid., 1:701. "Molière. Mon opinion sur *Tartuffe* est que ce n'est pas une comédie, mais un pamphlet."]

19. [Ibid., 1:703. "La gloire du comédien. . . ."]

20. [Ibid., 1:657. "Je ne prétends pas que la Joie ne puisse pas s'associer avec la Beauté, mais je dis que la Joie [en] est un des ornements les plus vulgaires."]

21. [Ibid., 1:656. "Ce qui n'est pas légèrement difforme a l'air insensible;—d'où il suit que l'irrégularité, c'est-à-dire l'inattendu, la surprise, l'étonnement sont une partie essentielle et la caractéristique de la beauté."]

22. [The translator has not been able to locate precisely Mallarmé's words

asserting that art is hyperbole. In Albert Thibaudet's book on Mallarmé, however, one finds the phrase "hyperbole de poésie pure." Considering the publication date of the book, it is possible that Nishiwaki read the passage. See Thibaudet 1926, 164.]

23. [Source not indicated by Nishiwaki.]
24. [Source not indicated by Nishiwaki.]
25. [Source not indicated by Nishiwaki.]

AMBARVALIA

Ambarvalia was published through Shiinoki sha in 1933. The title is in Latin and not transliterated. "Ambarvalia" denotes a Roman festivity, a joyful procession around the plowed fields in honor of Ceres, the goddess of corn. Nishiwaki most likely found the word in *Marius the Epicurean* by Walter Pater (1834–94), one of his favorite writers. Also, a description of ambarvalia appears in an elegy written by Tibullus, a Roman poet of the Augustan Age contemporary with Ovid. Nishiwaki translates the elegy in the "Latin Elegies" section of *Ambarvalia*, entitling it "Ambarvalia." I have omitted from my translations the entire "Latin Elegies" section except his own poem "Elegy," for it consists of Nishiwaki's translations of Latin poems by Catullus, Tibullus, and several anonymous poets. None of Nishiwaki's translations in *Ambarvalia* was indicated as such in the text. Thus, an ordinary reader would have had no way of knowing that these translations were actually not Nishiwaki's original writings. Similarly, there were no notes provided with the original text to explicate the numerous allusions Nishiwaki employed throughout the text. Therefore, the notes assembled here may create a new reading of Nishiwaki's poetry. Whether it will be a better reading than a reading done without the knowledge of authorial as well as intertextual origins remains debatable. My notes to Nishiwaki's poems rely heavily on Niikura Toshikazu's study *Nishiwaki Junzaburō zenshi inyu shūsei* (Niikura 1982). For this work, I use the abbreviation "*IS*."

TITLE. "The song of Choricos": *korikosu no uta*. "Choricos" is the title of a poem by Richard Aldington (1892–1962) (*IS*, 157). See Aldington 1919, 7. The Latin word *choricus* is an adjective, pertaining to a chorus.

1. "The Abydos": *abidosu jin*. The people of Abydos. Abydos was an ancient city of Egypt. There is a poem by George Gordon, Lord Byron (1788–1824) entitled "The Bridge of Abydos" (*IS*, 157).

2. "Like an upturn'd gem": *kutsugaesareta hōseki no yōna*. A translation of the phrase "like an upturn'd gem" in *Endymion*, book 3, line 777, by John Keats (1795–1821) (*IS*, 157).

3. Nishiwaki uses two different words for "someone" and "somebody." The first one, *nanpito*, is an archaic, literary word, whereas the second, *dareka*, is a more colloquial expression.

4. "Karumojin": *karumojiin*. A fabricated name (*IS*, 158). See chapter 4 for more details.

5. "Damson": *sumomo*. A Japanese plum (*Prunus salicina*). Usually it is

written either in *hiragana* or in *kanji*, indicating the word's native origin, but here it is written in *katakana*. See my commentary on Nishiwaki's use of *katakana* in chapter 4.

6. "Dolphin": *dorufin*, transliterated from English.

7. "The twilight of gems": *hōseki no tasogare*. An echo of Keats's line, "One faint eternal eventide of gems," in *Endymion*, book 2, line 225 (*IS*, 158).

8. "Smyrna": *sumiruna*. A seaport town of Ionia in Asia Minor. In mythology, the daughter of Cinyras, king of Cyprus, who gives birth to Adonis by an incestuous union with Cinyras.

9. "Maud": written in English, not transliterated. It is taken from the poem "Maud" (1885) by Alfred, Lord Tennyson (1809–92) (*IS*, 158).

10. "Bliss, Carman": *buris, kāmen*. Bliss Carman (1861–1929), Canadian poet (*IS*, 159).

11. "Bliss": *yorokobi*. The correspondence with the above "Bliss" is not so conspicuous as in the translation.

TITLE. "The Head of Callimachus and Voyage Pittoresque": *karimakosu no atama to* Voyage Pittoresque. Callimachus was an ancient Greek poet (ca. 305–ca. 240 B.C.).

12. "Tanagra": city of ancient Boetoia, Greece.

13. "Terra-cotta dream": *terakota no yume*. Tanagra is known for the lively Hellenistic terra-cotta figures of women and groups from daily life found in its graves.

TITLE. "Latin Elegies": In this section, Nishiwaki included his partial translations of three Latin texts found in *Catullus, Tibullus, Pervigilium Veneris*, Loeb Classical Library (Cambridge: Harvard University Press, 1913): a selection from the poems by Catullus, a poem entitled "Ambarvalia" by Tibullus, and a selection from "Pervigilium Veneris" (The Eve of St. Venus). Here I translate only the last poem in this section, "Aika" (Elegy), first written in Latin and freely translated into Japanese by Nishiwaki himself. In the original text, Nishiwaki places this Japanese translation first, followed by the Latin original, and then by a more literal translation of the Latin text.

14. According to Niikura (*IS*, 160), this line means "The beautiful poet died," referring to the death of Keats.

15. "Ptolemy": a celebrated astronomer who lived in Alexandria in the second century A.D. (*IS*, 160).

16. "Triton": a reference to Keats's *Endymion*, book 3, lines 888–89: "They stood in dreams / Till Triton blew his horn" (*IS*, 160).

17. This line refers to the first line of a poem by Keats, "To Autumn": "Seasons of mists and mellow fruitfulness" (*IS*, 161).

18. A reference to Keats's *Endymion*, book 2, line 610: "Haply, like dolphin tumults" (*IS*, 161).

19. A reference to Keats's *Endymion*, book 2, line 913: "My silent thoughts are echoing from these shells" (*IS*, 161).

20. "Quercus infectoria": *mosshokushi*. A type of gall that infects oak trees.

21. "Velázquez and game birds": an allusion to Diego Rodríquez de Silvay Velázquez (1599–1660), a major Spanish painter, and to his painting *Philip IV at Fraga* (1644) (*IS*, 161).

22. "Viewing the Acropolis in the far distance": an allusion to "Prière que je fis sur l'Acropole quand je fus arrivé à en comprendre la parfaite beauté" in *Souvenirs d'enfance et de jeunesse* (1883) by Ernest Renan (1823–92) (*IS,* 161).

23. "A visit by Angelico": an allusion to *The Annunciation,* a fresco by the Italian artist Fra Angelico (ca. 1400–1445) (*IS,* 161).

24. "Kariroku": an East Indian tree (*Terminalia Chebula retz*) from which myrobalan is produced.

25. "Gillyflower": *araseitō* (*Matthiola incana*).

26. "The bishop Benbo": Pietro Benbo (1470–1547), Italian poet (*IS,* 162).

27. "Amarante": *amarante,* transliterated from French. It denotes the amaranth flower or its violet color. It appears in a poem, "Bruxelles," by Arthur Rimbaud (1854–91), and was used by Nishiwaki as an epigraph to *Chōgenjitsushugi shiron* (Surrealist poetics): "Plates-bandes d'amarantes jusqu'à / L'agréable palais de Jupiter."

TITLE. "A Picture Card Show, Shylockiade": *kamishibai* Shylockiade (written in English, not transliterated). A parody of Shakespeare's *Merchant of Venice* (*IS,* 162).

28. "Saxpere": *sasupēru.* An old spelling of Shakespeare (*IS,* 162).

29. "Digitalis": *jikitarisu.* Bellflower (*Digitalis purpurea*), *kitsune no tebukuro* in Japanese.

30. "Applis": *apuri,* Middle English for "apples" (*IS,* 163).

31. "Monkshood": *torikabuto* (*Aconitum chinense*).

32. "Legenda Aurea": not transliterated. A thirteenth-century hagiology compiled by Jacobus de Voragine (1230–98). Also called *Golden Legend.*

33. "Its eternal riddle": The Sphinx's riddle was as follows: "What creature walks on four legs in the morning, two at noon, and three in the evening?" Oedipus solved the riddle with this answer: "Man walked on his hands and feet when he was young, at noon in middle life he walked erect, and in the afternoon of life he walked with the aid of a walking stick." Water as a metaphor for man's life appears repeatedly throughout Nishiwaki's later poetry. For example, see the first poem in *No Traveller Returns.*

34. "Hélas, hélas, hélas": *hēra, hēra, hēra* (in *katakana*). Niikura states that *hēra* was a coinage from the French word *hélas* (*IS,* 163). It may also be related to the Greek goddess Hera, queen of the gods and of heaven.

35. "The tragedy of King Oedipus": a parody of *Oedipus at Colonus* by Sophocles (496–406 B.C.) is to follow.

36. The beginning scene of *Oedipus at Colonus,* here translated into Japanese by Nishiwaki.

37. "Thou shalt be a breeze": See *Iphigenia in Aulis* by Euripides (480–406 B.C.), in which Artemis transforms Iphigenia into a breeze and brings her to the country of Tauris (*IS,* 164).

TITLE. "Paradis Perdu": *shitsurakuen.* The title is based on *Paradise Lost* (1667) by John Milton (1608–74). "Shitsurakuen" is actually Nishiwaki's free translation of his own French poem written for the literary periodical *Mita bungaku* (June 1925), published by Keiō University. The original is now in *NJZ* 9:688–98.

38. "A singular object": *ikko no*. Nishiwaki replaces the counter for trees (*hon, pon,* or *bon*: counter for long cylindrical objects) with the counter for pieces of solid objects (*ko*). Thus modified, the tree gains the sense of a singular, solid object, such as a rock.

39. "Talipot palm": a type of palm tree (*Corypha umbraculifera*).

40. According to Niikura (*IS*, 164), this is a parody of "The Night Song" in *Thus Spoke Zarathustra* by Friedrich Nietzsche (1844–1900): "Night has come; now all fountains speak more loudly. And my soul too is a fountain" ([1954] 1959, 217).

41. "Golden Bat": a brand of cigarettes.

42. "Single": *ikko no*. See note 38.

43. "Thomas Caldy": a play on Thomas Hardy (1840–1928) (*IS*, 165).

44. "Perennial blue": *omoto*, a type of lily (*Rhodea japonica*).

45. "Singular": *ikko no*. See note 38.

46. "Luca della Robbia": Italian sculptor (1399–1482). Here Nishiwaki refers to the *cantoria*, the "singing gallery," in the Museo dell' Opera del Duomo. It consists of ten figured reliefs. Walter Pater has a chapter on him in *The Renaissance*.

47. An allusion to Baudelaire's "Mon coeur mis à nu": "Le Dandy doit aspirer à être sublime sans interruption; il doit vivre et dormir devant un miroir" (1975, 1:678) (*IS*, 165).

TITLE. "Journaux Intimes": *naimenteki ni fukaki nikki*. Based on Baudelaire's "Journaux intimes." This is section 2 of "Paradis Perdu."

48. "Singular": *ikko no*. See note 38.

49. "Isarago": a district in Tokyo.

50. "The afternoon of shepherds": an echo of "Après-midi d'un faune" by Stéphane Mallarmé (1842–98).

51. "Within a piece of sweet bread": *Amaki pan no naka*. A possible pun on "pan." It can be either Pan, the god, or *pan*, bread.

52. An echo of "Le balcon" by Baudelaire: "Et les soirs au balcon, voilés de vapeurs roses" (1975, 1:36) (*IS*, 165).

53. "Scarlet toy-Daruma": *okiagarikoboshi*. A toy figure so contrived as to right itself when knocked down.

54. "Singular": *ikko no*. The usual counter for houses is *ken*. See note 38.

55. "Singular": *ikko no*. See note 38.

56. "Bread": *pan*. Again, this might refer to the Greek god Pan. See note 51.

57. "Comellon": *komeron*. Niikura states that *komeron* is a play on "Solomon" and this passage is a parody of the Gospel of Matthew 6:29, "yet I tell you, even Solomon in all his glory was not arrayed like one of these" (*IS*, 166).

58. An allusion to *Bells and Pomegranates* by Robert Browning (1812–89) (*IS*, 166).

TITLE. "Rose des Vents": *kaze no bara*. In French, it means "compass."

59. "Ramune": Japanese soda pop.

60. "Kléber": a street in Paris.

61. "Dead wine": a play on the Homeric epithet "wine-dark sea" (*IS*, 166).

62. "Demeter": the Earth Mother goddess of the Greeks. The subject of

ambarvalia rites. Here Nishiwaki refers to her statue in the British Museum (*IS*, 167).

63. "Coquelicot": *kokuriko*, transliterated from French, meaning "poppy."

64. "Ravenalas": *ravunarasu*. "Ravenala" is the French for "traveller's palm." But when transliterated into Japanese (with the final plural "s" transliterated as "su"), a possible play on words seems to occur. *Ravu* can be read as a transliteration of "love." *Narasu* means "to bear (fruit)." Thus it can be read as "love-bearing tree," which connects nicely to the next line. This wordplay does not occur in Nishiwaki's original version in French. In "Gerontion" by T. S. Eliot, we find "the wrath-bearing tree."

65. "Bergamot": *kunenbo* (*Citrus bergamia*).

66. An allusion to "The Night Song" in *Thus Spoke Zarathustra*. See note 40.

TITLE. "Roman de la Rose": *bara monogatari*. The title is based on a medieval French poem, *Roman de la rose*.

67. "John": John Collier (b. 1901), English novelist whom Nishiwaki befriended during his sojourn in London (*IS*, 167). This poem is partly autobiographical.

TITLE. "May": *go gatsu*. This poem (a section of "Paradis Perdu") is based on Nishiwaki's English poem "Ode to the Vase" in *Poems Barbarous*.

68. "Themistokles": Athenian politician and naval strategist (ca. 524–ca. 460 B.C.).

69. "Akebi": *akebi* (*Akebia quinata*).

TITLE. "The Primitiveness of a Cup": *koppu no genshisei*. Niikura states that this poem is based on a painting, *Tōbi* (transliterated), by Botticelli (*IS*, 168). However, there is no painting entitled *Tobias* or dealing with the subject of Tobias and the Angel attributed to Botticelli, except a free imitation by Botticelli of Tobias and the Angel by Andrea Verrocchio (1435–88). See Wilhelm Bode, *Sandro Botticelli*, translated by F. Renfield and F. L. Rerdston Brown (New York: Charles Scribner's Sons, 1925), 107. Walter Pater in his *Renaissance* also mentions a painting by Botticelli depicting Raphael walking with "Tobit" ([1893] 1977, 37). This section is based on Nishiwaki's English poem "On a Primitive-Painter" in *Poems Barbarous*.

70. "Red-belly": *akahara*, a kind of dace (*Tribolodon hakonensis*).

TITLE. "Barber": *rihatsu*. This section is based on Nishiwaki's English poem "The Zinc Mine" in *Exclamations*.

71. "Corbière": Tristan Corbière (1845–75), French poet.

72. "Penang": *penan*. A leading port of Malaysia; or betel nut, the fruit of the areca palm.

NO TRAVELLER RETURNS

Tabibito kaerazu was published in 1947 through Tokyo shuppan. The English title "No Traveller Returns" had appeared as the title of an essay Nishiwaki published in the periodical *Tsuda bungaku* (February, 1930). It was originally taken from Shakespeare's *Hamlet*: "The undiscover'd country, from whose bourn / No traveller returns" (3.1.80). Also, Nishiwaki's friend John Collier wrote a novella with the same title, published in 1931.

1. According to Niikura (*IS*, 173), the beginning of this poem is based on a poem by the seventeenth-century English poet Sir Edward Sherburne:

The Fountain

> Stranger, whoe'r thou art, that stoop'st to taste
> These sweeter streams, let me arrest thy haste;
> Nor of their fall
> The Murmurs, (though the Lyre
> Less sweet be) stand t'admire:
> But as you shall
> See from this Marble tun
> The liquid Christall run;
> And mark withall,
> How fixt the one abides,
> How fast the other glides;
> Instructed thus the Difference learn to see,
> 'Twixt Mortall Life, and Immortality.   (Sherburne [1651] 1961, 101)

Also, there may be an echo of "What the Thunder Said" in *The Waste Land* by T. S. Eliot:

> Here is not water but only rock
> Rock and no water and the sandy road
> The road winding above among the mountains
> Which are mountains of rock without water
> If there were water we should stop and drink
> Amongst the rock one cannot stop or think   (Eliot 1971, 47)

2. "Illusion": *utsutsu*. A classical, literary word originally meaning "reality." It has, however, gained the opposite meaning of "unreality," albeit mistakenly, through its connected usage with the word *yume* (dream), as in *yume utsutsu*. Therefore, it presents an unusually antithetical ambiguity to the reader. The reader must decide its meaning from the context or allow the indeterminacy of its meaning.

3. "Water-sprite": *kappa*. An amphibious supernatural creature said to inhabit Japan's waters. Thought to be a transformation of a water deity.

4. "Sorrel": *yabugarashi* (*Cayratita japonica*).

5. "Autumn bellflower": *rindō* (*Gentiana scabra*).

6. "Zelkova": *keyaki* (*Zelkova serrata*).

7. "Nagoe Mountains": small mountains in the city of Kamakura, where Nishiwaki spent a few years during World War II.

8. "Thistle": *azami* (*Cirsium*).

9. "Spearflower": *yabukōji* (*Ardisia japonica*).

10. "Floating weeds": *ukikusa* (*Spirodela polyrhiza*).

11. "Lonely is my life": *samishiki mono wa wagami narikeri*. According to

Niikura (*IS*, 174), this phrase comes from a famous *waka* by Fujiwara no Kintsune (1171–1244), no. 96 of *Hyakunin isshu*, compiled by Fujiwara no Sadaie (1162–1241):

Hanasasou	It is not snow
Arashi no niwa no	In the garden where the storm
Yuki narade	Entices the blossoms
Furi yuku mono wa	What drifts by
Waga mi narikeri	Is my life

12. An allusion to "Renouveau" by Mallarmé (*IS*, 174).

13. "Maupassant": Guy de Maupassant (1850–93), French short-story writer, novelist, and literary journalist. Here Nishiwaki refers to Maupassant's collection of travel sketches, *Sur l'eau* (1888) (*IS*, 174).

14. According to Niikura (*IS*, 174), this refers to Yoshida Issui (1898–1973), a Japanese poet.

15. "Eventide of gems": *yūgure no yōna hōseki*, a phrase by Keats from *Endymion*, book 2, line 225 (*IS*, 174).

16. According to Niikura (*IS*, 174), this is a playful allusion to the story "Azuma no kata ni yuku mono kabura o totsugite ko o shōzuru koto dai ni" in *Konjaku monogatari*, vol. 26, no. 2 (compiled in the early twelfth century). The story is as follows. A man is suddenly assailed by an uncontrollable sexual desire on his way to the eastern countries. He finds a large radish in the fields, bores a hole, and uses it as a substitute for a woman. After he has left, a young maiden finds it and eats it. Consequently she becomes pregnant and gives birth to a beautiful boy. The man comes back and finds out what has happened, and happily marries the girl. See *Konjaku monogatari shū*, 1970–73, 513.

17. A reference to *The Razor's Edge* (1944) by William Somerset Maugham (1874–1965) (*IS*, 175).

18. "Cockscomb": *keitō* (*Celosia cristata*).

19. "Kamakura": a city in southeastern Kanagawa Prefecture, 45 kilometers southwest of Tokyo. Its historical importance dates to the twelfth century, when it became the seat of the Kamakura shogunate. Nishiwaki lived in Kamakura for two years (1943–45) in order to evade the bombing of Tokyo during the war.

20. "Jizō": one of the most popular bodhisattvas in Japanese Buddhism. *Jizō* is usually represented as a monk with a jewel in one hand and a staff in the other. Its images are often placed along roadsides.

21. "Cézanne": Paul Cézanne (1839–1906), French painter. Here Nishiwaki refers to Cézanne's *Still Life with Apples and Oranges*.

22. "Deutzia": *u no hana* (*Deutzia crenata*). Since "u" signifies the fourth lunar month, it can be translated as "April flower."

23. "Horse chestnuts": *tochi* (*Aesculus turbinata*).

24. "Oak": *kunugi* (*Quercus acutissima*).

25. "Spikenard": *udo* (*Aralia cordata*).

26. "Hazel eyes": *hashibami no me*. According to Niikura (*IS*, 175), the English essayist William Hazlitt (1778–1830) called the eyes of John Keats

"hazel eyes." Niikura, however, does not state the source. "The day of truth" (*makoto no hi*) in the last line, then, recalls Keats's "Ode on a Grecian Urn": "Beauty is truth, truth beauty . . ." (Keats, 1966, 253).

27. "Nettle-flower": *irakusa* (*Urtica thunbergiana*).

28. "Konpira": the guardian deity of seafarers.

29. "Reality": *utsutsu*. See note 2.

30. "Reality": *utsutsu*.

31. "Indian lilac": *sarusuberi* (*Lager stromia indica*).

32. "Holly": *umemodoki* (*Ilex serrata*).

33. "Noborito": a district in the city of Kawasaki, Kanagawa Prefecture. "Chōfu": a city in Tokyo.

34. "The Musashi Plain": it extends from Tokyo to Saitama Prefecture, southwestern Kantō Plain, surrounded by the Tama River, the Irama River, and the Ara River, and by Tokyo Bay.

35. "Sagami": old name of a land, now Kanagawa Prefecture.

36. "Kodaira": a small town in Tokyo. Nishiwaki taught at Tsuda Eigaku Juku (now Tsuda Women's University) in Kodaira from 1934 to 1942.

37. "An unbelievably impertinent woman": *ito hashitanaki onna*. A parody of a line from *Ise monogatari* (Tales of Ise): "sono sato ni, ito namameitaru onna harakara sumi keri" (*IS*, 175). *Ise monogatari* 1970–73, 133.

38. "Tsuda bungaku": literary periodical published through Tsuda Eigaku Juku.

39. "Bats": *batto* (transliteration from English). A brand of cigarettes, "Golden Bat."

40. "Kunugi and nara": types of oak, *Quercus acutissima* and *Quercus serrata*.

41. "Mogusaen": a town and a park in the city of Hino, Tokyo.

42. "White magnolia": *kobushi* (*Magnolia kobus*).

43. "Knotweed": *inutade* (*Polygnum blumei*).

44. "Foxtail": *enokorogusa* (*Setaria viridis*).

45. This poem is based on a famous *waka* by Fujiwara no Yoshitsune (1169–1206), no. 91 of *Hyakunin isshu* (*IS*, 176):

Kirigirisu	Crickets cry
Nakuya shimo yo no	In this frosty night
Samushiro ni	Over the chilly mat
Koromo katashiki	Why must I spread only one side
Hitori kamo nen	Of my robe for me alone?

46. "Lady-flower: *ominaeshi* (*Patrinia scabiosaefolia*). "Lady-flower" is a direct translation of the *kanji* adopted for "*ominaeshi*."

47. "Honey locust": *saikachi* (*Gleditschia japonica*).

48. According to Niikura (*IS*, 176), this poem is based on a poem in *Man'yōshū* (vol. 12, no. 3137), the earliest surviving anthology of Japanese poetry, compiled in the eighth century:

Tōku areba	Since you are far away
Katachi wa miezu	You remain invisible, yet

Tsune no goto	As if nothing had changed
Imo ga emai wa	Your smile looms out
Omokage ni shite	In a shadowy image

49. "Dayflower": *tsuyukusa* (*Commelina communis*).

50. "Chitose": a village in Tokyo. *Chitose* means "one thousand years old."

51. "An ancient savage god": *inishie no Kōjin*. *Kōjin* (savage god) is a category of folk deities. It is said to cast evil spells on people and expose them to dangers unless properly revered.

52. "Ginger": *myōga*. There is a pun on *myōga* (Japanese ginger) and *myōga* (divine protection by *Kōjin*).

53. "Yose": town in Kanagawa Prefecture, now called Sagamiko machi.

54. According to Niikura (*IS*, 176), this poem is based on Shakespeare's *Macbeth*: "Lady Macbeth: I heard the owl scream and crickets cry" (2.2.17).

55. See the beginning of *Macbeth*, act 1, scene 7: "Hautboys and torches. Enter, and pass over the stage, a Sewer, and divers Servants with dishes and service. Then enter Macbeth [who is now determined to assassinate the king, Duncan]."

56. Niikura sees an echo of "Autre éventail" by Mallarmé (*IS*, 176). The second stanza:

> Une fraîcheur de crépuscule
> Te vient á chaque battement
> Dont le coup prisonnier recule
> L'horizon délicatement.   (Mallarmé, 1945, 58)

57. "Evening-face": *yūgao* (*Lagenaria leucantha*). "Evening-face" is a direct translation of *yūgao*. It is a type of bottle-gourd. It is also a prominent flower (associated with a lady) in *The Tale of Genji*.

58. "Damson": *sumomo* (in *kanji*).

59. "Novel": According to Niikura (*IS*, 177), this refers to *Eyeless in Gaza* (1936) by Aldous Huxley (1894–1963).

60. "Purple-willow": *kawayanagi* (*Salix gracilistyla*).

61. "Katsura": *Cercidiphylum japonicum*.

62. "Book": According to Niikura (*IS*, 177), this refers to section 139 of *Tsurezuregusa* (ca. 1330) by Yoshida Kenkō (1238–1350). See Yoshida 1967.

63. "Sane-kazura": *Kadsura japonica*.

64. According to Niikura (*IS*, 177), this poem is based on a poem by Johann Wolfgang von Goethe (1749–1832). The poem appears as an epigraph to book 3 of his novel *Wilhelm Meisters Lehrjahre*. The following is an excerpt from the English translation by Michael Hamburger:

> Do you know the land where the lemon trees flower,
> Golden oranges glow in the dark-leaved bower,
> Where a gentle wind blows from an azure sky,
> Unruffled the myrtle grows and the laurels rise high—
> Do you know the land?
> > There, only there
> With you my beloved, I long to go.   (Goethe 1983, 29)

65. "Koma": a town in Saitama Prefecture.

66. "Sumac": *nurude* (*Rhus javanica*).

67. "Knotweed": *itadori* (*Polygonum cuspidatum*).

68. "Tiger lilies": *oniyuri* (*Lilium lancifolium*).

69. "Yōgō Temple": a temple in the city of Kawasaki, Kanagawa Prefecture.

70. "Yakushi": the Buddha of healing.

71. "Pampas grass": *susuki* (*Miscanthus sinensis*).

72. "Kasuri": a kind of cloth, typically of hemp, ramie, or cotton, with hazed patterns of reserved white against a deep indigo-blue ground, popular for farmers' and merchants' clothing from the mid-eighteenth century to the beginning of the twentieth century.

73. Bindweed": *kohirugao* (*Calystegia hederacea*).

74. "Mugwort": *yomogi* (*Artemisia vulgaris*).

75. "Soba": Japanese buckwheat noodles.

76. "The Sun and the Moon": *nitten getten*, Buddhist terms for the deities of the sun and the moon.

77. "Red knotweeds": *akanomanma*, same as *inutade* (note 43). *Akanomanma* means "red rice."

78. "Irreality": *utsutsu*. See note 2.

79. "Shiba": a district in Tokyo.

80. "Kunisada": Utagawa Kunisada (1786–1864), an ukiyo-e woodblock print designer and book illustrator, specializing in figures of women and portraits of Kabuki actors.

81. "Chinese bellflower": *kikyō* (*Platycodon grandiflorum*).

82. "Sangen Teahouse": *Sangen jya ya*, a district in Tokyo.

83. "Doppo": Kunikida Doppo (1871–1908). Here, Nishiwaki refers to Doppo's text *Musashino* (The Musashi Plain).

84. "Jōdo Lost": a play on *Paradise Lost* by Milton, who became blind. *Jōdo* means "pure lands" in Buddhism. They are realms of purity, the residence of Buddhas and bodhisattvas.

85. "Stinking bark": *hekusokazura* (*Paederia scandens*).

86. According to Niikura (*IS*, 178), there is an echo of "Astrophel" by Edmund Spenser (1552?–99):

> Her yellow locks that shone so bright and long,
> As Sunny beames in fairest somers day;
> She fiersly tore, and with outragious wrong
> From her red cheeks the roses rent away.
> And her faire brest the threasury of joy,
> She spoyld thereof, and filled with annoy.
>
> His palled face impictured with death,
> She bathed oft with teares and dried oft:
> And with sweet kisses suckt the wasting breath,
> Out of his lips like lillies pale and soft.   (Spenser 1943, 183)

87. "Hills of Tama": a hilly area in southern Tokyo. It used to be a natural forest area; now it is a residential area.

88. "Kiso": a district in southern Nagano Prefecture, famous for its mountains and forests.

89. "Fudō": (Sanskrit, *Acalanatha*) a type of *Myōdō*; the god of fire. The third ranking category in Japanese Buddhist iconography.

90. An allusion to a *waka* by Fujiwara no Toshinari (1114–1204):

Yū sare ba	As evening deepens
Nobe no akikaze	Autumn winds blow through the fields
Mini shimite	And through me—
Uzura nakunari	A quail cries
Fukakusa no sato	In the village of Deep Grass

(The Japanese text is in *Senzaiwakashū* 258, in Matsushita and Watanabe 1951, 147.)

91. "Shimada coiffure": *shimada*, a type of chignon usually worn by unmarried women.

92. "Fringed pink": *nadeshiko* (*Dianthus superbus*).

93. "Muku": a type of elm (*Aphanathe aspera*).

94. "They get together and again they part": *issho ni nari mata wakareru*. A Japanese translation of the title of a novel, *Together and Apart* (1937), by Margaret Kennedy (b. 1896). I have retranslated the Japanese in order to retain the effect of the phrase being not the title of a novel but a part of the ongoing narrative.

95. "Avoid evil spirits": *akurei o sakeyo*. Retranslation of *The Devil and All* (1934) by John Collier.

96. "Difficult predicament": *kurushiki tachiba*. Retranslation of *Of Human Bondage* (1915) by William Somerset Maugham.

97. "Lemon farm": *remon batake*, a novel by Martin Boyd (b. 1893).

98. "Razor teeth": *kamisori no ha*, a play on the *The Razor's Edge* by Maugham.

99. "His monkey wife": *saru nyōbo*, a novel (1932) by Collier.

100. According to Niikura (*IS*, 179), this poem is based on a passage from a novel by Richard Aldington, *All Men Are Enemies* (1933, 152):

> To his surprise, Scrope was not in his favourite eighteenth-century room, but in the tapestried Elizabethan hall, sitting in front of a fire of smouldering elm-logs, a plaid over his knees and a screen behind his back. Only later did Tony discover the reason for this change of habits—coal was almost unobtainable, and the small grates would not burn these long rough branches which rested on the iron dogs in the huge fireplace. Yet even as he entered the door, Tony was seduced by the charm of this ordered, seemingly untroubled life—here, at least, was something uncrushed by the tanks of war. But that happy feeling lasted only the time from the door to the fireplace. It went as soon as he saw his old friend, and tried to keep from his own face any expression of his startled pity. Scrope's body seemed to have shrunk inside his tweeds, his face was sunk and wrinkled, his voice had developed the slight quaver of age, and as he looked up with the pathetic try-not-to-hurt-me expression of very old people, Tony saw in his eyes for a second the strange dull gleam he knew only too well—the eyes of those about to die. Antony was so much shocked that at first he had some difficulty in talking coherently, and was glad when lunch was announced.

101. "Maeterlinck": Maurice Maeterlinck (1862–1949), Belgian poet, dramatist, and essayist. Here Nishiwaki presumably refers to Maeterlinck's *La vie des abeilles* (1901) (*IS*, 180).

102. "Pink": *nadeshiko*.

103. "Irreality": *utsutsu*. See note 2.

104. According to Niikura (*IS*, 180), this poem is based on the beginning of *Divine Comedy* by Dante (1265–1321):

> Midway the journey of this life I was 'ware
> That I had strayed into a dark forest,
> And the right path appeared not anywhere.   (Dante 1947, 3)

105. "Shūzenji": Izushūzenji, a town in eastern Shizuoka Prefecture. Situated on the Kano River, it developed as a hot-spring resort in the Edo period (1600–1868).

106. Niikura informs us that there is a story about a monster-dipper from the Muromachi period (1386–1573), but does not specify the source (*IS*, 180).

107. According to Niikura (*IS*, 180), this refers to a novel by D. H. Lawrence (1885–1930).

108. "Goldenrod": *kirinsō* (*Sedum kamtschaticum*).

109. Heraclitus (540–475 B.C.), Greek philosopher of Ephesus, who maintained that everything is in a state of flux; change is the only reality; fire is the origin of all things; nothing is born and nothing dies; birth and death are but rearrangements.

110. "Bergson": Henri-Louis Bergson (1859–1941), French philosopher. Presumably, here Nishiwaki refers to Bergson's *L'evolution créatrice* (1907), in which biology, theories of evolution, and the notion of "la durée réelle" are discussed.

111. "Chavannes": Pierre Puvis de Chavannes (1824–98), French painter.

112. "Mandala": It is possible that here Nishiwaki was thinking of *mandarage*, a fictitious flower said to bloom in heaven; *mandarage* could also be another name for the wild flower *chōsen asagao*(*Datura metel*).

113. "Tenjin": literally, "the heavenly god(s)." Usually, it refers to the deified spirit of Sugawara Michizane (845–903), a leading court scholar and political figure of the Heian period (794–1185).

114. "The philosophy of clothes": an allusion to *Sartor Resartus* (1837) by Thomas Carlyle (1795–1881) (*IS*, 181).

115. "Nettle": *enoki* (*Celtis sinensis*).

116. According to Niikura (*IS*, 181), this poem refers to a *waka* by Masaoka Shiki (1867–1902):

Waga niwa no	In the hedge
kakine ni ouru	Of my garden
bara no me no	A rose bud
tsubomi fukurete	Swelling
natsu wa kinikeri	Summer is here (Masaoka 1969, 2:21)

117. "Peony": *shakuyaku* (*Paeonia albiflora*).

118. "Althea": *mukuge* (*Hibiscus syriacus*).

119. Niikura (*IS*, 181) suggests a possible allusion to the ending of "Lycidas" by Milton: "At last he rose, and twitch'd his Mantle blew: / To morrow to fresh Woods, and Pastures new" (Milton 1950, 80).

120. "Mokkei": (Chinese, Muqui or Mu-chi), a thirteenth-century Chinese Zen monk-painter.

121. Cf. "The Primitiveness of a Cup" in *Ambarvalia*.

122. "Morning-Glories": *asagao* (*Pharbitis nil*).

123. "Mandin": *nanten* (*Nandina domestica*).

124. "Field horsetail": *sugina* (*Equistetum arvense*).

125. "Camellia": *sazanka* (*Camellia sasanqua*).

126. "Amer": French, transliterated in *katakana*.

127. According to Niikura (*IS*, 181), this is a parody of a section in *La culture des idées* (1901) by Remy de Gourmont (1858–1915): "L'homme malgré sa tendance au mensonge, a un grand respect pour ce qu'il appelle la vérité; c'est que la vérité est son bâton de voyage á travers la vie, c'est que les lieux communs sont le pain de sa besace et le vin de sa gourde" (Gourmont, "La dissociation des idées" [(1900) 1964, 66]).

128. Niikura informs us that this refers to the Japanese novelist Tayama Katai (1872–1930) carrying around *Une vie* (*Onna no isshō* in Japanese translation) by Maupassant as the bible of naturalist novels (*IS*, 182). *Jōshū* is the previous name of the land now called Gunma Prefecture.

129. "Revolutionary": According to Niikura (*IS*, 182), this refers to Oliver Cromwell (1595–1658).

130. "Shimousa": previous name for the land that is now occupied by northern Chiba Prefecture and southwestern Ibaragi Prefecture.

131. "Poet": According to Niikura (*IS*, 182), this refers to Shelley.

132. "Portrait": *Dōjo zō* by the Japanese painter Kishida Ryūsei (1891–1929).

133. According to Niikura (*IS*, 182), the first three lines of this poem are based on the Prologue of *The Vision Concerning Piers the Plowman*, presumably written by William Langland (1330?–1400?):

> In a summer season, when soft was the sunlight,
> I shook on some shreds of shepherd clothing,
> And habited like a hermit, but not a holy one,
> Went wide in this world, watching for wonders.   (Langland 1949, 1)

134. "Irreality": *utsutsu*. See note 2.

135. "Spears rusted": *Yari sabi* may denote a type of ditty, a short love song.

136. "Ovarian orchid": *ransō*. A play on the word *ransō* written in the *kanji* for the orchid plant, but the trace of its homophone meaning "ovary" is undeniable.

137. "Hiroo Field": a reference to a landscape Hiroo depicted in *Edo meisho zue* (Pictorial descriptions of noted places in Edo) (1829) by Saitō Yukio, Yukitaka, and Yukinari. See Saitō, Yukitaka, and Yukinari 1967, 58–67.

138. "Irreality": *utsutsu*. See note 2.

139. See note 90.

ETERUNITASU

Eterunitasu is the transliteration of *aeternitas* (Latin for "eternity") in *hira-gana*. Ususally transliteration is done in *katakana*. Thus, the title appears to be doubly removed from the original Latin. This poem is taken from Nishiwaki's eighth book of Japanese poetry, *Eterunitasu* (Tokyo: Shōshin sha, 1962), which contains two other long poems, *Saien no yōjutsu* and *Oto*.

    1. "Autumnal face": According to Niikura (*IS*, 265), this is an allusion to an elegy, "The Autumnall" by John Donne: "No spring, nor Summer Beauty hath such grace, / As I have seen in one Autumnall face" (1968, 113).

    2. According to Niikura (*IS*, 265), this alludes to a haiku by Matsuo Bashō (1644–94):

Tsuki izuko	Where is the moon	
kane wa shizumite	The bell is sunk	
umino soko	To the bottom of the sea	(Matsuo 1972, 41:186)

    3. "Seven lamps of ambiguity": a play on the title of the book *Seven Types of Ambiguity* (1930) by William Empson (b. 1906).

    4. "Pound": Ezra Pound (1885–1972).

    5. "Nipplewort": *tabirako* (*Trigonotis peduncularis*).

    6. "Dorothy Osborn": wife of Sir William Temple (1628–99) (*IS*, 266). Dorothy's letters to Temple were published in 1888.

    7. "Poussin": Nicolas Poussin (1594–1665), French painter.

    8. "Phocion's funeral": *Funeral of Phocion* by Poussin.

    9. Allusion to the painting above.

    10. "Bindweed": *sankirai* (*Smilax glavra*).

    11. "Fearful Joy": *kyōfu no yorokobi*, title of a novel by Joyce Cary (1888–1957) (*IS*, 266).

    12. "Cottonweed": *hahakogusa* (*Gnaphalium multiceps*).

    13. According to Niikura (*IS*, 266), this alludes to Baudelaire's "Mon coeur mis à nu": "Plus l'homme cultive les arts, moins il bande. Il se fait un divorce de plus sensible entre l'esprit et la brute. La brute seule bande bien, et la fouterie est le lyrisme du peuple" (1975, 1:702).

    14. "The Dutchess of Ormond": taken from the title of a poem by John Dryden (1631–1700), "To Her Grace the Dutchess of Ormond" (*IS*, 266).

    15. "Epos": *eposu*, transliterated from Greek, meaning "heroic poem."

    16. "Taranbō": written in *katakana*. Its meaning is unknown. It might be a combined pun on *taran* (lacking) and the poet's name "Rimbaud."

    17. According to Niikura (*IS*, 267), this is a borrowing from the ending of "Lycidas." See note 119 *No Traveller Returns*.

    18. "Akebi": see note 69 on *Ambarvalia*.

    19. "Priapus": in mythology, the god of procreation.

    20. Niikura (*IS*, 267) suggests that this passage is a parody of *Die Welt als Wille und Vorstellung* (1819) by Arthur Schopenhauer (1788–1860), but does not elaborate.

21. "Amanda": *amanda*, written in *katakana*. Niikura (*IS*, 267) suggests that this is Nishiwaki's neologism coined from the Latin *amando*.

22. "Copulation": *kopyurashon*, transliterated from French. This alludes to Baudelaire's passage in "Mon coeur mis à nu." See note 13.

23. "Table": This passage alludes to Plato's *Republic* 10:596b.

24. A play on Keats's "Ode on a Grecian Urn": "Heard melodies are sweet, but those unheard / Are sweeter" (1966, 252) (*IS*, 267).

25. "Toynbee": Arnold Joseph Toynbee (1889–1975), historian.

26. A play on the title of *Gone with the Wind* by Margaret Mitchell (1900–49) (*IS*, 268).

27. "Cynara": taken from a poem, "Non sum qualis eram bonae sub regno Cynarae," by Ernest Dowson (1867–1900): "I have forgot much, Cynara! gone with the wind" ([1934] 1967, 52). The title of Mitchell's novel also derives from this line (*IS*, 268).

28. "Sesame and lilies": the title of a book by John Ruskin (1819–1900) (*IS*, 268).

29. Allusions to Ruskin's *Stones of Venice* (1851–53) and to the descriptions of clouds in the poetry of Gerard Manley Hopkins (1844–89), such as in "Pied Beauty" (*IS*, 268).

30. "Japanese pepper": *sansho* (*Xanthoxyum piperitum*).

31. An allusion to Baudelaire's "La beauté" (*IS*, 268): "Je suis belle, ô mortels! comme un rêve de pierre" (1975, 1:21).

32. "Chinese milk-vetch": *rengesō* (*Astragalus sinicus*).

33. "Rape blossom": *nanohana* (*Brassica campestris*).

34. "Sorrel": *sukanpo* (*Rumex acetosa*).

35. "Briar": *noibara* (*Rosa multiflora*).

CHAPTER ONE
MODERNIST POETRY IN JAPAN

1. For a detailed account of this natural as well as human disaster, see Yoshimura 1977.

2. Itō Noe was well known for her editorship of a feminist journal, *Seitō* (Bluestocking).

3. On *Shi to shiron*, see Lower 1987. The entire set of *Shi to shiron* (including *Bungaku*, to which the journal changed its name after no. 14) is now reprinted and published by Kyōiku shuppan sentā.

4. The journal was established by Miyoshi Tatsuji (1900–1964), Maruyama Kaoru (1899–1974), and Hori Tatsuo (1904–53). It continued until 1944 and included works by Ibuse Masuji (b. 1898), Hagiwara Sakutarō, Takenaka Iku (1904–82), Tachihara Michizō (1914–39), and Nakahara Chūya, among others.

5. There were around that time three other translations of Marinetti's manifesto into Japanese, demonstrating an unusual interest in futurism. See Chiba 1971, 42.

6. Though he is not considered a modernist poet, Takamura was keenly interested in modernism. Takamura reportedly wrote a letter to Marinetti,

soon after Ōgai's translation appeared in *Subaru*, and received much information on futurism from Marinetti himself. See Chiba 1978, 104.

7. Kinoshita Mokutarō was a poet, playwright, novelist, artist, historian, and medical doctor. He was known for his association with the aesthete poet Kitahara Hakushū (1885–1942), the novelist Mori Ōgai, and the journals *Myōjō* and *Subaru*. His book on modern art, *Inshōha igo* (1916; After impressionism), as well as his translation of writings by Wassily Kandinsky (in *Bijutsu shinpō*, February, March, and June 1913), was influential in introducing modernism.

8. Yosano Hiroshi was known as a tanka poet and the husband of Yosano Akiko (1878–1942), another superbly talented tanka poet. His collection of translations *Rira no hana* (1914; Lilac flowers), completed after his sojourn in Paris, included poems by Marinetti and other futurist poets.

9. Horiguchi Daigaku was an influential poet and translator. His collection of French poetry *Gekka no ichigun* (1925; A moonlit gathering) included such avant-garde poets as Guillaume Apollinaire, Max Jacob, Jean Cocteau, Francis Picabia, Yvan Goll, and Philippe Soupault. Horiguchi's elegantly translated French poetry had an enormous effect in shaping modern Japanese poetry as well as the literary taste of the general reader of poetry.

10. Moriguchi Tari was an art critic. His *Itan no gaka* (1920; Heretical artists), which included chapters on futurism, became a best-seller.

11. The ardent futurist Kanbara later turned to communism and became critical of modernism.

12. Both articles are reprinted in Takahashi 1982, 4:173–79.

13. On Takahashi, see M. Ueda 1983, 335–79; Ko 1977; and Stryk 1971. Takahashi often claimed that he had nothing to do with dada after 1924.

14. Quoted in M. Ueda 1983, 337–38. Translation by Ueda.

15. For an exhaustively detailed study of Kitasono and modernism in Japan in general, see Solt 1989.

16. See Nakano 1975, 17–68.

17. Tsuboi was later sternly criticized for his essays published in *Bungei kaihō*, which was judged pro-Marxist. He was then severely beaten up by a group of anarchists. The incident made him convert to communism. Later he went through *tenkō* (apostasy) in prison.

18. Only one issue was published, due to the embezzlement of funds by the accountant. See Chiba 1978, 134.

19. One of the most important avant-gardists in Japan, Murayama studied in Germany from 1921 to 1923 and brought back theories of expressionism and constructivism. Later he became a proletarian playwright who went through *tenkō* in prison.

20. "Shokuyō gaeru," in Ōoka et al. 1975, 8:138–39.

21. For the English translation of his poetry, see Kusano 1969.

22. .Miyazawa Kenji was one of the most important poets of modern Japan. For the English translation of his poetry, see Miyazawa 1973. On the poet, see M. Ueda 1983, 184–231.

23. It renamed itself Nihon proretaria geijutsu renmei (Japan proletarian arts league) after purging the anarchist faction at the meeting.

24. On Nakano, see Silverberg, 1990.

25. The cover of *Gunkan mari* was illustrated by Marjorie Biddle and the title was handwritten by Nishiwaki.

26. "Haru" in Ōoka et al. 1975, 10:264.

27. "Haru," ibid.

28. "Odarisuku," ibid., 10:280.

29. "Zetsubō no uta," ibid., 10:246.

30. "Rasshu awā," ibid., 10:248.

31. "Tsubaki," ibid., 10:251.

32. "Uma," ibid., 10:252.

33. One may see Nishiwaki's influence on Haruyama's insistence on methodology when one considers that Nishiwaki's theoretical papers on poetic methodology were published before *Shi to shiron* started. Especially important in this regard is Nishiwaki's "Esthétique Foraine," which appeared in the May 1927 issue of *Mita bungaku* and was later collected in *Chōgenjitsushugi shiron*. A careful reading of Nishiwaki's papers reveals that Nishiwaki was never a part of the rigid formalism that Haruyama ardently advocated.

34. *Shururearisumu no tenkai* 1981, 214. Forty years after this critique, Nishiwaki and Kanbara met at a mutual friend's wake. Kagiya recalls the scene:

> "Mr. Kanbara, I'll never forget that. Your attack was too severe!"
>
> "No, Sensei. That's not right. I was praising you there. If you read it carefully you'll see I was praising you there."
>
> "Really?" We [Kagiya and a friend] had a hard time suppressing our laugh watching the scene.
>
> "I see, Mr. Kanbara was really praising me. For a long time I thought I got blasted by you." (Kagiya 1983, 60–61)

35. See Yoshimoto, 1970.

36. For example, Donald Keene writes: "His [Kaneko's] fame today rests largely—but by no means exclusively—on the fact that he alone of the Japanese poets expressed opposition to the policies of the militarists in the 1930s." Keene 1984, 358.

37. Prompted by the secession of Kitagawa and others from *Shi to shiron*, the most topical issue for the writers contributing to *Shi to shiron* as well as to *Shi • genjitsu* became that of *actualité* and "reality."

38. "Hinomaru no hata," partially quoted in Sakuramoto 1983, 20.

39. "Shingapōru otsu," partially quoted ibid., 10.

40. *Chōgenjitsushugi shiron* (Surrealist poetics) was published in 1929 through Kōseikaku shoten, where Haruyama Yukio was employed. When this book was reissued by Arechi shuppansha in 1954, Nishiwaki added the following introduction:

> On the occasion of the reissuing of *Chōgenjitsushugi shiron*, which I wrote a long time ago, I was asked to add some kind of introduction. When I was still abroad, people like Reverdy and Yvan Goll published a small magazine called *Le surréalisme* in Paris. I encountered this term "surrealism" for the first time when I read this magazine. As a matter of fact, since I had already known Baudelaire's remark that the two primary factors of literature are irony and the supernatural, I wanted to use the word *chōshizen* (supernatural) for the title. But the editor at that time [Haruyama] chose

the newly coined term "surreal." In short, this book attempts to introduce a poetic theory that has been extant for a long time in Europe: "The essence of poetry is what becomes harmonized by linking contrary elements." I still believe in this theory. The way to poetry is long. We must wander around a hedge in the country and seek a *delectable* woman. Moreover, it is difficult to meet a man who weeps at a festival. (*NJZ* 4:678–79)

CHAPTER TWO
PURE POETRY AND REALITY

1. See Barthes 1974.
2. See Bataille 1955.
3. *NJZ* 4:8. It is interesting to note that Kanbara Tai took this passage as an expression of a *surrealist* position in his critique of Nishiwaki. See chapter 1 above.
4. One may recall how insignificant objects (indifferent material) held an important role in Freud's theory of dreams. See Freud 1965, 197–221.
5. See "The Octopus that Does Not Die," in Sato and Watson 1981, 484–85.
6. A term proposed by Derrida. It combines the sense of difference and differing at once already present in the ground of signification. The French verb *différer* means both "to differ" and "to defer." Yet the noun *différence* (with an *e*) does not have the sense of deferring. By replacing the ending *-ence* with *-ance*, Derrida inserts an inaudible but graphic difference (between *e* and *a*) and thus creates an effect that is essentially indecisive as to its being linguistically active or passive, or being a "difference" as spacing or postponement. In Alan Bass's words, "it defers differing, and differs from deferring, in and of itself" (Alan Bass, translator's note, to Derrida 1982, 8). See Derrida, "Différance" (1982, 3–27).
7. Unless otherwise stated, all citations from Derrida in this chapter are to Derrida 1976. It is hereafter abbreviated *DG*.
8. Saussure writes:

A language and its written form constitute two separate systems of signs. The sole reason for the existence of the latter is to represent the former. The object of study in linguistics is not a combination of the written word and the spoken word. The spoken word alone constitutes that object. But the written word is so intimately connected with the spoken word it represents that it manages to usurp the principal role. As much or even more importance is given to this representation of the vocal sign as to the vocal sign itself. (Saussure 1986, 24–25)

CHAPTER THREE
THE DETOUR OF TRANSLATION

1. The peculiar difficulty of this text is almost legendary. Even as brilliant a reader as de Man has to admit, "Whenever I go back to this text, I think

I have it more or less, then I read it again, and again I don't understand it" (de Man 1986, 92). Robert Alter expresses his bewilderment: "Although it has become fashionable to cite and celebrate Benjamin's most vatic pronouncements as his greatest profundities, I frankly don't know what to make of this, however arresting it may be as a poetic image, and I am inclined to see it as the evocative, ultimately incoherent extravagance of a lyric literary imagination conjuring with mystical ideas" (1991, 46). Facing the peculiar difficulty of this text, which seems to incorporate esoteric paradoxes freely, one needs to devise a special strategy of reading. Benjamin himself devised a mode of reading (writing) that may offer us an example to follow: a type of "collage text" in which disparate fragments of thought as well as quotations are allowed to collide. It becomes absurd to summarize Benjamin's flow of thought in this essay. It is, more than anything else, a textual performance, an experiment in thought. Thus what follows also takes the form of a collage to a certain degree: a collage of quotations from Benjamin, Derrida, Nishiwaki, and my inevitably fragmentary responses. Hence the incorporation of an unusually large number of quotations. See a similar claim made by Susan Handelman (1991, 23).

2. Ironically enough, for the student of translation, this peculiar textual difficulty becomes most visible in the translations of this text on translation. Paul de Man finds that the scandalousness of the text is such that even the most admired translators of the text (Harry Zohn in English and Maurice de Gandillac in French) seem to have been led astray into making some blatant mistranslations. See de Man 1986, 79–81.

3. All citations from Benjamin's text are to Benjamin 1969. It is hereafter abbreviated *BJ*. The original text can be found in Benjamin 1972.

4. Carol Jacobs points out that the translator's doom is already inscribed in the title of the essay "Die Aufgabe des Übersetzers": "The translatability of the text excludes the realm of man and with him the translator, the figure to which Benjamin's essay is devoted. The 'Aufgabe' of the translator is less his task than his surrender: he is 'aufgegeben,' given up, abandoned" (Jacobs 1975, 765).

5. Paul de Man points out a significant mistranslation in this passage: "if they are referred exclusively to man," is indeed the opposite of what the original says, "Wenn sie nicht . . . auf den Menschen bezogen werden," "if you *do not* relate them to man" (de Man 1986, 85). The marked significance of this lapse in the translation emerges when we consider the moment of its occurrence. It occurs exactly when language supersedes man. The scandalousness of Benjamin's assertion momentarily blinds the translator. The translator struggles against his own death by mistranslating the death sentence.

6. Unless otherwise stated, all citations from Derrida in this chapter come from Derrida 1985. It is hereafter abbreviated *DD*.

7. Derrida cites Voltaire: "I do not know why it is said in *Genesis* that Babel signifies confusion, for *Ba* signifies father in the Oriental tongues, and Bel signifies God; Babel signifies the city of God, the holy city" (*DD*, 166).

8. We must note here that in the kabbalistic view of language, which seems to have influenced Benjamin greatly via Gershom Scholem, the Name of God is the metaphysical origin of all language. Richard Wolin quotes the thir-

teenth-century Spanish kabbalist Abraham Abulafia: "the Name of God, which is something absolute, because it reflects the hidden meaning of the totality of existence; the Name through which everything else acquires its meaning" (Wolin 1982, 40).

9. Zohn's rendering of *Überleben* as "afterlife" here reveals an interesting (unconscious?) interlingual shift of meaning. *Überleben* is usually translated as "survival" or more literally "(over)/outliving." "Afterlife" in turn should be translated as *zukünftiges Leben* in the sense of "later/future life," or as *Leben nach dem Tode* in the sense of "life after death." But the French equivalent of *Überleben, survie*, does mean "survival" as well as "afterlife," that is, "more life" and "more than life."

10. A question of "totality" must be addressed here. Benjamin indeed seems to be saying that pure language constitutes a totality of mere earthly languages. But what kind of totality is it? Is it God or the Name of God? A few pages later, Benjamin writes (in Zohn's translation): "Fragments of a vessel which are to be glued together must match one another in the smallest details, although they need not be like one another. In the same way a translation, instead of resembling the meaning of the original, must lovingly and in detail incorporate the original's mode of signification, thus making both the original and the translation recognizable as fragments of a greater language, just as fragments are part of a vessel" (*BJ*, 78). Carol Jacobs takes issue with Zohn's translation and points out that the last phrase of the above passage should be rendered: "just as fragments are the *broken* part of a vessel" (Jacobs 1975, 762). De Man seizes this point and asserts that the fragments will not be redeemed by a totality; they will remain "broken." See de Man 91.

11. *BJ* 82. The original reads: "Aber es gibt ein Halten. Es gewährt es jedoch kein Text auaer dem heiligen, in dem der Sinn aufgehört hat, die Wasserscheide für die strömende Sprache und die strömende Offenbarung zu sein" (Benjamin 1972, 4.1:21).

12. In the handwritten version copied at the beginning of this chapter, the parentheses that appear in *Ambarvalia* are eliminated. Thus there is a slight modification in the translation.

13. See *Endymion*, book 3, line 666, by John Keats.

CHAPTER FOUR
AMBARVALIA TO ETERNITY

EPIGRAPH: The shiny furniture / Polished by the years / Would decorate our chamber / The rarest flowers / Mingling their odors / With the amber's vague scent / The rich ceilings / The profound mirrors / The splendor of the Orient / All would speak / Secretly to the soul / The sweet native tongue.

1. See, for example, Inoue Teruo, "Nishiwaki Junzaburō to Bōdorēru," in *Gendaishi tokuhon 9* 1979, 114–23.

2. For a discussion of these translations, see Soviak et al. 1975. Also, for a comprehensive study of the history of modern Japanese poetry, see Keene 1984.

3. These foreign texts are now included in *NJZ*: "Paradis Perdu" 9:688–99, *Une montre sentimentale* 3:590–530, *Spectrum* 3:544–486, *Poems Barbarous* 3:482–475, and *Exclamations* 11:610–562.

4. The revelation of this fact most likely came from Nishiwaki himself. One of the earliest source studies is Kinoshita 1966.

5. For example, Kitagawa Fuyuhiko praised the poem "Ambarvalia" in his essay "Nishiwaki Junzaburō" (1957) without knowing that the poem was actually Nishiwaki's translation, and wondered why nobody had yet written on this poem. When the essay was reprinted in *Gendaishi kanshō* (Tokyo: Yūshindō, 1970), he added a note: "I must add here that when I was informed by Kinoshita Tsunetarō that Nishiwaki Junzaburō's "Ambarvalia" was, except the last five lines, entirely his translation of a Latin poem, I felt as if my soul were expiring" (Fukuda, Murano, and Kagiya 1971, 146).

6. Nishiwaki Junzaburō, *Amubaruwaria* (Tokyo: Tokyoshuppan kabushikigaisha, 1947), now included in *ZS*.

7. His *Zenshishū* (Collected poems) includes 1,257 pages of poetry written in Japanese.

8. One should be careful not to confuse the notion of the "author" with that of a "person." I am here concerned only with a textual status named the "author," not with the person named Nishiwaki Junzaburō.

9. "Sakutarō's naturalism?" So one may ask, for Hagiwara is considered the champion of an antinaturalist movement called "Romanticism." Yet the poet Miyoshi Tatsuji, like Nishiwaki, seemed to detect a naturalist propensity in Hagiwara's employment of the grotesque. See Ōoka 1978.

10. Yura Kimiyoshi recounts the scene when he learned the origin of "Karumojiin": "About the 'Karumojiin' at the beginning of the poem, once I heard this from Nishiwaki himself: 'Well, I just made an association out of Calmotin.' The revelation made me jump out of my chair. Nishiwaki put down his cigarette. But his look immediately turned from that of mischievousness to boredom. He asked, 'Have you ever taken Calmotin?'" (Yura 1984, 47).

11. In the original Japanese syntax, the subject *hibari* comes *before* the negative verb *inai*.

12. See Shea 1964, 338–39.

13. See Kitasono 1971.

14. *Mujō*: the inconsistency, transience of the phenomenal world. It is a central notion in Buddhism. The court literature of the Heian period (794–1192) had its counterpart in *hakanasa*.

15. *Sabi*: the desolation and beauty of loneliness; solitude, quiet. It was introduced as a positive ideal for *waka* by Fujiwara Shunzei, and thereafter developed variously by subsequent writers, notably Matsuo Bashō.

16. *Renga*: linked poetry. It developed from a pastime in the twelfth century into a serious art. In effect, successive *kami no ku* (5–7–5-syllable stanzas) and *shimo no ku* (7–7-syllable stanzas) of tanka were joined in sequence such that each made an integral poetic unit with its predecessor (and therefore its successor) without having a semantic connection to it.

17. *IS*.

18. See the first note to *No Traveller Returns* above for more details.

19. See Imoto 1970.

20. This introductory passage by Bashō is in turn based on a text by the famous Chinese poet Li Po (701–62). See Abe Kimio 1979, 77.

21. No. 96 of *Hyakunin isshu*. See Shimazu 1969, 202–3.

22. See *NJZ* 4:77.

23. In Japanese, unlike English, the modifier must come before the modified. Here we may detect an invasion of English syntax, whose unnaturalness Nishiwaki exploited in *Ambarvalia*.

24. Citing Kafka, Foucault speaks of the source of writing as "this disquieting sound which announces from the depths of language" that survives man as well as his impotence of speech. See Foucault 1977, 53–67.

25. For the semantic instability of the word *utsutsu*, see note 2 to *No Traveller Returns*.

26. Niikura states that the teacher in this section refers to an actual acquaintance of Nishiwaki, Ōtsuka Takenobu. See *IS*, 175.

27. See Barthes 1974.

28. Bataille 1957, 32. (It is found again. / What? Eternity. / It is the sea / Merged with the sun. . . . Poetry leads us to eternity, to death, and through death to continuity: poetry is eternity.)

29. For selected translations of poems from these works, see Claremont 1991.

Bibliography

Abe Kimio. 1979. *Shōkō: Oku no hosomichi.* Tokyo: Nichiei sha.

Abe Takeshi. 1980. *Kindaishi no haiboku: Shijin no sensō sekinin.* Tokyo: Ōhara shinsei sha.

Adams, Hazard, ed. 1971. *Critical Theory since Plato.* New York: Harcourt Brace Jovanovich.

Akiyama Ken, et al., eds. 1970–73. *Nihon koten bungaku zenshū.* 51 vols. Tokyo: Shōgakkan.

Aldington, Richard. 1919. *Images.* London: Egoist.

———. 1933. *All Men Are Enemies.* London: Chatto and Windus.

Alter, Robert. 1991. *Necessary Angels: Tradition and Modernity in Kafka, Benjamin, and Scholem.* Cambridge: Harvard University Press.

Andō Ichirō. 1971. "Nishiwaki Junzaburō no shiteki sekai." In *Nishiwaki Junzaburō kenkyū,* pp. 9–48. See Fukuda 1971.

Andō Yasuhiko. 1978. "Chō to bakudan." In *Gendaishi monogatari,* edited by Fundō Junsaku and Yoshida Hiroo, pp. 2–28. Tokyo: Yūhikaku.

Bacon, Francis. 1908. "The Tvvo Bookes of the Proficience and Advancement of Learning Divine and Hvmane." In vol. 1 (1605–50) of *Critical Essays of the Seventeenth Century,* edited by J. E. Spingarn, pp. 1–9. London: Oxford University Press.

———. [1908] 1936. *The Essays of Francis Bacon.* Edited by Clark Southerland Northup. Boston: Houghton Mifflin.

Bahr, Hermann. 1925. *Expressionism.* Translated by R. T. Gribble. London: Frank Henderson.

Banville, Théodore de. 1872. *Petit traité de poésie française.* Paris: Bibliothèque de l'Echo de la Sorbonne.

Barthes, Roland. 1974. *S/Z.* Translated by Richard Miller. New York: Hill and Wang.

Bataille, Georges. 1955. "Hegel, la mort et le sacrifice." *Deucalion* 5. Paris: Neuchâtel.

———. 1957. *L'erotisme.* Paris: Editions de Minuit.

Baudelaire, Charles-Pierre. 1975. *Œuvres complètes.* Edited by Claude Pichots. 2 vols. Paris: Bibliothèque de la Pléiade, Gallimard.

Benjamin, Walter. 1969. "The Task of the Translator." In *Illuminations,* edited by Hannah Arendt, translated by Harry Zohn, pp. 69–82. New York: Schocken Books.

———. 1972. "Die Aufgabe des Überstzers." In vol. 4.1 of *Gesammelte Schriften,* edited by Theodor Adorno and Gershom Scholem, pp. 9–21. Frankfurt: Suhrkamp Verlag.

Blanchot, Maurice. 1963. *Lautréamont et Sade.* Paris: Editions de Minuit.

Borges, Jorge Luis. 1964. "On Rigor in Science." In *Dreamtigers*, translated by Mildred Boyer and Harold Morland. Austin: University of Texas Press.

Bosschère, Jean de. 1917. *The Closed Door.* Translated by F. S. Flint. London: John Lane, The Bodley Head.

Breton, André. 1969. *Manifestoes of Surrealism.* Translated by Richard Seaver and Helen R. Lane. Ann Arbor: University of Michigan Press.

Brooke, Rupert. 1918. *The Collected Poems of Rupert Brooke, with a Memoir.* London: Sidgwick and Jackson.

Chiba Sen'ichi. 1971. "Shiron no hatten to ryūha no tenkai: Shōwa ki." In *Nihon kindaishi: hikaku bungaku teki ni mita*, edited by Nakajima Kenzō et al., pp. 34–92. Hikaku bungaku kōza 2. Tokyo: Shimizu kōbundō.

———. 1978. *Gendaibungaku no hikakubungaku teki kenkyū: Modānizumu no shiteki dōtai.* Tokyo: Yagi shoten.

Claremont, Yasuko, trans. 1991. *Gen'ei: Selected Poems of Nishiwaki Junzaburō, 1894–1982.* University of Sydney East Asian Series, no. 4. New South Wales: Wild Peony.

Claudel, Paul. 1929. *Art poétique.* Paris: Mercure de France.

Cocteau, Jean. 1925. *Poésie, 1916–1923.* Paris: Librairie Gallimard.

Coleridge, Samuel Taylor. 1983. *The Collected Works of Samuel Taylor Coleridge.* Vol. 7, *Biographia Literaria*, edited by Kathleen Coburn and Bart Winer. Bollingen Series 75. 2 vols. in 1. Princeton: Princeton University Press.

Crimp, Douglas. 1979. "Pictures." *October* 8: 75–88.

Dante. 1947. *The Divine Comedy.* In *The Portable Dante*, translated by Laurence Binyon. New York: Viking Press.

De Man, Paul. 1986. "Conclusions: Walter Benjamin's 'Task of the Translator.'" In *The Resistance to Theory*, pp. 73–93. Minneapolis: University of Minnesota Press.

Derrida, Jacques. 1976. *Of Grammatology.* Translated by Gayatri Chakravorty Spivak. Baltimore: Johns Hopkins University Press.

———. 1978. "From Restricted to General Economy: A Hegelianism without Reserve." In *Writing and Difference*, translated by Alan Bass, pp. 251–77. Chicago: University of Chicago Press.

———. 1982. "Différance." In *Margins of Philosophy*, translated by Alan Bass, pp. 3–27. Chicago: University of Chicago Press.

———. 1984. *Signéponge/Signsponge.* Translated by Richard Rand. New York: Columbia University Press.

———. 1985. "Des Tours de Babel." In *Difference in Translation*, edited by Joseph F. Graham, pp. 209–48; translated by Graham, pp. 165–207. Ithaca: Cornell University Press.

Deutsch, Babette, and Avrahm Yarmolinsky, trans. 1927. "A Russian Song," by Igor Severyanin. In *Russian Poetry: An Anthology*, p. 160. New York: International Publishers.

Donne, John. 1968. *The Complete Poetry of John Donne.* Edited by John T. Shawcross. New York: New York University Press.

Dowson, Ernest. [1934] 1967. *The Poetical Works of Ernest Dowson.* Edited by Desmond Flower. London: Casell.

Eliot, T. S. 1971. *The Complete Poems and Plays, 1909–1950.* New York: Harcourt, Brace, and World.

Foucault, Michel. 1977. *Language, Counter-Memory, Practice: Selected Essays and Interviews.* Translated by Donald F. Bouchard and Sherry Simon. Ithaca: Cornell University Press.

Freud, Sigmund. 1965. *The Interpretation of Dreams.* Translated by James Strachey. New York: Avon Books.

Fukuda Rikutarō, Murano Shirō, and Kagiya Yukinobu, eds. 1971. *Nishiwaki Junzaburō kenkyū.* Tokyo: Yūbun shoin.

Garrod, H. G. 1924. *The Profession of Poetry: An Inaugural Lecture.* Oxford: Clarendon Press.

Gendaishi tokuhon 9: Nishiwaki Junzaburō. 1979. Tokyo: Shichō sha.

Goethe, Johann Wolfgang von. 1983. *Goethe: Poems and Epigrams.* Translated by Michael Hamburger. London: Anvil Press.

Goll, Yvan. 1968. *Œuvres.* Edited by Claire Goll and François Xavier Jaujard. 2 vols. Paris: Editions Emile-Paul.

Gourmont, Remy de. [1900] 1964. *La culture des idées.* Paris: Mercure de France.

Hagiwara Sakutarō. 1917. *Tsuki ni hoeru.* Tokyo: Kanjōshi sha.

———. 1934. *Hyōtō.* Tokyo: Daiichi shobō.

———. 1978. *Howling at the Moon.* Translated by Hiroaki Sato. New York: Columbia University Press.

Handelman, Susan A. 1991. *Fragments of Redemption: Jewish Thought and Literary Theory in Benjamin, Scholem, and Levinas.* Bloomington: Indiana University Press.

Harazaki Takashi. 1980. "'Shi to shiron' oyobi 'Bungaku' no seiritsu to tenkai oboegaki." In *Shi to shiron: Gendaishi no shuppatsu.* Edited by Ginyū henshūbu, pp. 83–131. Tokyo: Tōji shobō.

Horiguchi Daigaku, trans. 1981. *Gekka no ichigun.* In vol. 2 of *Horiguchi Daigaku zenshū,* pp. 7–264. Tokyo: Ozawa shoten.

Imto Nōichi, ed. 1970. *Hyōhaku no tamashii: Bashō no hon 6.* Tokyo: Kadokawa shoten.

Ise monogatari. 1970–73. Vol. 8 of *Nihon koten bungaku zenshū. See* Akiyama 1970–73.

Jacob, Max. N.d. *Art poétique.* Paris: Chez Emile-Paul.

Jacobs, Carol. 1975. "The Monstrosity of Translation." *Modern Language Notes* 90:755–66.

Jespersen, Otto. [1894] 1909. *Progress in Language, with Special Reference to English.* London: Swan Sonnenschein.

Johnson, Samuel. [1783] 1890. *The Lives of the Most Eminent English Poets with Critical Observations on Their Works.* Edited by Mrs. Alexander Napier. 3 vols. London: George Bell and Sons.

Kagiya Yukinobu. 1971. *Nishiwaki Junzaburō ron.* Tokyo: Shinchō sha.

———. 1983. *Shijin Nishiwaki Junzaburō.* Tokyo: Chikuma shobō.

Kant, Immanuel. 1929. *Immanuel Kant's Critique of Pure Reason*. Translated by Norman Kemp Smith. New York: Humanities Press.

Karatani Kōjin. 1990. "Murakami Haruki no fūkei." In *Shūen o megutte*, pp. 75–113. Tokyo: Fukutake shoten.

Keats, John. 1966. *The Selected Poetry of Keats*. Edited by Paul de Man. New York: New American Library.

Keene, Donald. 1984. *Dawn to the West: Japanese Literature of the Modern Era, Poetry, Drama, Criticism*. New York: Holt, Rinehart, and Winston.

Kinoshita Tsunetarō. 1966. "Amubaruwaria, Nishiwaki Junzaburō." *Kokubungaku: Kaishaku to kanshō* (January): 95–103.

Kitagawa Fuyuhiko. 1971. "Nishiwaki Junzaburō." In *Nishiwaki Junzaburō kenkyū*, pp. 123–45. *See* Fukuda 1971.

Kitasono Katsue. 1971. "Tabibito kaerazu e no tegami: Kaze o hiita makibito." In *Nishiwaki Junzaburō kenkyū*, pp. 113–22. *See* Fukuda 1971.

Kodama, Sanehide, ed. 1987. *Ezra Pound and Japan: Letters and Essays*. Redding Ridge, Conn.: Black Swan Books.

Konjaku monogatari shū. 1970–73. Vol. 23 of *Nihon koten bungaku zenshū*. *See* Akiyama 1970–73.

Ko Sung-Won. 1977. *Buddhist Elements in Dada*. New York: New York University Press.

Kusano Shinpei. 1969. *Frogs and Others*. Translated by Cid Corman and Kamaike Susumu. Tokyo: Mushin sha/Grossman.

Langland, William. 1949. *Visions from Piers Plowman*. Translated by Nevill Coghill. London: Phoenix House.

Lautréamont, Comte de [Isidore Ducasse]. 1963. *Œuvres complètes*. Paris: Librairie José Corti.

Lower, Lucy Beth. 1987. "Poetry and Poetics: From Modern to Contemporary in Japanese Poetry." Ph.D. diss., Harvard University.

Mallarmé, Stéphane. 1945. *Œuvres complètes*. Edited by Henri Mondor and G. Jean-Aubry. Paris: Bibliothèque de la Pléiade, Gallimard.

Marvell, Andrew. 1898. *Poems of Andrew Marvell*. Edited by G. A. Aitken. London: Lawrence and Bullen.

Masaoka Shiki. 1969. *Masaoka shiki, Takahama Kyoshi*. Vol. 2 of *Nihon shijin zenshū*, edited by Kamei Katsuichirō et al. Tokyo: Shinchō sha.

Matsuo Bashō. 1966. *The Narrow Road to the Deep North*. Translated by Nobuyuki Yuasa. Harmondsworth: Penguin Books.

———. 1972. *Matsuo Bashō shū*. Vol. 41 of *Nihon koten bungaku zenshū*. *See* Akiyama 1970–73.

Matsushita Daizaburō and Watanabe Fumio, eds. 1951. *Kokka taikan: Ka shū*. Tokyo: Kadokawa shoten.

Milton, John. 1950. *Complete Poetry and Selected Prose of John Milton*. Edited by Cleanth Brooks. New York: Modern Library.

Miyazawa Kenji. 1973. *Spring and Asura*. Translated by Hiroaki Sato. Chicago: Chicago Review Press.

Murano Shirō et al., eds. 1961. *Gendaishi zenshū*. 10 vols. Tokyo: Kadokawa shoten.

Murasaki Shikibu. 1977. *The Tale of Genji*. Translated by Edward G. Seiden-sticker. New York: Alfred A. Knopf.

Naka Tarō. 1979. "Nishiwaki to Sakutarō." In *Gendaishi tokuhon 9: Nishiwaki Junzaburō* 172–78.

Nakano Kaichi. 1975. *Zen'eishi undōshi no kenkyū*. Tokyo: Shinsei sha.

Nietzsche, Friedrich. [1954] 1959. *Thus Spoke Zarathustra*. Translated by Walter Kaufman. New York: Penguin Books.

Nihon kindai shiron kenkyūkai. 1974. *Shōwa shiron no kenkyū*. Tokyo: Nihon gakujutsu shinkōkai.

Niikura Toshikazu. 1982. *Nishiwaki Junzaburō zenshi inyu shūsei*. Tokyo: Chikuma shobō.

Nishiwaki Junzaburō. 1929. *Chōgenjitsushugi shiron*. Tokyo: Kōseikaku shoten.

———. 1933. *Ambarvalia*. Tokyo: Shiinoki sha.

———. 1947. *Tabibito kaerazu*. Tokyo: Tokyo shuppan.

———. 1962. *Eterunitasu*. Tokyo: Shōshin sha.

———. 1981. *Teihon, Nishiwaki Junzaburō zenshishū*. Tokyo: Chikuma shobō.

———. 1982–83. *Nishiwaki Junzaburō zenshū*. Edited by Kagiya Yukinobu et al. 12 vols. Tokyo: Chikuma shobō.

Omokage. 1969. In *Yakushishū*, pp. 5–19.

Ōoka Makoto. 1978. "Tōji no kakei." In vol. 7 of *Ōoka Makoto chosakushū*, pp. 55–74. Tokyo: Seido sha.

——— et al., eds. 1975. *Nihon gendaishi taikei*. 13 vols. Tokyo: Kawade shobō.

Pater, Walter Horatio. 1885. *Marius the Epicurean: His sensations and ideas*. London: Macmillan.

———. [1893] 1977. *The Renaissance*. Chicago: Academy Press.

Poe, Edgar Allan. [1902] 1965. *The Complete Works*. Edited by James A. Harrison. 17 vols. New York: AMS Press.

Reverdy, Pierre. 1969. *Plupart du temps*. 2 vols. Paris: Editions Gallimard.

———. 1975. *Nord-sud: Self-defence et autres écrits sur l'art et la poésie, 1917–1926*. Paris: Flammarion Editeur.

Rimbaud, Arthur. 1972. *Œuvres complètes*. Edited by Antoine Adam. Paris: Bibliothèque de la Pléiade, Gallimard.

Romains, Jules, and G. Chennevière. 1924. *Petit traité de versification*. Paris: Librairie Gallimard.

Saitō Yukio, Yukitaka, and Yukinari. 1967. *Edo meisho zue*. Edited by Suzuki Tōzō and Asakura Haruhiko. 6 vols. Tokyo: Kadokawa shoten.

Sakuramoto Tomio. 1983. *Kūhaku to sekinin: Senjika no shijin tachi*. Tokyo: Mirai sha.

Sato, Hiroaki, and Burton Watson, trans. and eds. 1981. *From the Country of Eight Islands: An Anthology of Japanese Poetry*. Seattle: University of Washington Press.

Saussure, Ferdinand de. 1986. *Course in General Linguistics*. Translated by Roy Harris. La Salle, Ill.: Open Court.

Selby, F. G. 1925. "Bacon and Montaigne." *The Criterion* 3, no. 10: 258–77.

Shea, George Tyson. 1964. *Leftwing Literature in Japan.* Tokyo: Hōsei University Press.

Shelley, Percy Bysshe. 1971. "A Defence of Poetry." In *Critical Theory Since Plato,* pp. 499–513. *See* Adams 1971.

Sherburne, Sir Edward. [1651] 1961. *Poems and Translations: The Poems and Translations of Sir Edward Sherburne.* Edited by F. J. Van Beeck. Assen: Van Gorcum.

Shimazu Tadao. 1969. *Hyakunin isshu.* Tokyo: Kadokawa shoten.

Shintaishi shō. 1882. Translated by Toyama Shōichi, Yatabe Ryōkichi, and Innoue Tetsujirō. Tokyo: Maruzen.

Shi to shiron/Bungaku. [1928–33] 1985. 10 vols. Tokyo: Kyōiku shuppan sentā.

Shururearisumu no tenkai. 1981. Shururearisumu tokuhon 2. Tokyo: Shichō sha.

Silverberg, Miriam. 1990. *Changing Song: The Marxist Manifestos of Nakano Shigeharu.* Princeton: Princeton University Press.

Sitwell, Osbert. 1921. *Who Killed Cock Robin?* London: C. W. Daniel.

Solt, John Peter. 1989. "Shredding the Tapestry of Meaning: The Poetry and Poetics of Kitasono Katsue (1902–1978)." Ph.D. diss., Harvard University.

Sontag, Susan. 1967. Preface to *Writing Degree Zero,* by Roland Barthes, pp. vii–xxi. New York: Hill and Wang.

———. 1981. *Under the Sign of Saturn.* New York: Vintage Books.

Soupault, Philippe. 1973. *Poèmes et poésie, 1917–1973.* Paris: Bernard Grasset.

Soviak, Eugene, et al., eds. 1975. "Toward a Modern Japanese Poetry." *Literature East West* 19: 7–120.

Spenser, Edmund. 1943. *The Works of Edmund Spenser.* Edited by Edwin Greenlaw et al. Baltimore: Johns Hopkins University Press.

Spingarn, J. E., ed. 1908. *Critical Essays of the Seventeenth Century.* 3 vols. London: Oxford University Press.

Stevens, Wallace. [1954] 1982. *Collected Poems.* New York: Vintage Books.

Stryk, Lucien. 1971. "Shinkichi Takahashi: Contemporary Zen Poet." *Malahat Review,* no. 18.

Takahashi Shinkichi. 1982. *Takahashi Shinkichi zenshū.* 4 vols. Tokyo: Seido sha.

Takamura Kōtarō. 1978. *Chieko's Sky.* Translated by Furuta Soichi. New York: Kodansha International.

———. 1988. *Chieko and Other Poems.* Translated by Hiroaki Sato. Honolulu: University Press of Hawaii.

Thibaudet, Albert. 1926. *La poésie de Stéphane Mallarmé.* Paris: Librairie Gallimard.

Tzara, Tristan. 1975. *Œuvres complètes.* Edited by Henri Béhar. 5 vols. Paris: Flammarion.

Ueda Bin, trans. 1969. *Kaichōon.* In *Yakushishū,* pp. 20–57.

Ueda, Makoto. 1983. *Modern Japanese Poets and the Nature of Literature.* Stanford: Stanford University Press.

Valéry, Paul. 1960. *Œuvres complètes.* Edited by Jean Hytier. 2 vols. Paris: Bibliothèque de la Pléiade, Gallimard.

Verlaine, Paul. [1890] 1973. *Fêtes galantes, romances sans paroles: Précédé de poèmes saturniens.* Edited by Jacques Borel. Reprint. Paris: Editions Gallimard.

Wolin, Richard. 1982. *Walter Benjamin: An Aesthetic of Redemption.* New York: Columbia University Press.

Yakushishū. 1969. Vol. 28 of *Nihon no shiika,* edited by Itō Shinkichi et al. Tokyo: Chūōkōron sha.

Yoshida Kenkō. 1967. *Essays in Idleness.* Translated by Donald Keene. New York: Columbia University Press.

Yoshimoto Takaaki. 1970. "Zensedai no shijin tachi." In vol. 5 of *Yoshimoto Takaaki zen chosaku shū,* pp. 38–55. Tokyo: Keisōsha.

Yoshimura Akira. 1977. *Kantō daishinsai.* Tokyo: Bungei shunjū.

Yura Kimiyoshi. 1984. "Nishiwaki Junzaburō: Ambarvalia." *Kokubungaku: kaishaku to kyōzai no kenkyū* (December): 44–49.

Index

STUDIES OF THE EAST ASIAN INSTITUTE

Selected Titles

Private Academies of Tokugawa Japan, by Richard Rubinger. Princeton: Princeton University Press, 1983.

Fragments of Rainbows: The Life and Poetry of Saito Mokichi, 1882–1953, by Amy Vladeck Heinrich. New York: Columbia University Press, 1983.

State and Diplomacy in Early Modern Japan, by Ronald Toby. Princeton: Princeton University Press, 1983 (hc); Stanford: Stanford University Press, 1991 (pb).

Japanese Culture, third edition, revised, by H. Paul Varley. Honolulu: University of Hawaii Press, 1984.

Japan's Modern Myths: Ideology in the Late Meiji Period, by Carol Gluck. Princeton: Princeton University Press, 1985.

Urban Japanese Housewives: At Home and in the Community, by Anne E. Imamura. Honolulu: University of Hawaii Press, 1987.

The Japanese Way of Politics, by Gerald L. Curtis. New York: Columbia University Press, 1988.

Neighborhood Tokyo, by Theodore C. Bestor. Stanford: Stanford University Press, 1989.

Suicidal Narrative in Modern Japan: The Case of Dazai Osamu, by Alan Wolfe. Princeton: Princeton University Press, 1990.

Sowing the Seeds of Change: Chinese Students, Japanese Teachers, 1895–1905, by Paula S. Harrell. Stanford: Stanford University Press, 1992.

Social Mobility in Contemporary Japan, by Hiroshi Ishida. Stanford: Stanford University Press, 1992.

The Writings of Kōda Aya, a Japanese Literary Daughter, by Alan Tansman. New Haven: Yale University Press, 1993.

Japan's Foreign Policy after the Cold War: Coping with Change, Gerald L. Curtis, ed. Armonk, N.Y.: M. E. Sharpe, 1993.